CLAPHAM
in the
Twentieth
Century

Edited by Peter Jefferson Smith and Alyson Wilson

Designed by Derrick McRobert MCSD MSTD

Published by The Clapham Society
22 Crescent Grove, London SW4 7AH

Printed by Cantate Battley
Parkfield Industrial Estate, Culvert Place,
Battersea SW11 5BA

ISBN 0 9500694 5 0

CLAPHAM
in the
Twentieth
Century

THE CLAPHAM SOCIETY

Contents

CLAPHAM IN THE TWENTIETH CENTURY

PEOPLE WRITE DOWN THEIR MEMORIES at times significant to them; but the end of a century also sparks off much recall of the past. Both factors gave rise to this book. We knew of a number of people who had recorded their lives in Clapham; in particular, one member of the Clapham Society, now aged 90, had written a long memoir of his family and his working life. We also knew of many contemporary accounts of life here, whether factual or incorporated in works of fiction by people who had lived here. There was a local business – the printers of this book - which had always taken a pride in Clapham and had encouraged its employees to write down their memories. The year 2000 prompted us to collect what we had, and see whether we could find or commission enough to give some sort of picture of how people lived here, right through the century.

The beginnings and ends of centuries mark off the passage of time in a quite arbitrary way: 1900 and 2000 were not significant in themselves, but they have marked each end of a century of immense change. In 1900, Clapham was changing very fast, and those living at the time knew that well; the same was true in 2000. In 1900, the first aeroplane had yet to fly. The electric underground train had just reached here, but it was still the age of the horse-drawn tram or bus. Correspondence was by letter, and telephones were rare. In 2000, the car dominated the roads, and it was the age of the internet and the mobile phone. Other changes are less obvious – to clothing, diet, and health for instance. Culture and leisure activities changed gradually; older people can often recall when their family first had a television, but other changes are harder to pinpoint – for example the point at which holidays abroad became accessible to most people. In this book, some contributors record changes, usually when they are looking back; but in most cases, the very different social circumstances of the earlier years have to be inferred and imagined from what the authors tell us.

We would not claim or pretend that this book gives a systematic or balanced account of the history over a century of our part of London; given its origins, it could not do so. While we make no apologies for our editorial choices, others would see the last century in quite different ways. No doubt there will be many more memories to come, and we hope this book will encourage people to record them. As to what is here, the words and opinions are those of their authors, and not those of the editors or of the Clapham Society. All we have tried to do is to see that the facts are correct, and we should be surprised if we have wholly succeeded in that.

We are very grateful to all who have given permission to reproduce copyright material. We have tried to obtain all permissions necessary, but if we have inadvertently failed, we apologise. We would like to thank most sincerely all who have helped compile this book – the other members of the Clapham Society's Local History Group, Annabel Allott, Eleanor Grey, Bernard Middleton and David Perkin; all who provided material, and above all, those who wrote specially for us. We have had the benefit once more of Derrick McRobert's design skills as well as his enthusiasm, energy and apparently endless forbearance. We also owe a debt of gratitude to our local printers, Battley Brothers. Not only have they undertaken the printing of the book with their customary expertise, but as both a family and a business based in Clapham for the duration of the twentieth century they have provided a significant amount of the material in the book.

Throughout the century, Clapham has been a place where some people have stayed a long time – often a lifetime – while for others it has been a place of passage. Memories may or may not be happy. Some contributors look back with nostalgia to better times, while others celebrate times in which they write. The Clapham Society exists both to preserve what is good in Clapham and to enhance it, and its members who have compiled this book like living where they do. On this, we cheerfully admit to lack of balance, and indeed to bias. We share the views of our youngest contributor:

"I like going to other places, but my favourite place is Clapham."

Clapham, July 2002   Peter Jefferson Smith
                                                     Alyson Wilson

World events	Science and technology
1900	
1902 Boer War ended	1901 Transatlantic radio signal transmi⟩
	1903 Flight of motor-powered aeropla⟩
	1905 Einstein's theory of relativity
1910	1908 Mass produced cars
1914-18 World War I	1915 Tanks invented
1917 Russian revolution	
1920	1919 First non-stop transatlantic flight
	1926 TV images transmitted
1930 1929 Wall Street crash; Depression	1928 Penicillin discovered
1933 Hitler came to power in Germany	
1940 1939-45 World War II	1938 Nylon invented
	1939 Nuclear fission discovered
	1944 First electronic computer
1946 Start of Cold War	1947 Supersonic flight made
1947 Independence and Partition of India	1948 Bic ballpoint pen
1950 1949 Communist victory in China	1952 First passenger jet flight
	1953 Discovery of DNA
1956 Suez War	1956 First oral contraceptives
1957 Start of European Common Market	
1960	
1962 Cuban Missile Crisis	1962 TV satellite relays live pictures
1963 US President J F Kennedy	
assassinated	1967 Successful heart transplant
1970	1969 Manned mission to the moon
	1971 Microprocessor chip invented
1973 UK joined European Economic	
Community	1978 Birth of baby conceived by IVF
1980	1979 Smallpox eradicated
	1981 Compact discs on sale
1982 Falklands War	1982 Video keyhole surgery
1990 1989 Berlin wall fell: Cold War ended	
1991 Gulf War	1991 Internet browser developed
1991 Break-up of Soviet Union	
	1997 Sheep produced by cloning
2000	

UK social and political events	London and Clapham
1901 Death of Queen Victoria	1900 Tube extended to Clapham Common
	1901 First electric tramway
	1906 Bus route numbers introduced
1908 Pensions for poor people over 70	
1911 National health insurance	1911 Last horsebus withdrawn
1918 Women over 30 given right to vote	
1922 BBC went on air	
1926 General Strike	1926 Tube extended to Morden and Clapham South station opened
1929 Poor law and workhouse abolished	
	1932 Public baths in Manor St. Clapham
1935 Compulsory driving tests	1933 Battersea Power Station built
1936 Accession and abdication of Edward VIII	1936 The Crystal Palace, Upper Norwood, burnt down
	1939-45 Clapham residents killed in air raids total 232
1944 Free secondary education for all	
1945 Labour landslide election	1948 Olympic Games in London
1948 National Health Service	1948 Arrival of Caribbean immigrants on the *Empire Windrush*
1952 Accession of Elizabeth II	1951 Festival of Britain
	1952 Last London trams
1958 First Motorway opened	
	1963 Clapham Society founded
1966 Britain won football World Cup	1965 London County Council replaced by Greater London Council
1966 Barclaycard first credit card	
1969 Capital punishment for murder ended	1965 Most of Clapham came under Lambeth Borough Council
1971 Change to decimal currency	
1972 "Bloody Sunday" in N.Ireland	1974 Clapham ceased to be a single parliamentary constituency
1979 Margaret Thatcher became Prime Minister	
1980 Council tenants given "right to buy"	1981 Brixton riots
1984 Pound note and halfpenny abolished	
	1986 Greater London Council abolished
	1988 Clapham rail crash
	1990 Inner London Education Authority abolished
1997 New Labour government elected	
1997 Death of Princess Diana	
1998 Good Friday Agreement in N.Ireland	
	2000 Greater London Authority set up and London Mayor elected

NOTES

THE TEXT. Each individual piece has a brief introduction in *Gill italics*. The text is then reproduced exactly as written by the contributor, with three dots ... to indicate omissions, and a short linking piece in *Gill italics* when there is a long break or a change of subject. Some editorial notes have been added within the text in square brackets [thus] to clarify points – usually names or abbreviations – which may not be readily understood by the reader today.

UK CURRENCY. Prior to decimalisation in 1971 the currency used in the UK was pounds (£), shillings (s) and pence (d). There were 12 pence (commonly called pennies) in one shilling, and 20 shillings in one pound. Amounts were written £1.2s.6d. or £1. 2/6. Halfpenny ($^1/_2$d) and quarter penny, known as farthing ($^1/_4$d) coins were also in circulation. To avoid repetition in the text we give an approximate exchange rate below.

1d. = 0.4 pence

6d. = 2.5 pence

1s. (12d.) = 5 pence

2s. (also known as a florin) = 10 pence

2s.6d. (also known as half-a-crown) = 12.5 pence

5s. (also known as a crown) = 25 pence

10s. = 50 pence

£1 (20s.) = £1 (100 pence)

£1.1s. (one guinea) = £1.05

VALUE OF MONEY. Throughout the century the value of the pound fell. £1 in 1900 had the same purchasing power as nearly £70 in 2000.

Purchasing power of £1 in year 2000 values

1900	£69.26	1950	£19.14		
1910	£62.79	1960	£13.49		
1920	£24.25	1970	£9.19		
1930	£38.17	1980	£2.55		
1940	£30.82	1990	£1.35	*Source*: National Statistics	

THE START OF THE CENTURY

Cecil J Cooper worked at Bon Marché, the department store in Brixton and lodged in a house off Brixton Hill. On 29 August 1900 he married Dora Davis and they went to live in their new house at 74 Crescent Lane. Dora's family lived in Denbigh and Cecil's letters to her at home during the last few weeks before the wedding describe in detail the decoration and furnishing of the new house.

23 July 1900

HAVE JUST BEEN TO CRESCENT LANE. Everything is going on splendidly. All the rooms are papered and the hall and stairs will be finished on Wednesday. Mr Peacock [the builder] is delighted with this hot weather and says the house will be perfectly dry. The dining, drawing, billiard and back bedroom papers look beautiful, but the front bedroom is just a little bit bright. Will no doubt look well though when the furniture and pictures are in. Have given Mr Peacock instructions to estimate for a conservatory from the drawing room and if the cost is not too high shall put it in hand as the room will then be much handsomer and larger. You will be charmed when you see the house finished.

25 July 1900

...Today I went to No 74 and put the conservatory in hand. It is to cost £11 including snow guards on the roof, and I have asked several people about it and everybody agrees that it is very cheap. As you say, dear, it will be a great improvement to the room. After leaving 74 I went to the City and visited the B[uilding] Society and informed them the house was ready for second survey. I had to pay £1.1.0 second survey fee and when the inspector has been down they will write me to say the cheque has been sent on to the solicitors. I shall then pay my second £75 and the solicitors fees and a new registration fee (just come into force) and if all is well shall be able to take possession on Wednesday next.

13 August 1900

Am pleased you like arms to the bedstead, as they do help to make the room look pretty when nicely draped, as they will be with you to see to them. I have chosen striped blinds drab [a type of linen cloth] with a little red scalloped & fringed edge. Plain dark green for kitchen and scullery. Mr Ellis is sending up tomorrow to measure the drawing room & two bedrooms for carpets. Which make do you like, pile or brussels? The billiard and Jayne's room and the maid's room had better be covered with linoleum with strips of carpet by bedside and dressing table. Bath Room and

Dora Cooper

usual offices also with linoleum. Solid walnut cornice in dining room stained ditto in all the other rooms except the drawing room where I propose to have a brass rail. I hope all this will meet with your approval, dear.

The stair carpets I am leaving to see a little later when all the furniture is in. Shall select nice wide brass stair rods. Dining & Drawing room overmantels are in hand also dining, drawing & bedroom suites, side boards &c... Have ordered the bedding today and for our own bed it will cost about £8. The dining room carpet is an Eastern make worth wholesale £10 or £11 and is really a very handsome present.

Extracted from letters of CECIL COOPER,
in the possession of his grand-daughter, Margaret Battley

Between 1889 and 1903, **Charles Booth** *(1840-1916)*
published his immense survey of Life and Labour of
the People in London. It was one of the first scientific studies
of poverty and the first attempt to map social conditions.
Booth used a team of researchers, who went round
interviewing and mapping each part of London.
A team was in Clapham in 1899 and 1900,
interviewing clergymen and going round the streets
with the local police. They made maps, as on the inside
front cover of this book, classifying the houses according
to their view of the wealth of the inhabitants.
The best houses were coloured yellow, and then they ran through
red, pink, purple and grey to reach dark blue and black,
for the very worst criminal areas.

On Sunday 1 July 1900
one of the researchers spent the afternoon in Clapham

WALKING ACROSS THE COMMON I fell in with two <u>Salvation Army</u> efforts, the one, the stronger of the two offered nothing but the most usual kind of gospel hammering – the other a very small affair armed only with cymbals which men and women alike used, sang verse by verse a hymn into the reading of which a strong featured, strong voiced, man threw a great deal of passion. "I saw one hanging on the tree, who fixed his dying eyes on me." On <u>me</u> he repeated & the words rang out. There was an anti-climax in the jolly tune to which the verse was set, hardly exceeded as a contrast by the gay fluting of a passing bicyclist who managing his machine with his feet, performed this tour de force at the head of a column of his friends rattling along the roadway by the side of which the little salvation party and their audience of half a dozen children were gathered.

Near the bigger group of salvationists in the centre of the Common I joined a party of men all close crowded round an elderly man seated on a chair who was I believe a secularist – and between him and some other men a very good humoured and courteous discussion was being carried on – as many had crowded in as could hear, for there was no speechifying nor raising of the voice. The men just talked as in a room with polite deference and without the least heat. The subject seemed to be the value of the Bible story of creation as compared to any other version we had.

This walk has given me a great idea of the new world being created in this part of London.

That afternoon, the researcher had been exploring the churches

At the South East corner of Clapham Common the <u>Catholics</u> have a large & beautiful church [St Mary's, Clapham Park Road] in which there was a good attendance of prettily dressed children for an afternoon service …

Clapham Parish Church, Holy Trinity which is also at the south east corner of the Common, I found filled with children and those accompanying them, not Sunday School children, (though they may have been) but the children of the congregation, small and large. The galleries were unoccupied but the whole body of the large old fashioned Georgian church was filled & the good old Rector was just finishing his address. It was on prayer – very simple very good…

St Barnabas [North Side] is a brand new spick and span church of the neat cyclopean stone work of which there are many specimens here about but this the best. "No expense spared" seems to be said – really beautifully finished as new, and likely to become increasingly beautiful with some age. When I passed, the special service for men on the first Sunday in the month was just ending &

I saw the men coming out. There might be about 70 of them perhaps – absolutely typical of the kind of man who takes to this kind of thing – not an inspiriting kind of man. I was told by the clergyman that the next service would be the 1st Sunday in September – August being missed & that they would be very glad to see me. I regretted having been late today.

The clergy told the researcher about their parishes and congregations.
The name of the church is followed by the member
of the clergy interviewed

St Paul's [Rectory Grove] <u>Danford</u> (curate). The vicar has for some years been a notorious dipsomaniac & some weeks since was under pressure from the bishop: resigned and retired to an inebriate retreat for a year. Bishop promising (Mr D says) to find some kind of work for him afterwards. Mr D here 18 months – came knowing nothing of the Vicar's habits and was so charmed with him and the parish that he bought a house. Mr Hughes (the vicar) a man of great ability & a magnificent preacher & great organiser... the church has always been full – well to do middle class cong[regation] drawn from all over Clapham by Mr Hughes' preaching. Population 8000 poor – 1500 lower middle and 500 middle cl[ass]. Poor nearly all north of Wandsworth Rd. Rashleigh St. desperately low and squalid & a criminal in almost every house.

Baptist, Victoria Rd [now Rise]. <u>Henderson</u>, here 27 yrs: Congreg[ation] mostly comfortable class – not so rich as formerly. Clapham going down socially – but not poor. Majority shopkeepers – bakers, butchers & a good many employed in Army and Navy Stores [in Victoria] – easy access. Some in City. Poorest are railwaymen in LC&DR works [London Chatham and Dover Railway works off Silverthorne Road]. Richest 2 retired; army doctor & a surgeon. The comfortable rich live between Wandsworth Road & Common and poor between Heath St. and Wandsworth Rd. Both becoming poorer. The rich have gone further out or further in. The young people when they marry go to Wimbledon – fashion has set that way and rents have fallen for good houses. New electric railway has brought the city very close...

Here as elsewhere the church fails to reach men – and the poor whether male or female – men will go to political or socialist meetings – church fails to attract...

John Burns [MP for Battersea] has a good influence though he has lost some of his popularity – can wake up the people – down on the treatment of wives, a teetotaller himself – seems somehow able to make the labourer ashamed of himself...

Clapham very conservative – No public hall – everything very slow and not much done. Battersea the other extreme – men on the vestry [the local council] there a low type – bear garden meetings – rates gone up by leaps and bounds – "those on the hill shall pay for us."

Drink the curse – all PHs [public houses] in poor streets thrive – women drink more [Henderson] puts it down to greater nervous strain of modern life & greater freedom...

Prostitution fearful on Common – you cannot cross without solicitation – a disgrace – more supervision wanted – lighting necessary, sexual intercourse a public exhibition – women haggard, dirty, diseased – a plague spot...

Union Tabernacle, Wandsworth Road, Cameron... most of the chapels in neighbourhood are nearly empty... in the new highly respectable working class streets scarcely a soul attends any place [of worship] – [Cameron] attributes decay of observance largely to bicycles, excursions, bands in park etc...

Holy Trinity – Greene "nearly 70, yellow white beard, tobacco stained, middle height, cultured quiet type of country rector". Here 15 years – 5 curates under him, will have 6. Large

Canon Greene

rectory, parish runs through all the grades, yellow to light blue, none are very poor. Old village type of long standing poverty. Great changes going on. Merchant princes left and place taken by rows of £40 [annual rent] houses. Old Clapham moved to Kensington or Surrey – new Clapham moved up out of Kennington – constant changes – the new streets on 3 year leases – a landlord does more for a new tenant than an old one and moving is thought nothing of. Eagle House and gardens that belonged to Mrs Edgar (Swan and Edgar) now covered with 600 pink or purple houses [Narbonne Avenue and adjoining streets] - a few large gardens remain – pop[ulation]. estimated 13000.

Religiously main feature today [is the] high church tone of its parish church & its Catholic surroundings. The old Clapham Sect influence is gone…

Baptist, Grafton Square. [now Peoples' Church] <u>Hanger</u>. There 14 years never met much success… reasons given (1) [Chapel] is hidden away in a quiet square (2) Clapham dead alive difficult to move in any way (3) Its sympathies so far as they can be moved are on the side of Roman Cath[olic] ritualism and conservatism. Greatest centre of Catholicism in London –

Congregational Church, Grafton Square

RC church the fullest in neighbourhood…

Referred to changes in Clapham especially Liston Rd and Grafton Sq which were "quiet respectable & even select" – now whole of south end let as flats and swarming with children – garden from being beautifully kept is filthy & unkempt & the old inhabitants remaining cannot stand it much longer… "my wife tells me we shall have to go."

Congregational Grafton Sq – [now United Reformed Church] <u>Guinness Rogers</u>. Resigned last Jan – was 35 yrs minister & has been 22 years in his house on North Side… Mr R expressed gloomy views – growing neglect of Sunday, denounced the bicycle and the 3 years lease system – Sunday more and more a day of pleasure and the "unattached" church going of those who went at all: 1st year trying round – 2nd year concentrating more or less – 3rd year breaking up for the move.

The choir at this church is a great point – it is the work of an enthusiast – one of the Colman (mustard) people who gives his life to it – ransacks a no.[number] of schools for voices and choir are repaid for their services by his teaching and training – some may be paid a little too.

St James. [Park Hill] <u>Gretton</u> – This is the great evangelical church of Clapham... Pres[ent] pop[ulation]. unknown - was 8000 at last census, now not less than 12000 – clerks, business men, civil servants etc. av[erage] income this class £800-£900.

Four or five very rich families left, but big houses falling vacant almost unlettable & taken at absurdly low rents for remainder of lease.

North of Clapham Park Rd. pop[ulation] working class with large theatrical & music hall element in Tremadoc Road, only poor bit near White Sq which had a very bad reputation, not safe there at night. Though much improved still very rough, scene of much drunken brawling. Costers and poor labourers and cadgers.

With Sgt Nunn, the researcher, Arthur Baxter, made three walks in Clapham in 1899: he summed them up as follows

Although it covers large area numerically [Clapham is] a small district. Even in older part – north of Common and High St the roads are so wide & widely spaced that pop[ulation] is scanty for area while south of the Common & High Street is still largely open ground – probably there is no district in London equally close to the centre which is less crowded.

But though it is not likely to become congested for many years its present supply of airiness and open space is not likely to last much longer: and to me it was a surprise to find that it had not changed more rapidly during the eight years which had passed since I lived in Bromfelde Road. Indeed there seems to have been a rush of change just before that period, when Clapham Park was cut into Abbeville Road and the Avenues [Lynette, Lessar, Cautley and Narbonne] then a long pause in the development, for though, as will be seen when I have chronicled a large number of new streets, they are of quite recent growth and many of them unfinished. I came back expecting to find Clapham Park almost gone or altered past recognition whereas the assault on it is only just beginning and the magnificent wide roads with their splendid trees and gardens and huge, solid Cubitt built houses remain almost as they were: but now that Lincoln House the largest of all the estates is closed [for building Rodenhurst Road], the change will probably be very rapid, and another ten years is scarcely likely to leave much of this delightful bit of London uncovered with streets of small and rather mean villas.

But for the disappearance of Eagle House and its large grounds the frontage of so much of the Common as is in Clapham [Parish] is quite unchanged and it still remains one of the most picturesque and charming pieces of London: with the possible exception of Cheyne Walk there is nothing in London more beautiful and interesting than the old Georgian terrace of Church Buildings and the other old group of Georgian houses facing Cock Pond.

He divided Clapham into four parts (modern descriptions used here)

North-east of Wandsworth Rd – Clapham High Street railway – but for Killyon Rd the new street running from Larkhall Lane to Wandsworth Road this bit is unaltered – it remains in the main good solid middle class people with a sprinkling of artisans and a few of the poorer classes to the extreme E[ast].

Between Wandsworth Rd, railway, High Street, Common and Cedars Rd. – again but for new roads on the west of rly line the changes are not extensive – but on the whole there is a downward tendency in better streets – Grafton Sq. South of North St. with quaint little courts off it on west – is and was poor – patch W[est] of Wirtemburg [Stonhouse] Street gone.

Between High Street Bedford Rd and Clapham Park Road – this area contains the nearest approach to any real poverty and squalor that can be found in Clapham. White Sq. Nelsons Row which as to poverty remain the same but from police point of view have improved. No arrests in White Sq. for 18 months – but the police leave it much alone. I imagine that if they arrested all the boys who gambled here their hands would be full, as it is an ideal place for the purpose and when I passed through alone a large number of lads were engaged with a pack of cards in the centre of the Square. Otherwise a decent working class quarter, but new streets look jerry built and may deteriorate.

All the area off South Side including Clapham Park – apart from the new roads on the site of Eagle House it remains wonderfully little altered: only four of the great houses have actually fallen into the builders' hands, and only in two places (Grove [now Weir] Road and Cavendish Road) has building actually begun – in the main the Park, I imagine, still remains the residence of people in the £1,000 to £20,000 a year – only two or three days since I saw the will of the last owner of a house in Poynders Rd was proved for over £350,000, though the presence of a considerable number of houses to let and of the girls' school in Atkins Road shows that the approach of the builder has made itself felt. The rapid change which will now come will probably be from yellow to pink... the newer roads in the same quarter of distinctly inferior quality: the Board School too in Bonneville Road indicates the character of the new inhabitants...

Clapham then remains on the whole an exceedingly prosperous district containing probably more wealth in proportion to inhabitants than any other suburb of the same distance from the centre – & it will probably prove a great church going district. New building appears unusually good – nothing like shoddy building which is rampant in Fulham. From police point of view uninteresting with exception of White Sq. and Orchard St. [now demolished and replaced by Saxby Road, off Lyham Road] district thoroughly law abiding. Clapham Common had a bad reputation but has improved – the LCC [London County Council] have cut down many of the bushes under the shelter of which the prostitutes used to carry out their trade.

Relative costs of housing

There are several poor streets in Clapham and some poverty, but not much overcrowding... the rents the houses in these districts range from £30 to £40 per annum... the type of house occupied by the poor of these districts is a 2-storied house, containing 4 to 6 rooms at a rental of 7/6 to 12/-. There are many streets with houses built on the flat system to accommodate two families, one family occupying the three rooms on the ground floor, the other living in the 3 rooms above – each pays rent of 6/6 to 7/6 a week.

White's Square, Four roomed houses 5/6 – 6/-: 2 room's 3/-. Very bad repair, condemned. No 25 family of 8 persons, rent 3/-. Ages 30, 34, 12, 10, 7, 5, 4, 7 months.

The Battersea side of the Common was little changed

— the general remarks refer to...

... the tardy demolition of the yellow west side of Clapham Common which has withstood the builder so much longer than the north and south – even now the greater portion remains intact. The only poor road in this otherwise well-to-do district is Chatham Road and the Street off it. In this short road is no less than four beer houses & one public house...

But further north

... Clapham Junction neighbourhood has an evil character – professional and non-professional prostitution are rife – Lavender Hill swarms with girls of loose character.

In July 1899 – Arthur Baxter took a walk with PC George on the West side of Clapham Common

*Around Northcote Road...*according to George's evidence there has been considerable decay in the streets between Wandsworth Common and Northcote Road: these on the map are red or purple but George says that they are now universally let to two families and are servantless: indeed in his opinion "there are not six families in Battersea that have a house to themselves".

Some of the roads close to Wandsworth Common were, and I think from George's tone, still are a good deal frequented by prostitutes, who ply their trade on the Common.

Between North Side and Lavender Hill. The great change in this district is the demolition of the bulk of the fine old houses facing Clapham Common and the formation of new roads on their sites: with the exception of the new houses actually facing the Common all the new building is of a high class pink character: the older roads between the Common and Lavender Hill (which too were built on the sites of the old houses with large gardens) were nearly all red when the map was made: but with the exception of Lavender Gardens, they have all decayed, and are now almost exclusively tenemented.

Extracted from the researchers' notebooks, in the archives of the British Library of Political and Economic Science, London School of Economics.

Patrick Spencer, now lives in Dulwich,
but his family once lived in Clapham
and are remembered
in a well-known local painting.
He wrote about his local connection
for the Clapham Society's newsletter
in 2000.

MATRIMONY PLACE, which runs from Rectory Grove down to Wandsworth Road alongside St Paul's Church, is the setting of a picture painted in about 1900 by C L Floris. It is now an unattractive footpath, far different from the scene painted in the picture, which depicts a newly married couple coming down the footpath welcomed by a happy band of onlookers. The cottages in the picture did actually exist then, but have since been demolished. The whereabouts of the original picture is unknown but engravings – of which I have one – sometimes come to light, and have been included in books on local history. My particular interest lies in the fact that my uncle, Alfred James Spencer (1877-1914), was the model for the bridegroom. No doubt this came about because the artist lived at 7 Fitzwilliam Road and my family at no. 3.

Amongst the family archives are letters of 1869-70 written by my grandfather in his courtship of his future wife. They are largely written on his employer's notepaper and during the working day (did the boss know this?); the romance is further curtailed by the cold and sombre name of the company: 'The British & Foreign Marble Galleries'. The early letters end 'Faithfully yours' but the final one 'Yours, that is to be'. There are many examples of the efficiency of the post: writing at 1 am 'I can't write much as my ink is low & the candle is going out. I have also to go & search for a letters pillar box so that your ladyship shall have this at breakfast time'.

They married in April 1870, and my grandfather's meticulously kept cash book records that he married on a wage of £1.10s.0d per week; the wedding ring cost 14s.6d, marriage fee 10/6d and 9 days honeymoon at Hastings £2.7s.6d. The time was well spent: 9 months and 3 days after the wedding the first of five children was born!

PATRICK SPENCER, 2000

OPPOSITE: Matrimony Place. Engraving of a painting by local artist, C L Floris

Frank Byford (1872-1952) was born in Broadhinton Road and educated at Durham House School, North Side and Christ's College in Rectory Grove. He was a talented musician and after an apprenticeship to Edward Phillips' music shop at 13 South Side, he moved to Dunkley's Music and Pianoforte Warehouse in Clapham High Street, where he spent all his working life. He lived for many years in Narbonne Avenue. Throughout his life he jotted down notes about his life and kept the scraps of paper in a box until as he said 'there were so many of them I decided to sort them out into some semblance of order and write them down'. The result, compiled in about 1940, is a delightful handwritten book illustrated with Byford's own pencil drawings. Sadly, a second volume to which he refers was either not completed or has been lost.

MY FATHER AND MOTHER attended Clapham Congregational Church in Grafton Square. [The church, on the site of the present United Reformed Church was demolished after war damage.] I was christened there by the pastor, Dr Guinness Rogers… Dr Rogers was a very eloquent preacher who attracted a large congregation. On his retirement in January 1900, he was presented with a purse of one thousand pounds, in recognition of his long ministry which he commenced in 1865. The Church was renowned for its choir, and Joseph Tapley (who afterwards became famous as a vocalist) was the leading tenor. The choir was under the direction of Mr Clement Colman, a member of the famous mustard firm…

…In Wirtemburg Street (now re-named Stonhouse Street) was Denny's Dairy, which had been in the same family for generations. A familiar sight was their milk cart, which carried a milk churn on a platform only a few inches from the ground so that the roundsman could step on and off while the horse was going at a moderate pace…

…Mr Percy Thornton, Clapham's popular M.P. used to ride horseback to visit his constituents and often called to see Mr. Dunkley, who was one of his staunchest supporters. Also Mr. Floris, the artist who painted the popular picture "The Wedding in Matrimony Place". Dan Leno, the celebrated comedian who lived at 345 Clapham Road, used to pass the shop driving his smart little dog cart. One day he stared at me while I was dusting a piano in the window. He opened the door, and looking round the corner, said: "Do you know who I am?" I replied: "Yes, I have seen you in many a pantomime at Drury Lane." "That's right," he said. "Is that a good piano?" indicating the one I was dusting, and as it happened to be one of our finest models, I could recommend it with confidence. He took me at my word, and immediately wrote a cheque for it – the quickest and easiest sale I ever made...

...The old South London Tramway Company always paid a good dividend to its shareholders, but the line was taken over by the L.C.C. [London County Council] in 1899 and I think I am right in saying that no further dividend has ever been declared. The line was electrified in 1903, and May 15th was a gala day for Clapham when the Prince and Princess of Wales (later King George V and Queen Mary) drove the first tram along the route. It was enamelled white all over, with gilded decorations and garlanded with flowers; it was kept in the Clapham Depot for a long time as a souvenir of the occasion. On this great day, the High Street was gaily decorated with flags and bunting and Mr Dunkley invited a good many of his prominent friends and customers to view the procession from the roof of the shop. There was a large skylight in the roof which gave light to the far end of the shop, and one of the ladies returning from the show, trod on one of the panes of glass, and her leg came through quite a long way. Inside the shop were many viewing the procession from the front

Denny's Dairy, Wirtemburg (now Stonhouse) Street

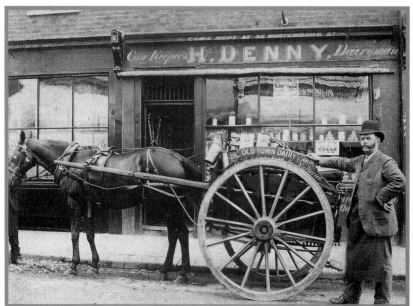

window, including the shop boy. He saw the accident and burst into such a fit of uncontrollable laughter that I thought he would never cease… Fortunately, the lady escaped with only a slight cut on the leg which was promptly attended to by her friends…

…Eagle House… the only remaining portion of the old house is known as "The Room" (the meeting house of the local branch of the Plymouth Brethren) which, I believe, was the old billiard room, shews how far back the house lay from the Common. [This building at the top of Narbonne Avenue was restored in 1989 for use as his own office by structural engineer, Sinclair Johnston]…
…The first Picture Palace was The Globe quite a small affair, at the corner of the Tram Depot; opened in 1910 & closed in 1915 owing to the competition of the Majestic. The second venture was the Electric Palace, also opened in 1910, and erected on the site of Tillings' stables in Venn Street. Later on an entrance was made in the High Street at the side of the Plough Inn [now The Goose and Granite]. It was on a larger scale than the Globe and enjoyed a fair amount of success, remaining open until 1920. The Clapham Pavilion, in the High

The Horse Ride, Clapham Common. Drawing by Frank Byford

Park Crescent Mews, Clapham Park Road. Byford

Street, near the Clapham Road Station arch, was opened in 1913 and still provides entertainments daily.

The outbreak of the Great War saw the opening of the present Majestic. Built on the stables of the large stores founded by E J Wright and opened by Miss Irene Vanbrugh on 27 August 1914. It was famed for its symphony orchestra, under the direction of the late George Pritchard, and later of M. Jean Michaud. I used to go sometimes on a Monday or Wednesday morning to help Michaud select the music for the films. We would sit in the front row of the balcony and the films would be run through in silence while we chose suitable music, (which used to include many pieces of my own composition). We timed the changes, made up our list, and afterwards looked out the necessary band parts from his huge library of orchestral music in a large room under the stage. Many people used to attend regularly, merely to listen to the music.

With the advent of sound films in August 1929, the orchestra was disbanded and a large theatre organ, supplying sound effects, was installed. This has now been replaced by a powerful gramophone, which can supply all the incidental music now required.

I vividly remember the sensational coup brought off by the then manager, Castleton Knight, (a big noise in the cinema world of today) who kidnapped Charlie Chaplin from an aerodrome and brought him to the Majestic by car, without Chaplin having any idea of his destination. It all passed off as a joke, and was a smart advertising stunt. [It is now thought that this incident is unlikely to be true. Castleton Knight was renowned for his publicity stunts and it is more likely that he employed a Charlie Chaplin "look-alike"]...

...When the 1914 war started all the men in Dunkley's piano factory had to join up immediately, as they belonged to the Volunteers, who were the first to be called up, and to supplement our stock of pianos, Mr Dunkley was in the habit of trading with a firm of piano makers in Camden Town, named T G Payne & Co., who made a very similar instrument to Dunkley. The name of the traveller was Coward, who turned out to be the father of the famous Noel Coward. Noel was only a boy then, but his father often talked to me about his clever son, and said he thought he had a great future as a dancer! In his autobiography Noel Coward mentions that his father travelled for a piano firm. When his father died, he and his mother took apartments in the house next door to Brook House, on the South Side opposite the long pond...[See Chapter 2 – where Noel Coward's autobiography mentions that his father also lived at this house]

...The Clapham Common Murder: Clapham has been particularly free from sensational incidents, but its quietude was rudely awakened on the morning of New Year's Day 1911, when the body of a man was found on the Common, near the path known as "The Bishop's Walk". It proved to be a Mr Leon Beron, a Russian Jew from Whitechapel. He had been stabbed to death, and a letter S was cut into the cheek. This led to the arrest of Stinie Morrison, an ex-convict on licence, who was arrested in a few days. After a sensational trial he was found guilty of the murder and sentenced to death, which was later commuted to penal servitude for life. He died in Parkhurst Prison in 1921, and thus ends Clapham's one and only murder in my time...[See Chapter 2]

... [one of the houses on North Side] was occupied by the Watson family, who were the proprietors of Watson's Magic Cleaners. The two sons were very gay, noisy young men; they each bought a sports motor car – one was painted a bright yellow, which was an innovation in those days, and they used to race each other round the Common. Anyone who lived in Clapham would remember them.

FRANK BYFORD, *Personal Reminiscences 1880–1914,*
Unpublished manuscript c1940
in the possession of Bernard Battley

PEACE AND WAR

Noel Coward *(1899-1973), the playwright and songwriter,*
was born in Twickenham, but the family moved to Battersea
when he was quite young. In his autobiography, he describes travelling
to the Chapel Royal choir school in Clapham.

A SHORT WHILE AFTER WE HAD SETTLED in Battersea Park... It was agreed that
I should go to the Chapel Royal school to begin with until I was old enough to
have my voice tried for the choir itself. The school was in Clapham [in Park Hill],
and was run by a Mr. Claude Selfe. It was small, consisting only of the twelve
Chapel Royal boys, and seven or eight outside pupils of whom I was one...

...I travelled to school daily by tram, or rather, two trams, as I had to
change half-way. The second one landed me at the 'Plough',[now The Goose and
Granite] Clapham, and from there I walked, in anguish in the mornings, and on
wings of song in the afternoons when I was on my way home, loitering on
autumn days to collect 'conkers,' and occasionally ringing a few bells just to
celebrate the joyful hours of freedom separating me from the next morning.
There was a second-hand book-shop on the way where I could buy 'back
numbers' of the *Strand Magazine* for a penny each, and I hoarded my pocket

money until I could buy a whole year's worth in order to read the E. Nesbit story right through without having to wait for the next instalment...

In about 1913 the family moved to live in Clapham

...While I had been away a long-discussed move had taken place, and the flat at Battersea Park had been left in favour of an upper maisonette on the south side of Clapham Common. It was a very tall house called 'Ben Lomond,' and was owned by a Mrs White and Miss Pitney, her sister, who inhabited the ground floor and basement while we had the rest of the house. The rooms were much bigger than those we had had in the flat, and looked straight out across the Common in the front, and on to a large private garden at the back. I had a tiny bedroom at the very top, situated next door to the kitchen in which we usually had our meals, because we couldn't afford a servant. Mother, I think, was unhappy but she didn't show it, and for my benefit treated the cooking and washing and floor-scrubbing as a lark. Eric, my brother, then aged eight, and I, helped with

The original 'padded cell' trains used on the City and South London Line, now the Northern Line, until the 1920s

the washing-up, and enjoyed it, anyhow for the first few days.

Clapham Common was a nice place to live. There was a pond opposite the house on which Father used to indulge his passion for sailing a model yacht in the intervals of travelling for Payne's pianos. He never succeeded in infecting me with enough enthusiasm to last out longer than a quarter of an hour. Eric, however, was more docile, and used to squat on the opposite side of the pond from Father and turn the boat round with a walking-stick every time it crossed successfully. We used to take our tea out under the trees during the summer and play bat-and-ball afterwards. There were pleasant walks in Clapham along tree-shaded roads, neatly spaced with refined suburban houses, secure in small prosperity with their conservatories and stained-glass windows and croquet lawns. From the 'Plough' onwards down the Clapham Road the atmosphere became palpably commoner, but it was very lively on Saturday nights, particularly at Christmas-time when the shop windows were gay with tinsel and crackers and paper-chains, and the poulterers' and butchers' and greengrocers' were glaring yellow caves of light, with the slow-moving crowds on the shining pavements silhouetted against them.

In order to get from Clapham Common to the West End you travelled either in a Number 88 bus, which took a long time, or in the City and South London Tube, changing at the Elephant and Castle into the Bakerloo, which was quicker.

The City and South London has now been transformed into a spacious network of efficiency, but then it was unique in uncomfortable charm. The trains were smaller than any of the other tubes and rattled alarmingly, and over it all there brooded a peculiar pungent stink which will live somewhere in the back of my nostrils for ever...

...I can close my eyes and ears now and conjure up completely the picture of Mother and myself late at night on our way from the theatre, Mother in a dust-coloured cloak over her evening dress, with a small diamanté butterfly in her hair, and me in a scrupulously pressed dinner-jacket suit (Lockwood and Bradley in the Clapham Road), rushing from the Bakerloo side at Elephant and Castle, down tiled passages with hot draughts flying up our legs until the well-known foetid City and South London smell met our noses and a distant screeching and rumbling soothed us with the knowledge that we had not, after all, missed the last train.

NOEL COWARD, *Present Indicative*, 1937

Frances Stevenson *(1888-1972) was a pupil at Clapham High School for Girls before the First World War. She later became the secretary, mistress and eventually, second wife, of the statesman, David Lloyd George, whose daughter had been her school friend. The school on Clapham Common South Side was demolished in the late 1970s and replaced by St Gerard's Close.*

AT CLAPHAM HIGH SCHOOL I tasted real happiness and a release from inhibitions. I thought it the most beautiful building I had ever been in, with its polished floors and staircases, its lovely central hall in which stood a statue of the Venus de Milo; the reproductions of Old Masters on the walls, and, above all, its opportunities for friendships with both girls and mistresses. There was an atmosphere of culture which my previous school had not possessed, and a regard for the individual which, to a certain extent, had been lacking there. One of my colleagues in the fifth form was Mair Lloyd George, the eldest daughter of the Liberal statesman. The family lived nearby. [In Routh Road, Wandsworth Common] Mair was a gentle and charming personality and I had particular reason to like her and be grateful to her, as she would often come to my help in my mathematical difficulties. She was good at mathematics: I was not, and she was always ready to explain away my problems. I liked her very much.

FRANCES LLOYD GEORGE, *The Years that are Past*, 1967

Percy Thornton *(1841-1918) was Unionist (i.e. Conservative) MP for Clapham from 1892 to 1910. The election of 1906 resulted in a landslide victory for the Liberals.*

THE DAY OF THE CLAPHAM ELECTION IN 1906 turned out far too exciting to attempt now to describe faithfully. I never realized that despite having been refused a hearing at a meeting in Nine Elms with Sir Samuel Hoare [a banker and Unionist MP] as a speaker, the friends of many years' standing, whose personal sympathy could scarcely have been alienated, had nevertheless repudiated the Unionist cause. Votes were going to that astute and able canvasser, my friend Mr. Frederick Low, K.C. [later Liberal MP for Norwich and a High Court judge], in shoals – men, many of whom had never voted Radical before, others previously classed as abstainers from all party politics, seemed then to have embraced enthusiastically the Radical programme. Personal and local influence was at its very "nadir," while the general trend of opinion over-whelmed Mr. Balfour's administration when the general election took place. And yet it is strange that these evident indications of "coming events" casting "their shadows before" never seemed to affect my inner confidence in the result at Clapham, the fact being that records of over 600, 2000 and 4000 majorities at three General Elections had seemed to mark the loss of Clapham as out of the range of practical politics, although on this occasion the chances were palpably equalized...

I was seldom out of the saddle on that cold, showery, and to me fateful day. Stones were thrown in the morning near the centre of New Road [now Thessaly Road], Nine Elms, and detecting an urchin nearly out of his teens with missiles in his hands I galloped the chestnut mare after him into Stewarts Road, where seeing me coming the youth fell prone on the ground crying "Oh, father! don't ride over me". But leaving him thoroughly well scared, I achieved the result that this form of annoyance ceased.

Late in the afternoon when crossing Clapham Common and in a bedraggled and tired state, both man and horse, I came up with my opponent in his carriage bedecked with Radical colours and asked how things fared with his campaign; to which query the reply came of a more than hopeful character. And very soon it was discovered what was the foundation for such assurance.

At the Battersea Town Hall were collected all the official Unionists to whose careful watchfulness, combined with unflagging energy, a smooth working of the local party organization had been due. But these popular experts were by no means sanguine as to the result, and one or two seemed really despondent. Nor were we encouraged as to the trend of events when, the counting for Battersea having concluded, John Burns marched triumphantly down the main staircase and announced in stentorian tones to the assembled municipal junto surrounding the Mayor "1600 majority," and this victory over such a strong assailant as Mr. Shirley Benn [Unionist candidate for Battersea, who later became an MP elsewhere and 1st Lord Glenravel] added to the already visible gloom on the faces of many Clapham Unionist supporters...

...Unable to gain outside information as to the progress made in the counting-room I asked Mr. Harnett [the Unionist agent] to find out and tell me how the fight went. Very soon he came down and suggested that I should go at once, and, as had been the case on former occasions, look after my own interests – voting seeming to be nearly equal and the last one or two boxes about to be counted. On arrival I found Mr. Low 30 ahead, and anxious glances were directed towards each batch of papers. Moreover a further slight Radical gain on the above figures was at the moment evident, when the officials placing the final box on the table, we all crowded round it. Its Thornton tendency was at once revealed, and the last turn of the political wheel of fortune restored their old Member to Parliament for the fourth time.

PERCY MELVILLE THORNTON,
Some Things we have remembered, 1912

Thornton's majority over Low was 96. Clapham remained a Conservative seat until John Battley won it for Labour in 1945 – see Chapter 5

Jack Hobbs

The cricketer, **Jack Hobbs** *(1982-1963) lived in Clapham for a time – first at 17 Englewood Road, where a blue plaque commemorates him, and later in Atkins Road in a house which has now been demolished. One brief passage in his autobiography relates an incident on Clapham Common in about 1906.*

A CURIOUS EXPERIENCE BEFELL ME at that time as the outcome of a visit to Clapham Common, where I went to watch a friend play. Some team or other had failed to turn up, and the rival team asked my friend and his party to make up a match. I was invited to join in, and I hit up a century, knocking some of the balls into the pond. Then I started to bowl and had the ill luck to smash the finger of a detective, who was in the opposing team. I approached to apologise, and, as we were standing around, he exclaimed: 'I've got you set; I know who you are.' His friends wondered what kind of criminal I might be, but he only told them my name at the end of the game, when they were as delighted as if I had been Crippen!

JACK HOBBS, *My Life Story*, 1935

At the end of 1910, there was public concern about violent crime by alleged anarchists among the immigrant community in the East End. The year had ended sensationally with the Houndsditch murders and the siege of Sidney Street. The murder of **Leon Beron** *on the Common on New Year's Day 1911 brought East End crime to Clapham.*

CLAPHAM COMMON MURDER MYSTERY. GRUESOME NEW YEAR'S MORNING DISCOVERY. EAST END LANDLORD'S TRAGIC FATE. New Year's morning brought to light the perpetration, under circumstances still shrouded in mystery, of a gruesome murder on Clapham Common, the victim of which has since been identified as Leon Beron (aged 47), a Russian Jew, who has been resident in the country for upwards of fifteen years, and last resided with one of his brothers at Jubilee Buildings, Jubilee Street, Mile End. The discovery was made at about 8 a.m. by a Cavendish Road constable, while patrolling "Bishop's Walk" – an asphalted pathway leading from the bandstand in a north-westerly direction towards Clapham Junction. Noticing something peculiar about the appearance of the furze bushes on one side of the path, the constable's further investigations disclosed the dead body of a respectably dressed man, to hide which most careful steps had been taken, the head resting on a pillow of dead leaves, whilst the face was covered with a coloured silk handkerchief. On this being removed, it was at once seen that the man's head had been battered in and was one mass of blood, whilst two stabs had been inflicted, after death had taken place, under the heart, whilst a number of similar injuries were found on the other side of the body. Apparently the corpse had been dragged some distance to its place of concealment, where those responsible for the outrage had proceeded methodically to cover up the traces of their crime, not only covering the face, as stated above, but also generally reposing the body as though for burial almost.

At once rumour, on account of the dead man's nationality, was inclined to associate the crime with the Houndsditch outrage, but the officials were at first more inclined to the theory of robbery, inasmuch as the deceased was known to have had something like £12 in his possession on Saturday night, besides a gold watch and chain, whereas only a halfpenny was found on the body, along with a bunch of keys and certain letters and papers which later served the purpose of establishing identity. Later the same day a working-man picked up, not far away from the spot, a pipe, which has since been identified as belonging to Beron, whilst a pen and a pocket handkerchief have also been found near by, the latter bearing different initials to those of the deceased man, whose father, it is said, was once a fairly well-to-do man, owning property in South London and other parts. Beron collected the rents of some of these properties and was said to have carried on a business as a "talleyman"; but as to how he came to be on Clapham Common is a matter which none of his friends and relatives are able to account for.

At the inquest the doctor who undertook the post-mortem examination gave a detailed and lurid description of the mutilated body, concluding:

Leon Beron... and his dead body on the Common

These [the wounds to the body] had apparently been inflicted after the head wounds, but while the deceased was still alive, though probably unconscious. The wounds on the head had apparently been inflicted by a blunt instrument of an angle-shaped character. It must have been a very deliberate thing, because there were certain distinct marks on the face which no ordinary murderer would have stayed to inflict. The principal of these were two 'S' shaped marks, one on each side of the face, which were too symmetrical to have been accidental, and for which there was apparently some motive.

THE CLAPHAM OBSERVER,
6 January 1911

Steinie
Morrison

Steinie Morrison, a Ukrainian
refugee living in the East End of London
was charged with the murder and a long
and complicated trial ensued.
*A key witness was **Andrew Stephens**,*
a cabman, whose evidence provides
a glimpse of London travel at those times.

ANDREW STEPHENS EXAMINED BY Mr MUIR [Prosecuting Counsel] – I am a hansom cab driver. In the early morning of 1st January I was with my cab on the rank at Clapham Cross [by the present entrance to Clapham Common Underground Station], and while I was there I picked up a fare. I first saw my fare walking round the palings from the Old Town, Clapham. As he walked by I asked him "Cab, sir?" He walked a little way on, and turned and came to the cab, and told me to drive to Kennington. I drove him to Kennington and set him down between the Hanover Arms and the Oval Station of the electric railway directly opposite the Kennington Church. He paid my fare, I had an opportunity of seeing what the man was like. It was the accused – I am quite sure.

Cross-examined he gave further details of his journeys during the night

I came out on 31st December between two and three in the afternoon, and I got off the cab at half-past six next morning, after a spell of about sixteen hours.

During these sixteen hours I had four fares with the first horse and I think eight with the second, about twelve or thirteen fares, but I cannot say exactly, nor can I tell exactly how much money I earned, but I had nineteen shillings at the end of the day. The last fare I had before picking up the accused was from the Royal Hotel, Blackfriars to Cedars Road, Clapham. I should think I took about half an hour. The fare I had before that was from Leicester Square to Clovelly Mansions, Gray's Inn Road. I am not exactly sure what time it was when I got to the rank at Clapham Cross, but I got there just before the last tram went to Tooting. I should think I got to the cab rank somewhere between half-past one and two o'clock. I picked the accused up about an hour after the last tram went, but I cannot tell the time exactly. There is a large illuminated clock quite near the cab rank at Clapham Cross.

[Mr ABINGER – Defending Counsel] Do you mean to tell the jury that with the clock so near that cab rank you cannot tell us what time you picked that man up?

[ANDREW STEPHENS] No, I did not look at the clock. I was on the ground when the accused came up, and I put my rug round me to jump up on my cab. It was not cold that night; it was a beautiful night. When I got to the cab rank there were a four-wheeled cab and a hansom cab there, but when I saw the accused coming along I was alone on the rank.

Stephens was persistently questioned about the exact time
he picked up the accused

[Mr MUIR] Did you say to Sergeant Cooper, "I arrived there about 1.30"?

[ANDREW STEPHENS] – I told him I did not know the time, and I put on there as the last tram went away, that was the way. I told him then there were forty or fifty people waiting for the last tram, and there were tram people waiting there on this morning. That was why I put on the rank, and it was just before the last tram went that I put on the rank, I saw the last tram go, also the staff tram that runs afterwards and that was how the time was first thought of. I said it was about half-past one.

H FLETCHER MOULTON (Ed.), *Trial of Steinie Morrison*, 1922

Despite the judge's belief that there was insufficient evidence
for a conviction, the jury found Morrison guilty.
Reprieved from the death sentence by the Home Secretary,

*Winston Churchill, Morrison died in prison after serving
ten years of his sentence, protesting his innocence to the end.
Most subsequent commentators believe that Morrison
was wrongly convicted. Among them was the son of a local tram
conductor,* **Charles Dunbar**.

MY FATHER WAS A TRAM CONDUCTOR and, as he had to work 12 hours a day without a break (eight on alternate Sundays) my mother had to meet him, at least once a day, with his tea-can and sandwiches…

…Sometime in the '60s there was a radio reconstruction of the trial of Steinie Morrison… and, as I could clearly remember the excitement at the time, I listened and was particularly careful to take note when I heard a reference to "the last tram", by the time of which a cab-driver claimed to identify Morrison. Which last tram? There might have been seven from different directions heading for the depot. At the Old Bailey the witness changed his evidence and said he meant a special car taking staff to Tooting. His Counsel, properly instructed, could have destroyed this man's evidence, and I am convinced, after reading the report of the trial in the British Museum Library, and knowing the tram times from my records, that, neither on his evidence, or that of other witnesses, could Morrison have committed the crime, although he was convicted.

CHARLES DUNBAR, *letter to Peter Jefferson Smith,* 22 April 1991

Against stern opposition from her family,
Maud Chadburn *(1868-1957) became one of the first women
to qualify as a doctor. A surgeon at the Elizabeth Garrett Anderson
Hospital in Euston Road, she saw the need for
another hospital for women.*

IT WAS DECIDED THAT THE NEW HOSPITAL would be most serviceable in South London, the opposite pole from the E.G.A. Hospital, and that, if a large house could be found, it could be the nucleus of the new hospital. So, towards the spring of 1911, three people combed South London, looking for this large and suitable house. By about September, 1911, suitable accommodation was found on the south side of Clapham Common, two large houses with a large area of garden. One was occupied by Bishop Hook (bringing in rent), the other empty and ready for occupation. The latter could take 20 patients in addition to nurses and administrative staff. The price of the whole freehold was about £5,000. Doctors waiting for hospital appointments (two physicians, two surgeons, and a pathologist) were invited to join Miss Chadburn. They each agreed to give £10 towards the propaganda expenses, and to work their friends as hard as they could. By August, 1912, nearly £5,000 had been collected and in that month the site on Clapham Common was bought for about that sum. By this time, the Executive Committee had exhausted all their friends and subscribers, so they

The opening of the South London Hospital for Women by Queen Mary, 1916

decided to appeal to the public through the Press. People having weight with various papers were chosen and approached to find out if they were willing to undertake an appeal.

Lady Robert Cecil wrote to *The Times* and her appeal produced opposition from a medical man. He said that the needs of women patients were sufficiently catered for, and if such a demand (as was indicated by the promoters of the hospital) did, in fact, exist, it was an artificial demand and would not have existed at all had not women forced their way into the medical profession. He said that there was nothing to justify the expense involved in building such a hospital, etc. Miss Chadburn replied to his letter and a short correspondence resulted in *The Times*. Other press cuttings at the time showed that adverse opinions were not universally shared.

At this crucial moment, Miss Chadburn's rejoinder caught the eye of some friends of medical women. The result was astonishing. A representative called on Miss Chadburn, asked her how much money she needed to build a hospital and whether it could be certain always to be officered by women doctors, and to admit only women patients (no males over the age of 6). These friends gave in all £53,000 for the building of the hospital and an additional £40,000 for endowment (the latter was presented on the day Queen Mary opened the hospital). Their only further condition was that they, the donors, should remain anonymous for ever.

On hearing this, the dumbfounded Executive Committee considered that an out-patient department should be opened as quickly as possible and two houses in Newington Causeway were found suitable for this purpose.

Arrangements were made with a Nursing home for the use of a large room containing 4 beds and in this ward 51 hospital surgical patients were treated during the last eight months of the year (1912). Owing to a dispute in the building trade, the in-patient building was not commenced until August, 1913, but progressed well after that date.

In 1915, owing to the war, there were delays in the building. It was noticeable that all the workmen on the building had white hair, the young ones having joined the Forces. On July 4th, 1916, H.M. Queen Mary opened the new building erected on the South Side of Clapham Common, having 80 beds.

MAUD CHADBURN *quoted in*
MISS MARGARET LOUDEN, *The South London Hospital
for Women and Children, 1958*

Dr Wilkins *(1858-1919) had a surgery on the corner of*
Wandsworth Road and The Chase, and lived at 66 Lillieshall Road,
where Mary, his second daughter, was born in 1908.
In 1919 Dr Wilkins retired due to ill-health and moved to
Westbrook, near Margate. He died two months later.
In 1987 Mary Wilkins wrote a slim volume of recollections
of her childhood in Clapham.

Mary Wilkins

LIFE WENT ON ITS EVEN COURSE until one day father came in exclaiming, 'I say we have declared war on Germany!' August 4th 1914 had arrived! Not that this news meant much to me at first – I was within easy reach of my sixth birthday. There was general dismay and bustle in the kitchen – the older boys talked for ages at the back door, and everyone said: 'It will be a walkover' etc., etc. The Kaiser had other ideas about it!

Christmas came and still the war went on. After breakfast each day we knelt down at our chairs and prayed for the soldiers: not that I did personally – my nose got rubbed by the seat of the chair and my knees ached, but that was the extent of my contribution!...

...One by one our younger doctor friends disappeared, and now and again came back to visit us in khaki. When I asked why father was not in uniform I was told that they would not accept him owing to his heart condition. I worked out in my mind that to go every day to the medical boards and do his own patients and as many of his absent friends as he could get in, was much harder work than putting on a smart uniform and 'Going to the front', wherever and whatever that was!

Gradually our staff and our young friends grew fewer – ammunitions factories, V.A.D. [Voluntary Aid Detachment] work and land work called them. Gracie Fields and other actors and actresses gave their time and talents to the troops – at home and overseas…

…Then came the air raids – the first daylight one came in the morning. My sister had gone to the bakers – Mr Dod rang up to tell us not to worry, he had 'put Miss Mildred down the cellar with the sacks of flour'. Mrs Wyatt who was cleaning the steps rushed indoors saying, 'Oh, Ma'am, oh Ma'am, those Germans are here'. Then she threw up her hands and said, 'Oh, me broom, me broom – I can't have they Germans bombing me broom', and rushed back up the area steps to fetch it…

…Then the Zeps [Zeppelins] started coming over – how well I remember father standing on the top of the garden steps with me in his arms watching this huge airship go over! It was dark and the searchlights made it look pink. Over our garden it went, quietly humming. Suddenly, there was a roar, a flash and a mighty explosion as a Zep burst in half. Resounding cheers rent the air. We had brought down our first German Zep – at Potters Bar. Food became short. You queued up for an hour or more outside the shop to buy your butter etc., and just as your turn came, the door was firmly shut and locked and a notice 'sold out' put up. Potatoes were scarce – the shop people appeared up at the house now and again with *our* potato –'For the Doctor's baby'. Though I was turned seven years old!

Meat was scarce but our friendly butcher did us as well as he could and mother, who had taken over the kitchen, made splendid concoctions with bones and vegetables and 'Edwards Dessicated Soup' and whatever she could get. Dumplings took the place of meat most days, but we usually had meat of some sort for Sunday dinner which we all had together, father being in. Now and again mother came by a tin of corned beef with which she made a really luscious stew, plus more bones and dumplings. Oxo cubes were the mainstay of our lives – and after all these years they are still in the shops.

Days came and days went, and nights too. During air raids at night I sat under the big billiard table in our basement dining room, accompanied by the dog and the cat, eating porridge with treacle on top. I was never frightened in the raids – was it the porridge and treacle, or was it that I had not the slightest idea of danger?

Father, of course, had to go out during the raids to help with the victims – there were victims although I was quite oblivious of the fact. By the time 1918 came, father's health was giving out. Well do I remember November 11th, 1918. It was a dark wet day. When the news came through and all the rockets went off, mother had to go up to the consulting room, where father kept his large collection of flags, and get out the largest Union Jack, plus a long thick bamboo curtain pole. Father sat in his chair by the dining room fire and fastened the flag to the end of the pole. He was too ill to go upstairs himself, so mother, accompanied by me and the dog, took it up to the top floor and hung it out of the window. It seemed quite unbelievable that war was really over.

Rejoicing went on everywhere by rich and poor alike – bands, good and bad, singing and inevitably pub parties ending with free fights all round.

MARY WILKINS, *Lillieshall & After,*
Recollections of the daughter of a Clapham doctor, 1987

During the First World War The Times *journalist,*
Michael MacDonagh, *lived in Abbeville Road in a house*
backing on to the grounds of the Notre Dame Convent.
The convent was demolished in 1947 and Notre Dame Estate
built on the site. He gives a vivid account of the bombing
of South London.

September 24, 1916 (Sunday)

I WAS SITTING IN MY ROOM READING about twelve o'clock last night when, through the slightly parted curtains of the glazed door (leading to a balcony which overlooked the grounds of the Notre Dame Convent, Clapham Common), there penetrated a ray of intense white light. Wondering what it could be I stepped out on the balcony, and saw the convent and its grounds made more vivid to the eye by a dazzling light streaming from the sky than I have ever seen them in sunlight. My conjecture that the light was associated with an air raid was confirmed by an explosion which had in it something of the roaring crackling of forked lightning. Then suddenly the strange light went out and the darkness of night enveloped the familiar scene...

...I went to the front door of my house, facing south-east, and again the light appeared, revealing a wide area, and I heard explosions of bombs in quick succession apparently near at hand. It then occurred to me that the mysterious light implied that the Germans with their devilish ingenuity had invented a bomb of a terribly destructive kind, which was being used by the raiders. But in this I was mistaken, as I found out afterwards. I caught no glimpse of the Zeppelin; and no wonder, for, by the use of flares, or Very lights – as was explained to me later – he hid himself behind a screen of dazzling and baffling glare which the searchlights that were probing for him could not penetrate. The explosions became fainter as the raider rapidly pursued into the distance his destructive way. Soon came the tremendous relief of silence, and the twinkling of stars in the darkened and empty void. Night was again upon us "with her train of stars," but not, as Henley adds, "with her great gift of sleep." We were all very much awake…

Some time later he had an alarming experience on his journey home to Clapham

…Arriving at the "Horns" public-house, at the end of Kennington Road, opposite Kennington Park, I was relieved to see a tram coming down Kennington Park Road, heavily curtained and almost noiseless. What luck – it was a Clapham tram too. It had about a dozen passengers. The conductor told

Zeppelin, German Naval Airship L13, 1916

me that he and the driver had left the tram and taken shelter from the raid in a tube station, and when the lull came, being anxious to get home, decided to take advantage of it to run their car to the Clapham garage. Our only comfort was the deep silence of the night. At Stockwell stopping point, which is about half-way, that silence was shattered by a sound that made us quake. It was a rocket signal that the raiders were returning to resume their devilish moonlight revels! It explained the long lull...

...Most of the passengers bolted for the Stockwell tube station. Only three girls – programme-sellers at a theatre – and myself were left in the car when it continued its journey. About five minutes later the guns began to roar. The conductor and driver decided to go on, and advised us to remain in the car until we got to Clapham Common, where we could take refuge in the tube station. It was, in fact, the only course open to us with any degree of safety. It would have been a crazy thing to have got out of the tram, as the girls thought of doing, on the chance of a door of a house being opened to our knock asking for shelter. When we reached Clapham Common I rushed the girls to the tube station. There I was confronted by a situation so extraordinary that it astounded me.

The iron lattice-door of the station was closed, and through its chequered bars I could see that the booking-hall was packed with men, women and children. Its congestion afforded no proper shelter from the raid – the people would have been better off in their homes – and its state could only mean that the safer places, the platforms below and the stairs leading to them, were so crowded as to be inaccessible. Two policemen were inside the gates, and what really staggered me was that one of them, when the girls and I asked for admission, lifted up a large piece of cardboard, on which was printed in bold lettering: "Full up; no more room." Two of the girls dropped to the pavement in hysterics. And no wonder, for the barrage was now terribly affrighting. There was not only a mobile field-gun blazing away on Clapham Common, close at hand, but from the neighbouring Wandsworth Common I could hear the roar of the great gun we of Clapham called "Big Bertha," joining in the thunder of the other artillery of the London defences, near and far off. The policemen, moved by the pitiable condition of the two girls opened the gates and helped them into the booking-hall. I looked round for the other girl and saw her coolly walking away, homeward bound.

MICHAEL MACDONAGH,
In London During the Great War, 1935

The noted historian of Clapham, **Eric Smith** *(1907-1990)*
attended Clapham Parochial Boys' School from 1916-1919.
In his history of the school he described life there during the
First World War. The school, now called Macaulay School, has moved to
Victoria Rise, while the former school building is a private house.

IT WAS AT THIS PERIOD THAT ONE SMALL BOY (who shall be nameless) crept unwillingly into the school in Macaulay Road in the spring of 1915. He was a very shy, small boy who has no real recollection of that first day, but remembers regularly during the period that followed hanging his coat and school cap in the little room near the entrance and then wandering off down the long corridor which ran the length of the building on the left hand side. On the right were four classrooms divided from one another by glazed partitions which could be folded back, so that on occasions the school could be made into one large hall. It was one of the minor enjoyments of school life to be allowed to do the folding and to crash the sections back against the wall. The desks were of the old-fashioned variety with hinged seats (very hard) and a hinged top which could be turned up, when not in use for writing. There was a ledge which contained a small china inkwell and a depression in which pens and pencils could be placed. For the senior class there was a school library of which the small boy, being a voracious reader even in his earliest days, made good use. But of his lessons or his school books, he now remembers very little.

In a sanctum near the front door lived the Headmaster, Mr. L. H. Pritchard, a kindly man, but one whom nevertheless the small boy avoided visiting if this was at all possible. School reports which have somehow survived show that his first teacher was Miss H. F. Clarke, who had been appointed in the same year as a result of Mr. Dormer being called up for military service. Alas, after 60 years or more, her feminine charms have left no impression on his mind. He has pleasant memories, though, of Mr. A. F. Bowyer who had joined the forces in 1916 but was discharged the following year owing to ill-health. It was he who, in 1919, pushed this no longer very small boy forcefully and with inexplicable success through the trials and tribulations of what was then known as a Junior County Scholarship. Classes were large in those days. Class 3B contained 56 boys of whom the subject of these paragraphs was number 10; 2B had only 30; 1B fluctuated between 29 and 32; and 1A, the top class, had 46 boys; and here, in his last term, he managed to be number 3 and a monitor, and no doubt he went home and was suitably pleased with himself when he saw Mr. Pritchard's "He has done well" on his last report.

What other memories come back? During the morning "break" the boys played on the Common in front of the Parish Church (the girls in those days were segregated far away in Old Town), and on Fridays there were games of cricket and football thereabouts. An ability to forget names, though not faces, is a trial that now besets him, but he recalls Chapman, James, Jackson, Phipps, Richards, Triggs and Tunesi among the many who have passed into oblivion. On special occasions (Ascension Day was one), there were services for the school at church and then a half holiday in the afternoon, and the highlight of the year was Empire Day when the children, with their parents and friends, gathered in the large garden of the vast Victorian rectory almost opposite the School. Each child had a Union Jack and there was much parading and singing of hymns and traditional songs and *Land of Hope and Glory*, followed by prayers and an address by the Rector. After the National Anthem came lemonade and buns beneath the shady trees on the lawns of that long departed pleasance. These were the days of the First World War, a catastrophe that signified little to a boy of eight, or even eleven. An occasional air raid meant lack of sleep and a search next morning on the way to school for pieces of shrapnel from the shells of anti-aircraft guns; and there are memories of watching from the Common what must have been one of the earliest daylight battles in the sky. And one night there was a fiery glow in the northern sky visible from the windows of his home, as an enemy Zeppelin crashed to the earth in flames. And then there was all the excitement of the first Armistice Day, on the eleventh hour of the eleventh day of the eleventh month [1918]. And that is all the old boy remembers.

ERIC E F SMITH, *Macaulay School,*
The Story of a Church School 1648-1987,
1988

LIFE BETWEEN THE WARS

*The novelist and critic, **Pamela Hansford Johnson** (1912-1981),
spent her childhood in Clapham. Her father, a colonial administrator
on the Gold Coast, was rarely home on leave, and she and her mother
lived with her mother's parents on Battersea Rise. Her grandfather,
once a musician and dancer, was for the last 25 years of his life,
Henry Irving's treasurer.*

OUR HOUSE, DESPITE ITS UGLY FAÇADE, had a bizarre attraction within. My grandfather had a charming taste in wallpapers: the drawing-room, deep blue and gold-flecked, was adorned in the middle by one of the innumerable perks that came from Irving – a chandelier from his production of *Henry VIII*. I cannot say the same of his taste for furniture: he brought some horrible rocking-chairs back from San Francisco, and some really dreadful pieces of yellow maple, including a desk that was also a souvenir cabinet, filled with such objects as emus' and ostriches' eggs.

The hallways were hung with Irvingiana: Beckett loomed just inside the door, Ellen Terry as Lady Macbeth, hung beside it. Satin programmes, from Royal performances at the Lyceum, abounded: I now regret that I have given so many away, kept so few, of those left to me by my Aunt Kalie. Though I could never have seen Irving or Terry, I was told so much about them, that I began to *believe I had*: they remain a cult with me. I especially love Ellen Terry, because she was so ginger-golden, and because she had been so kind with gifts of toffees to my mother and my Aunt Kalie who, as children, had been at school at Eecloo, in Belgium.

But I was most permanently impressed by the books in my grandfather's library, mostly Irving's rejects. There was, above all, the Irving edition of Shakespeare, enthrallingly illustrated by Gordon Browne: it was from this that I learned my Shakespeare at a very early age, just spelling out the captions and then seeing where they fitted into the text. I had read the whole canon by the age of eight, though with what degree of comprehension I shouldn't like to say. Then there was *The Life of Sir Stamford Raffles* (dull), *The Arabian Nights* (expurgated), the complete works of Washington Irving, a few volumes of Dickens, and a medley of other books.

One book we did not have, was one grandfather had destroyed in a rage. He had always detested Irving's secretary, Bram Stoker. One day he came home with a greyish volume in his hands, and said to his children, 'Stoker has written a beastly book. It's all about people who suck other people's blood and lunatics who eat flies.' He put it straight on the fire. It was, of course, the first edition of *Dracula*...

Her father, who spent rather too much time drinking whisky and playing poker, died relatively young while home on leave, leaving the family nothing but debts

...It was some time before my father's death that we began to feel the pinch. No more were we able to keep open house, as my grandmother had done, on Sunday nights, the table covered with roast chickens, pies, jellies and wonderful trifles. Our 'musical evenings', which we much prized, became fewer and fewer. (They were somewhat better than average, because we were able to draw on many professionals.) My mother and I left our flat at the top of the house to make way for lodgers, and shared the semi-basement sitting-room as a bedroom. All manner of lodgers passed through our hands: one was speedily removed, being suspected of sleeping sickness: one, a rubicund Welshman, got into fights on the stairways with my Uncle Charlie: one, who posed as a doctor living with his sister, sat quietly upstairs manufacturing pornographic literature, until the police caught up with him.

All this seemed to me great fun, and I was surprised to hear my Aunt Kalie mourn that my grandmother, could she see, would be deeply distressed by the relative poverty indicated by the state of the larder.

But when my father died, things had to alter more radically. I was then at Clapham County Secondary School [now Thomas's Preparatory School], for which my mother paid fees of £5 a term. She had to plead with an acquaintance among the governors that this should be remitted, which it was. She took in typing, to bring a little money into the house, for R.K.'s [her late husband's] debts lingered on, and death did not appear to cancel them. She had some interesting clients, among them Mr Hsiung, author of *Lady Precious Stream*, and the son – or grandson – of Buffalo Bill. To see the last coming down our area steps on Battersea Rise, with Stetson hat and long white flowing locks, was something of an experience.

And I – few clothes, and meagre pocket money. But I adapted to all this without pain. I had my own plot in our long back garden, with poplars and a cherry tree, and had cultivated it as I pleased, never at a loss for bedding out plants and packets of seed. Now, at times, my mother would find me a hard-to-spare twopence, and I would go out in a delight hitherto unfelt to buy a root of pansies, or of pink-tipped daisies: to put in this one plant gave me more pleasure than putting in all the plants previously at my disposal. Poverty was rather fun, though it was nicer whenever it stopped hurting, like the old story of the lunatic banging his head against the wall because it was such a joy when he ceased to do so...

Her paternal grandparents also lived close by just off Broomwood Road

...On my way home from school, I would call in once a week at Grandmother Johnson's house; usually, with great laboriousness, she would extract from the reticule beneath her skirt, a sixpence. I did sense that she could ill-afford it, and indeed, when she continued the practice after my adolescence, was very embarrassed...

...When I was born in 1912, the Johnson side of the family had left the country and had created a curiously countrified atmosphere about them in a small villa off Broomwood Road, where I was later to go to school. The house was rather fusty, smelling of lavender, biscuits, and something quite indefinable.

Grandmother Johnson and Aunt Minnie provided enormous high teas for me and my two cousins: ham, salad, pears and custard, and cream cakes. Outside was a small garden with a laburnum tree. My cousin Kenneth and I used to go and pop the pods. It never occurred to us to eat their contents, which I now know was lucky for us.

The poet,
Dylan Thomas
(1914-1953),
had a romance with
Pamela Hansford Johnson
and came to stay at her house
in Clapham on two occasions.
The proposed marriage
did not take place.

Pamela Hansford Johnson and Dylan Thomas

In February 1934 I invited him to stay with us for a few days in the house on Battersea Rise. This time we were, of course, fully prepared to fall in love.

He arrived at the door, palpably nervous. After a brief exchange of courtesies, his first words to me were 'Have you seen the Gauguins?' There was a Gauguin exhibition in London at the time. He afterwards told me that he had been rehearsing his query, which seemed an appropriate form of opening an exchange between artist and artist, all the way in the train from Swansea.

He was smallish: and looked smaller than he was because his clothes were too big. A huge sweater exaggerated a boyish frame. His trousers were baggy. (Though a maudlin Welsh friend who saw them hanging on a clothes-line, was once heard to drool – 'such *little* trousers!') He wore a pork-pie hat, revealing, as he took it off, the most beautiful curling hair, parted in the middle, the colour in those days – when he washed it – of dark gold. But in the curiously-shaped face, wide and strong at the top, tapering to weakness at the mouth and chin, there were those marvellous eyes, dark brown, luminous, almost hypnotic.

Then, there was the magnificent organ voice. At that time, it had lost all the Welsh lilt: Dylan, like his father, spoke standard English. He was to recover the lilt later on, when it came in useful.

My mother was as enraptured with him as I was, and spoiled him as though he had been a child. He didn't in the least appear to mind this; even, he welcomed it. He would offer no resistance when, going off to meet friends, she suggested that he might wash his neck. Dylan and I talked late into the three or four nights that he stayed with us. About art. About music. About the novel. About poetry.

He knew all about the last. Otherwise, he was inclined to stupendous bluffing. He did not, I think, know much about the classic novels, except in the most surface fashion. Of painting, very little. Of music, very little too: though he chided me for admiring Wagner. But he could hold forth, in that resounding voice, upon all these things, and he did. After all, he was only nineteen.

Between these sessions of one-upmanship, we played the gramophone: Dylan particularly liked an old 78 record of a then popular, but now forgotten, favourite: a jolting tune, with the rhythm of a train, called 'The Beat of my Heart'. I cannot pretend that whenever I hear it I think of him: because I never do hear it.

We drank a little beer, which Dylan fetched from the off-licence. I must emphasise that at this time, and for some time afterwards, whatever he himself said, he was not a habitual drinker. It was true that he arrived at our house with a quarter bottle of brandy in his pocket, but that could not be expected to go far. Drinking was, for him, one of the great romantic necessities of the poet's image: he fantasticated his drinking. Later, tragically, the fantasy became the reality. The other two necessities were, to become tubercular, and – extremely oddly – to get fat.

The few days drew to an end, with tension between us, but nothing said. The letters went on: Dylan wrote to me that he loved me. In the spring he came back to stay with us. I don't know how long the stay was scheduled to last this time, but in fact it lasted about six weeks. We were deliriously happy. We talked of marriage, certainly we would marry some day, when Dylan had a job. He talked of becoming a bicycle salesman, doing his rounds in yellow rubber hood, cape and boots. 'When bicycles hang by the wall,' he would sing blithely.

We would make trips across the river to Chelsea – to both of us having an aura of high romance – and sit in the garden of the Six Bells, near the little fountain that dripped its tears, while we watched the shadows of the players on the bowling-green grow longer as the sun fell. (A part of the Six Bells, including the fountain, was destroyed in the war. On my sixtieth birthday the Manager – prodded, I think, by an imaginative friend of mine – sent me a piece of that fountain as a present, in memory of Dylan and myself. It is in my own small garden now.) We had great walks over Clapham Common, over those vast fields above which the stars were clear and the lovers lay in the dark – it was hard not to tread on them – to a favourite pub. It was about that period, or before it, that Dylan wrote 'Altarwise by Owllight'. An American critic bemused me by saying that it revealed Dylan's deep knowledge of astronomy. All Dylan knew about the subject was that he could recognise the Plough. 'Look!' he would say, pointing ecstatically upwards, 'I do know that. That's Charles's wain, "over the new chimney!"' [The chimney was that of the recently built Battersea Power Station]

PAMELA HANSFORD JOHNSON,
Important to me: Personalia, 1974

James and Anne Lamb married and raised a young family in Clapham between the wars. Their elder son, **John Lamb**, *writing in 2001, recalls his childhood.*

THE TWENTIES WERE NOT AN EASY TIME for many families, but my mother Anne, a nurse, had her banns called at Chelsea Old Church and married my father, James Charles Lamb, in St James' Church Clapham Park in June 1926. The wedding breakfast (reception) was held at Carpenters a well-known local restaurant, bakers and caterers on The Pavement (the space now occupied by Iceland supermarket). Many years later my brother David and Annemarie had their reception at the same place after their wedding at Holy Trinity.

I was born in June 1927 in a nursing home in Bolingbroke Grove, Wandsworth Common, and in April 1930 my brother David followed in a nursing home in Cedars Road, adjoining St Saviours', the daughter church of Holy Trinity, later destroyed in the bombing.

As was the custom of the time, we lived in flats in various parts of Clapham. I remember especially our move to 109 Elms Road [now 42 Elms Crescent] in Clapham Park. This was in February 1936 when stories of the Spanish Civil War were making the headlines in the national newspapers. For us schoolboys, this was a very happy period. We played with our friends in local roads, and often ventured on to the Common with its boats on the Eagle Pond, opportunities for tiddler fishing, climbing trees and playing football on the wide grassy areas.

The side roads were almost completely free of motor traffic, although our next door neighbour owned a car and a local doctor actually owned two identical cars. Most delivery vehicles were horse drawn. Carter Paterson, Pickfords, the Anglo-American Laundry and numerous coal merchants had sturdy single animals. The refuse collection contractors had large shire horses or percherons for their van type vehicles. When the van was fairly full a fresh van would arrive on a large pick-up lorry with ramps, the refuse horse was detached and harnessed to the new van; the full van was taken away to the wharf in Wandsworth, a neat and interesting operation to little boys.

Lighter "vanner" horses were used by greengrocers, bakers and other traders including the cats' meat (horse meat) man. Perhaps most numerous were the Welsh cobs used by the United Dairies for their milk floats. These milk float horses were real characters who got to know the roads on their rounds, and the best stopping points for titbits from customers. Equally the milkmen were characters in the local fabric of the community, who kept an eye on the well-being of their elderly customers, sounding the alarm if milk was not taken in.

At Christmas time there were the Christmas boxes and drinks. As each round served a great many households, it sometimes happened (after a long hard day) that the milkman would fall asleep as he drove back to the depot. The horses, however, were determined to get back home, which they did on their own, and later when traffic lights were introduced, they stopped at red lights, only moving on the green.

Some of the lightest horses in use were those of Doubleday's Pies in Acre Lane, who distributed the firm's products in high two wheeled carts, returning at great speed along Abbeville Road. The more daring of the schoolboys attempted a ride on the back of the Doubleday carts. The cart drivers had whips to encourage their horses and drive off schoolboys, so those unsuccessful in securing a hold would call out to the driver: "Whip up behind, governor!" which usually had some effect.

Man power instead of horse power brought Walls ice cream by the "Stop me and buy one" tricycles, always a welcome sight in the summer. There were also French and Spanish onion sellers who came on their bicycles with long strings of onions, a lively young salesman with a hand barrow, pushing chairs around the roads singing at the top of his voice something that sounded like "Hi tiddly hi tie I have chairs to buy", and in the summer young women selling lavender and pegs. In the gaslit late afternoon in winter one heard the bell of the muffin man with his white cloth-covered tray on his head. There were also knife grinders who sharpened knives, shears, etc. and chair menders.

My brother and I went to Bonneville Road School, a large two storey building erected by the School Board for London following the 1870 Education Act. Boys were on the first floor and girls on the ground floor with separate playgrounds. There was also a single storey block for younger children. I can only remember one classroom painting (a seaman pointing out a sailing ship to two small boys) and there was far less colour in the classrooms. The desks (perhaps the original ones?) complete with inkwells and the carvings of generations of past boys were arranged in stepped tiers. A firm hand was maintained by use of canes and book.

A memorable occasion was when Queen Mary came to South London to open the new Municipal Building at Wandsworth in 1937, with school children lining the route along South Side. The Queen was in a closed car sitting bolt upright without a royal wave to anyone. We did get some time off from school!

Cover of a 1939 catalogue of Claud Butler bicycles

For transport there was the Southern Railways Station fully manned at the north end of the High Street, from whence local manufacturers' products like the famous Claud Butler bicycles were despatched [Claud Butler made racing bicycles at a works in Clapham Manor Street]. There was also a goods yard for timber and coal. There was, of course, the Underground which originally terminated at a station on the corner of the High Street and Clapham Park Road. Clapham entered the Thirties served by London County Council trams and the London General Omnibuses. A strange police ruling prevented wind-screens for years, leaving the drivers exposed to the weather; the effect after a snowstorm was extraordinary. This unease by the police meant the late fitting of covered tops to the buses. I can remember travelling up Clapham Park Road on an open top bus with its garden type seats and their mackintosh covers. With the coming of London Transport we had covered in trams and more modern buses.

The trams had a simple controller with power on one side and a strong brake on the other. There is a story of a tram following a brewer's dray along Long Road across Clapham Common. The driver of the dray was slow to respond to the tram's warning bell and, as the vehicles closed together, the tram driver mistakenly turned on more power resulting in the two great dray horses going like race horses to give the drayman the ride of his life!

Clapham had a large tram depot on the site now occupied by Sainsburys with entrances in the High Street and Clapham Park Road. The drivers and conductors, many of them weather-beaten ex-servicemen, were smart in collars and ties and silver buttoned uniforms with white tops to their caps in summer. The drivers often helped the washerwomen and flower sellers by taking their baskets into the front platform.

Summer holidays really started as we boarded the Eagle paddle steamers at Tower Pier. My parents always paid the supplement for seats on the upper deck, leaving my brother and me free to wander round the ship and visit the engine room to watch the great machinery driving the paddles. The first stop was North Woolwich where we were joined by crowds of jolly East-Enders followed by a quieter lot at Tilbury. It was then on to Southend Pier. After leaving the pier there were two routes for paddle steamers, one to Margate and Ramsgate and the other to Clacton and Walton-on-the Naze.

One year we went to Clacton when my father could only get away from work for a brief visit. He had worked on the trams for many years, in later years as a Regulator. He came down in his city suit and bowler hat and, listening to our pleas (or persuading) for a ride on the Big Dipper, found that on the first dip our car went down while my father's bowler hat flew straight on! With a hunt it was found below.

On our last holiday before the war in 1939 we travelled by the *Crested Eagle* from Ramsgate. A crowd of Cockneys got on board and in no time they were singing and dancing The Lambeth Walk and the popular song which included "We'll hang out the washing on the Siegfried Line while the Siegfried Line's still there". [The Siegfried Line was a defensive line built by Germany along the border with France.]

As well as the big shops in the High Street, far more and better than they are now, for people in Clapham Park there was Abbeville Road where the group of shops had an almost small town atmosphere. One of them was a grocer's shop run by the Lambert family who installed one of the early grocery vending machines. Each compartment was lit up and contained items like cheese, sugar, tea etc. to help the late shopper.

Other memories I have of the Thirties include seeing the glow in the sky when the Crystal Palace burnt down in 1936, and the biplane sky writer telling those on the ground to buy Persil and other products.

The last great personal event from the Thirties was my joining of the 21st Clapham Scouts based at High Street Methodist Church. I was taken to the Scout shop in Buckingham Palace Road, leaving with a green jersey, mauve scarf and a Baden Powell hat. My first trip out was with a group of scouts collecting old newspapers on Crescent Lane. I was placed to hold the end of the shaft of the two wheeled truck cart. Out of sight two fellow scouts had staggered out of a nearby house with one of the old tin baths filled with newspapers which they managed to place on the tailboard. The result was dramatic! I rose in the air and the contents of the cart ended up in a pile on my misguided companions!

Towards the end of the Thirties there was a general feeling of unease with memories of the First Great War. My father had volunteered with a large group of friends and had fought on the Somme and in Salonika, having problems with his wounds for the rest of his life. Like many who survived the War, he would never talk about his war experiences.

The horrors of the Spanish Civil War added to his distress. The Territorial Army had recruiting drives with demonstrations on the Common, showing off the latest weapons which included Bren guns and carriers (light armoured vehicles on which the guns could be mounted) There was much digging of trenches around shelters and plans for the evacuation of school children.

Looking back Clapham was beginning to change in the Thirties with a number of new buildings. The new building of the South London Hospital for Women, fully and professionally staffed by women, was built with money raised mainly by women, including my mother. A very enterprising lady built Halliday Hall on South Side as a hotel, which after the war became a residential place for Kings College students. [It was demolished in 1997 and replaced by Charleston House and Wakeford Close]. Blocks of flats were built facing the Common which included Woodlands and Okeover on North Side, Windsor Court and Trinity Close on The Pavement, Hightrees House and Thurleigh Court in Nightingale Lane and Westbury Court over Clapham South Station. The Trade Union headquarters for the Post Office Workers and the Building Trades Workers were erected in Crescent Lane and there were another six trade union headquarters in Clapham.

The London County Council, under the energetic leadership of Herbert Morrison, had started a big slum clearance programme in South London with the building of estates consisting of blocks of flats in Macaulay Road and Poynders Road, to house those displaced from Elephant and Castle. These newcomers produced mixed feelings and were not always made welcome. It was rumoured that this was part of a deliberate policy of putting likely Labour voters into previous Conservative areas, but these were the areas with space for new estates.

JOHN LAMB, 2001

Pamela Turner recalls her early school days
at Bonneville Road School in the 1930s

A BIRTHDAY IN NOVEMBER meant that I went into the Bonneville Road Infants' School in September 1933, some two months before becoming five years. As an 'only one' I was quite advanced for my age, so I by-passed the reception class and went straight into the one above. Hence I appeared in the group illustrating an African Kraal on Empire Day, 1934.

Our classrooms were 'stepped', each row of desks being one step higher than the row in front with the back of the class having the highest row of all.

Thus the teacher could easily watch each child - a real aid to class control! We sat two to a desk, but the reception class had little chairs. The hall had an open fire at one end around which was a high guard upon which the under clothes of those who had 'accidents' were dried after being washed through.

The school day ran from 9 am to 12 noon and 2 pm to 3.30 pm for Infants or 4 pm for the 'Big' children. We had chanting of tables and simple addition , learning to read and to write (with a pencil at first), we sang nursery rhymes and singing games and did physical training and craft work. The latter involved weaving coloured paper strips to make patterns and, later, learning to knit (boys as well!). We also made the usual drawings of family, house and friends, common to all generations of children.

There were coloured dots, black, white and red marked in rows on the parquet flooring of the hall, and we did our gymnastic exercises on these spots: legs apart, arms out to the side, bending and stretching, and 'running on the spot'. Lunch was from 12 noon to 2 pm and we all went home for it. The teachers cooked their own lunches in the Staff Room which was provided with a sink and a gas stove as well as a staff toilet. The childrens' toilets were across the playground in a shed and were cold and damp in winter, but at least they were water closets. My country friends had earth ones! At first we were put down to sleep after lunch, but as we grew older this custom was withdrawn, much to my relief.

The class photograph was taken in April 1936 prior to our 'going up' into the 'Big School' where we were segregated into 'Big Boys' and 'Big Girls'. Here we sang national songs as we marched in to and out of morning assembly.

Bonneville Road Infants School. April 1936

We learned all manner of skills and facts throughout both schools. I can still reproduce a map of a medieval village showing the manorial system of farming. Friday afternoons were the weekly relaxation time and we were allowed to take a toy or game into school or do some quiet craft work. While this took place we were read to by our teacher: stories from Hans Andersen, Millie Mollie Mandy, The Little Prince, Alice in Wonderland – a wide range which founded our interest in reading for ourselves.

Our games were seasonal in the playground and out of it; whips and tops, hoops and skipping ropes in spring and into summer, when we also played marbles and five-stones and chasing games of the 'He' variety in winter. Important occasions such as royal jubilees and coronations were marked by an extra half-day holiday, as was Empire Day on 24 May when the Brownies, Cubs and Boys' Brigade members could come to school in their uniforms. I remember standing on Clapham Common South Side with my little Union Jack to greet King George and Queen Mary on their Jubilee Progress through South London. Our teachers were largely women, all of them single unless widowed, as once married they had to leave the profession. They were a dedicated group, kindly but firm, who cared deeply for their pupils' welfare and educational growth. I still have this poem which was sent to me by my first teacher in 1933 when I was ill on my birthday:

> *'Once a little maiden (Pamela was She)*
> *Met a little measle, asked him home to tea.*
> *Foolish little maiden, from that thing begone.*
> *Don't you know one measle never comes alone?*
> *Every little measle, when he makes a call*
> *Brings all his relations, uncles, aunts and all.*
> *Little brother measles camp out on your chest;*
> *Little sister measles like your back the best.*
> *Little cousin measles climb up both your arms*
> *Blotch your face all over, spoiling all your charms,*
> *Till the doctor's physic, taken every day*
> *Makes those naughty measles scamper all away.'*

How many teachers these days, with the best will in the world, have the time to write to one very new little pupil? Thank you Miss G W Knight, Bonneville Road School and the old LCC.

PAMELA TURNER, 2001

George and Zette Cattermole, *both born in the area, married and lived in Clapham in the 1930s. It is tempting to think George might be descended from* **George Cattermole** *(1800-1868), the artist and illustrator of Dickens' novels, who also lived in Clapham.*

GEORGE: I was born at 126 Coldharbour Lane on 26 June 1910. It was a big ten-roomed French style house, which my parents ran as a boarding house.

Charlie Chaplin was boarding there the night I was born. My father was showing him the rowing cups he had won when they heard my first cries. Of course, most people were born at home then. At the time, Chaplin was playing a barber in a revue at the Camberwell Palace called Fred Karno Hummingbirds. He paid 12/6d a week for board and lodgings and he stayed there for two weeks. There were a lot of actors and actresses staying around Clapham and Brixton and it was very respectable and very sociable in those days.

At 16, George became an apprentice at a metal printing business where his father worked and he commuted to Shoe Lane off Fleet Street on the Underground

ZETTE: My mother had scarlet fever when I was born on 27 July 1914 and so did I, we were at the Fever Hospital in Landor Road. I lived at 87 Acre Lane, with my parents who were both French. He was a waiter at the Savoy and neither of them spoke English. I learned English at school of course, at a Catholic school. When I left school I worked for the soft furnishing company run by my mother and stepfather in Acre Lane.

GEORGE: We met in 1935 at a hotel workers' ball held in a hotel on the Embankment. A young, unknown Italian musician was playing with his band. He had slicked-back black hair and played my favourite *Diane* and I knew he would do well – Mantovani was his name. [He did later become a well-known bandleader] I saw Zette and was smitten. At the end of the ball I wanted to impress Zette so I offered to take her home to her mother's in Northbourne Road in a taxicab.

ZETTE: My mother had told me I must not get into a car or a taxi cab by myself or with anyone but that I must use public transport. Of course, in those days it was safer with all the other people travelling. So George escorted me home on the tram from the Embankment and we walked up Acre Lane to Northbourne Road.

We married in St James Church, Park Hill in 1936, one of the last couples to be married on a Sunday. The Dean of Clapham conducted the service at the church, not the one there now though. It was destroyed by a bomb in 1940. GEORGE: I was doing well in business then, earning £7 a week. I remember giving the Dean £2 after the Service which was a lot when you think that a coal miner earned £2. 5/- a week then. He was impressed and pleased. We had a lovely day, 20 people came back to Northbourne Road for a sit down lunch which Zette and her mother had prepared in the morning. We rented a top floor flat in Northbourne Road for £1. 6/- per week.

GEORGE AND ZETTE CATTERMOLE *interviewed by Annabel Allott*, 2001

In 1937 they left Clapham and went to introduce photo-gravure into New Zealand. The war stopped supplies, so George spent the war working in hotels and on hospital ships and Zette joined the Air Force. They returned to England after the war. (See Chapter 6)

Lord Callaghan of Cardiff *(b.1912), Labour politician, Chancellor of the Exchequer (1964-67), Home Secretary (1967-70), Foreign Secretary (1974-76) and Prime Minister (1976-79) lodged in Clapham as a young man.*

I LIVED AT NO 36 THE CHASE, which was a turning off the Common, half way down on the right hand side. One or two of us who were in the Inland Revenue used to frequent the café near the clock tower and take coffee and play chess, but I cannot recall whether it was a Lyons Café or a Kardomah, but at any rate we spent many happy hours there. The café used to provide the chess board and the set, but I cannot think that they did very well from one cup of coffee.

The Board of Inland Revenue transferred me from Maidstone to London in 1934, which is when I first stayed at No 36 The Chase, which was a semi boarding house with about seven or eight residents, and provided dinner at night. I lived there for only a matter of months before moving on. The reason I chose Clapham was that my wife was at that time living in a student hostel at 46 North Side. When she ceased to be a student, I left also and moved to

Lewisham. The house was run by a husband and wife who fiercely quarrelled and had the most furious disputes after we had gone to bed, during which they threw plates at each other, and we used to stand at the top of the stairs and listen.

At that time, the Common was much more peaceful than it is nowadays, and two or three of us who had been transferred to London from various places in the provinces by the Inland Revenue used to meet and sit there at the weekends because we had no money to do anything else after we had paid for our lodgings. What a far cry from the young people of today.

We also planned meetings there of the young people who were members of the Inland Revenue Staff Federation, in order to alert the union to our problems. We did this with some success.

One other feature I recall in passing is that at that time we were posted to a tax office near Tower Bridge and I once bet one of my young colleagues half a crown that I could walk from Tower Bridge to Clapham in under an hour. I won – half a crown was quite a lot of money in those days.

LORD CALLAGHAN OF CARDIFF,
letter to Peter Jefferson Smith, 2001

*Before the First World War, the Georgian terrace on North Side,
nearly opposite Holy Trinity, had been bought by the Westminster Hospital,
which was planning to rebuild there. After 20 years of neglect,
an advertisement appeared in* The Times*:*

> .... Lane, W.C.2.
> **66 "A WREN ROW," North Side, Clapham Common.
> —PURCHASERS for THREE HOUSES
> NEEDED to SAVE THIS TERRACE under a mainten-
> ance covenant ; five houses already secured under like
> terms.—Apply Society Protection Ancient Buildings, 20,
> Buckingham Street, W.C.2.**
> RUSSIA and THE LEAGUE of NATIONS .....

*Agnes Crosthwaite was one of the purchasers,
as her grandchildren,* **Susan Schlaefle-Nicholas**
and **Frances Blackhurst***, recall.*

SUSAN: Captain Dadd, Jock and Eve Le Maitre, Mr and Mrs Derry, Granny and Capt Dadd again, bought nos. 21, 20,19,18, 17 looking at the row from left to right, in December 1934. They all knew each other and told each other about the row being up for sale for demolition for more flats on the lines of Macaulay Square to be built, or for restoration.

FANNY: One of the reasons my grandmother chose Clapham was because she was not in the slightest bit conventional and was totally oblivious to fashion (she went to visit one of her husband's cousins, Margaret Kennedy the writer who lived in Kent, and caused a stir because she wasn't wearing stockings).

SUSAN: No 18 was done up in 1935 by Uriel Kahana and John Hilton who were in partnership as architects at that stage. Uriel was a qualified architect and still practising in Tel Aviv when I stayed with him there in the 60s. They designed the attic completely fitted out with Alvar Aalto stuff which was spot on avant garde of course in 1935. It was Granny's workroom. Moore [her brother, later Sir Moore Crosthwaite, UK Ambassador to Sweden] was nowhere on the scene by then as his first foreign posting was Baghdad in 1932, having come down from Oxford and spent the best part of a year in Berlin before joining the Foreign Office. By December 1936 the house must have been finished as I was christened in Holy Trinity Clapham on 12 January 1937.

FANNY: John Hilton, who built the wing of three bathrooms on the back of No 18, was a family friend; he had been at Oxford with Moore. We still have some of the blond furniture in use here in my house. I think Granny had been to America sometime in the early 30s to see psychiatric social work in action and because she had experienced US plumbing, wanted the same for No 18. She also had a very good Westinghouse electric fridge, which came back to No 18 in 1952 from our parents' house in Gloucestershire and lasted until 1976; my husband Jim remembers it well! She was given a replacement Electrolux (because of Moore's connection with Sweden) as an 80th birthday present.

I vaguely remember Betty Stucley [a novelist] who lived in No 13, the house with the lovely magnolia tree, but I don't know if she'd been one of the original group. Jock Le Maitre dabbled in oil paints and allowed me to join him on Sunday mornings. The Le Maitre front room in the basement was very exotically decorated. I can't remember why – was the original boiler a feature? I think he was developing Gatwick airport in the 50s. [Sir Alfred Le Maitre was a senior civil servant in the Ministry of Transport and Civil Aviation.]

SUSAN: I have war time memories of barrage balloons on the Common, of going by tram with Granny from Clapham to a bakery called Jeffreys in Lower Sloane Street where she used to buy the most delicious brown bread. I remember being taken, aged 5 or 6, on the 88 from Clapham to Whitehall and seeing Moore come out of the FO for lunch before he was posted to Moscow. 1942? – must have been before the end of the war. Also of playing with Michael Davidson from 17 blissfully exciting games of submarines in the wreckage in their garden. His mum must have been Capt Dadd's caretaker there and when Granny bought her Dolphin Square flat Mrs Davidson used to clean for her.

FANNY: Mrs Abbott cleaned No 18 before I arrived there. She lived in Macaulay Square and when she retired her daughter Mrs Harris took over and carried on until Alice sold up in 1984. [Alice Crosthwaite was the authors' aunt and guardian, distinguished as one of the first women to be a Factory Inspector and an indefatigable worker for social justice.] Mrs Harris told me that during the war they kept hens and a cockerel on the balcony outside her flat. Consequently she was able to advise me on hens' laying habits in wintertime when I moved to the country.

SUSAN: I also remember hearing Haydn's incredibly exciting *Surprise Symphony*, those electrifying bangs from it, emanating from a radio playing in the kitchen while I was playing on the steps around the statue. I think at that stage the upstairs bit of the house had already fallen through as a result of a V1 as it was all dark up there and no one went up. After that the house became unliveable in until repaired after the war. But Granny never lived there again, she gave it to Moore, who very generously gave it to Alice for her to provide a home for her three wards on our parents' death in 1952.

SUSAN SCHLAEFLE-NICHOLAS and FRANCES BLACKHURST, 2002

Giles Le Maitre believes that No. 20 had been restored before his parents bought it, and that they paid £1,500. He adds:

I fell off the garage roof while playing there with my elder brother Andrew at the age of about 3 or 4. We used to clamber up by a ladder which doubled as a slide. I remember the instant of falling vividly. Luckily I fell into a bush, and must have screamed because shortly afterwards my father appeared and carried me through to Captain Dadd's house.

The oil painting in our basement passage was our trompe d'oeil, which was meant to make people think the steps were much steeper and longer than they really were. I think I remember some other painting in the kitchen, covering up the marks made by an exploding "toffee pudding" of my mother's. The whole house was long and narrow, but very nice indeed. The garages were rather ugly: concrete and brick. I had steam trains in ours (we did not have a car until 1951). They ran right the way round, crossing the door on shelves. The "concrete" ended outside our garage, and Captain Dadd didn't have one. I used to play cricket by myself for hours with a bat and tennis ball, but never got to be as good as Don Bradman (can't think why!).

Betty Stucley is a name I remember though I cannot put a face to her. Other names were Hephzibah Menuhin and Graham Greene, who I remember as people who lived in North Side, though we never met them.

We all loved Clapham; and it is good to see that North Side is apparently quite unchanged. I wish I could find the photo album I'm sure I kept from my mother's things.

GILES LE MAITRE, 2002

Graham Greene (1904-1991) whose novel, The End of the Affair, is set in Clapham lived at 14 North Side in the 1930s.
Greene's biographer tells how Graham and Vivien Greene came to rent the house and of how much they liked both the house and Clapham.

HE DID FEEL THAT HE NEEDED TO LEAVE OXFORD and live in London, the centre of the publishing world, and he went to look at flats and houses at Clapham Common. 'I was terribly struck by the place,' he wrote to his mother, 'most beautiful, of the Hampstead period, with lovely air and nice shops and only about twelve minutes from Leicester Square by tube and close to Aunt N [ora].' He went to see Derek Verschoyle's sister. She and her husband had bought 'a most beautiful Queen Anne house in a lovely row opposite the Common and done it up absolutely like a museum piece; the most beautifully decorated house I've ever been in.' The Robertsons (the owners) wanted to let the house furnished from the end of July as Mr Robertson had given up a business job in town in order to become a master at Sherborne. The rent was £5 a week, quite a substantial sum in 1935, and beyond Greene's means, but

Mrs Robertson was so taken with him that she promised that, if he could get rid of his flat in Oxford and if she had found no suitable tenant, she would let him have the house for the same rent he was paying at Oxford. And it turned out that way.

He had decided on the house without Vivien's help, but when, arriving with Lucy and the luggage she first saw No.14 North Side, she was delighted with his choice. [Vivien described the house in an interview in 1983]

'It was almost entirely panelled throughout – mostly pale grey, except the bedroom and the front sitting room. There was a big square entrance hall of stone . . . there was a room where we kept china and things in. The kitchen and an adjoining room were semi-basement and a door from the kitchen (glass) led into a small garden, part paved, quickly turned into a sand pit and garden slide. And then there was this wonderful staircase which is called a flying staircase. Someone said the flying staircase might be by Vauban but this seems unlikely. On the first floor there was a drawing room (pale grey panelling) and I got stripes – cherry and white – for the chairs and sofa. I had some papier mâché tables. And then the front was a sort of living room, sitting room and very pretty. The curtains were pale green with lilies of the valley on

Card sent by Graham Greene with directions to find his house

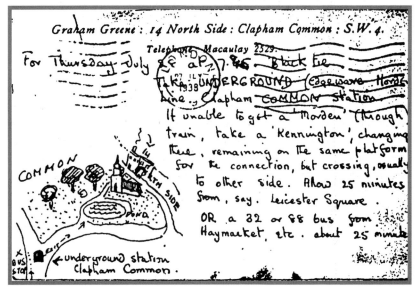

them. It was very elegant. Most of the rooms had shutters and window seats. And then, on that landing, there was a room for the maid and a bathroom. And the nursery. Oh, yes, and then next to the nursery was the night nursery. That's it.' ...

...Greene wrote to his mother: 'The whole appearance of Clapham Common is lovely, like a wide green plateau on a hilltop above Battersea, with the common stretching out of sight in one direction, and on three sides surrounded by little country-like shops and Queen Anne houses, a pond and in the middle of the Common, the 18th century church to which the Clapham set [sic] belonged. The house was built in 1730 [it was actually built from 1714 -1720] and was used by Macaulay's father as a school for black children.'

Something of his pride in the house is shown when, in 1938, having decided that his American publishers, Doubleday, were not selling enough copies of his books and he moved to Viking, he invited his contact with them, director Ben Hubsch, at that time staying at 55 Jermyn Street, to a party at his home. He sent Hubsch the ... neat sketch and accurate directions (though printed the handwriting is recognisably Vivien's) as to how to find 14 North Side – and reminding him to wear a black tie!

Several visitors to Graham Greene's house wrote about their impressions of the writer's life in Clapham.
Arthur Calder-Marshall *regarded Greene as the epitome of the 'Established Writer' with his stylish home in Clapham Common*

I was particularly impressed by Vivien's behaviour as the Protective Wife. One could not telephone Graham in the morning, because he was writing. Messages would be taken and passed on at more convenient times.... Yet, at the same time, when we met (preferably in pubs) I was conscious that there was another part of Graham which felt imprisoned by the comfort of the house in Clapham and his protective wife, which yearned for the seedy, the dangerous and the uncomfortable...

Another visitor, **Julian Maclaren-Ross,** *gained a similar impression*

...An elderly housekeeper treated him on the doorstep as if he were a salesman: I said, "Could I see Mr Graham Greene please?" She said, "We don't want anything today, thank you." I said: "He's expecting me to lunch." She said, "Oh. Well why didn't you say so then. Come in."

The housekeeper pointed to the drawing room at the top of the Adam staircase and left saying "He's out. You'll have to wait." Maclaren-Ross waited upstairs for a while and glanced round, and as he did so Greene appeared quite silently in the open doorway... "I hope you haven't been waiting long," he said. He had a spontaneous pleasant smile. "Nobody told me you were here. Would you like a cigarette? Something to drink?" "Something cold if possible," I said accepting the cigarette avidly.

There was no beer in the house and so they set off to the pub on the other side of the Common, each carrying a large jug... He also began to understand Greene's obsessive search for useful experience and copy – in the pub he attempted to smoke a Menzala to get used to Mexican tobacco as he was going out there, but he let it burn out in an ashtray on the bar.

NORMAN SHERRY, *The Life of Graham Greene*, 1989

AT WORK BETWEEN THE WARS

Bob Pethurst's *father kept a boot maker's shop at 12 The Polygon. There was much in the Old Town area to fascinate a small boy growing up in and just after the First World War. Written in 2000, his description starts with the baker at 1-3 Old Town and runs along the eastern side of Old Town and The Pavement to the junction of Clapham High Street and Venn Street.*

IN OLD TOWN, CLAPHAM I remember Dods the baker. Mr Harvey with his grocery store. He drove a pony and trap; he was a small man with a neatly clipped beard. Further along was a sweetshop which sold quite a variety of toffee. The toffee was sold broken up with a small metal hammer. The price was four ounces for a penny. Then the fire station, looking through the huge doors, you could see a row of about eight brass helmets and a wonderful fire engine. I used to get a great thrill to see the fire engine pulled along by two white horses. I think that because the turnout was so spectacular, it registered so deeply on my mind. When the fire engine was motorised it was still a wonderful sight, with the firemen hanging on. I can recall the thump of the solid rubber tyres on the bumpy roads. It fair shook our house. I think I was about seven.

The next interesting place which attracted me was a timepiece repairer and antique dealer. His name was Creed. It was a double fronted shop on the corner of Grafton Square. The antique shop was a boy's delight with its spears, swords and other oddities which had been collected from all over the world. Suits of armour, pictures of wild animals...

...At 61 Old Town was Johnsons the bakers. It was a very old building – I believe seventeenth century. It was built below street level, therefore one had to go down two steps to enter the shop. Inside you would be greeted by a queenly looking lady. I remember her smile and her gentleness. The window was packed with all kinds of fancy cakes. The aroma of newly baked bread filled the air. Mr Johnson had a bakery next door, where he also kept a delivery cart which used to be pulled by a moustached old man by means of a rope round his waist. Next door was a treble fronted showroom. The name was 'Harris and Others'. Large fold back doors when opened would reveal a Rolls Royce, a Bentley, a Benz or a Daimler, all luxury cars at that time. Next there was Watts the grocer. He had a large white beard. An incident happened inside his shop. Mrs Garrud, the Polygon tea shop man's wife, was sitting at Mr Watt's counter having a chat, when a mouse dropped from the shelf above her and went down the back of her dress. She screamed and Mr Watts with great presence of mind gave her several

Pethurst's Boot Makers shop in The Polygon

smacks on the back, killing the mouse. Mr Garrud was sent for and he escorted her home. I did not see this happening, it was told to me by my mother...

...[Now replaced by Trinity Close was] a block of good class flats called 'The Sweep'. They were I should think a nice place to live in if you had money. In those days, it seems that all middle class and rich had a servant or two. The lack of lifts in the large buildings posed a problem for people living on the upper floors, especially the old or disabled. Women's clothes were very long in those days, which made it very hard for women to negotiate the stairways. It seemed that once people moved into an upper floor flat they were trapped. I did see a sedan chair arrangement being used; also servant labour was in abundance and cheap. To mention myself as helping in this matter I was an errand boy and used to earn a few coppers. The aroma in some of these flats was indescribable, I think it just belonged to those days. The blessing was that these flats were on the borders of Clapham Common, which helped to air them...

...[At The Pavement was] the original 'Outsize House' started by a Mr Laming, usually to be seen wearing a frock coat. One or two small shops, I cannot recall their names, one of which was a long established men's outfitters. Then Carpenters, a high class bakers and speciality cake shop which had a large restaurant with high class clientele. Then a photographers. Then a large shop, Davies, which stretched from the Pavement through to Bromells Road. It sold everything to do with house building and hardware for the same. Next door was a printers, Bachoffeners. Next was Birdseyes, a long narrow draper's shop, which nearly always gave pins instead of the farthing change. Next was an archway leading to a tram yard. Trams used to enter, get on to a revolving tram track to reverse the way it was going.

Next the Plough Inn [now The Goose and Granite], then a picture palace which in 1914 was called the 'Better Hole'. The fascia was made up of bags of sand to copy the dugouts of the trenches in France. On Saturday it used to be threepence to go in. It seated a few hundred children. It was silent films, but not silent audience. It used to have a pianist and a violinist, who played music to suit the tempo of the situation which was arising. It was crazy. All in all these cinemas which were springing up all around were a blessing, a kind of release valve from the tension of war and near starvation. Try to imagine hundreds of grubby little hands clutching their few pennies for the pictures. For most of them this was the only treat they had through the week.

BOB PETHURST, 2000

Stevens Bros. *was a major Clapham business.
Famous for its annual Christmas 'Big Cake', it had a large bakery
between Bromells Road and The Pavement, where there was also
a retail shop and showrooms. The founder of the firm,*
Samuel Stevens, *died in 1933.*

IT WAS MR. STEVENS WHO ORIGINATED THE IDEA of building up a large iced cake each year, and this became a feature of Clapham life. Photographs of the big cakes went out all over the world. His first big cake was made at Gauden-road, and weighed over 300lb., but the last was about one ton in weight. The first one will be recalled by older residents of Clapham, as it had a small train running round it...

...He began business as a baker at Fenwick-place over fifty years ago [in 1876], working on his own, making the bread at night and delivering it on a barrow in the daytime... [The business grew. After Mr. Stevens retired] the old gentleman was always there to back up the efforts of his sons. He was adept at putting the icing on the cakes, and up to a week before his illness (a fortnight before his death) he was engaged in decorating wedding cakes, which was one of his hobbies.

Mr. Stevens was born in Chelsea, and came to live in Manor-street, Clapham, at the age of four years. He used to delight to recall the coming of the railway to Clapham-road [now Clapham High Street] and the arrival of the Tube, and often spoke of the time when picnic parties used to go to the countryside of Streatham and Brixton. He had seen Clapham grow, and would often refer to the old days when Manor Farm was situated on the north side of Clapham Common.

A thorough Christian, he was a deacon of the Ebenezer Strict Baptist Chapel, Stonhouse-street [now Cubitt Terrace], Clapham, and had been a regular attendant at the services every Sunday for over fifty years. For thirty-seven years he was superintendent of the Sunday School connected with that church...

From a newspaper cutting 13 May 1933

*A bakery trade paper in 1927 described "The 'Big Cake' House"
and how it came to The Pavement from Gauden Road.
The article shows how modern standards of hygiene and packaging
caused the business to expand.*

...just as it had risen to an output of 25 sacks per week, the Underground Bakehouse Act required so many alterations in the premises that a further move to The Pavement became a necessity. It was a great stroke of fortune that [20] The Pavement was unoccupied at that time, because the tide of affairs had commenced to turn and since then it has never looked back. All the sons at this time were in the business, and everything was progressing favourably until in 1911 Mr. Stevens lost his wife, which, coupled with the outbreak of war and failing health, caused him to leave the business entirely in the hands of the sons.

The brothers have always worked well together, and this, together with their thorough knowledge of the trade, both from within and without, has been responsible for the rapid strides forward during latter years of a concern that

'The Big Cake' at Stevens Bakery

practically started from nothing. In the first place, with the trade increased above the capacity of the original bakery, a temporary building was erected on the garden at the back of the premises, and this was soon working night and day. The next move was the erection of a bakery to deal solely with the steadily increasing trade for wrapped bread... Purchasing some adjoining property which gave the firm an outlet into Bromells Road, this was adapted to the wrapping and despatching of confectionery, a wedding cake decorating department, with dressing rooms and a reception hall on the floor above. ...The last venture was a large modern bakery with the very latest machinery, including ten new patent ovens, and finding employment for 104 hands...

...Before commencing a

general and detailed description of the bakeries as they are today, we should mention that the firm have experienced revolutionary increases from the wrapping of their products. Further, that the most happy relationships exist between themselves and the employees, who are paid good wages, who are often entertained at the firm's expense, and who derive the benefits of a splendid commission scheme. The employees have taken up with enthusiasm the scheme of the Hospitals' Saving Association [one of many medical insurance schemes, important before the coming of the NHS], to which Messrs. Stevens contribute monthly...

[The modern machinery is described at length...]... In the old bakehouse are to be seen ovens of an earlier type, which although less efficient than those of latter years, have splendid baking characteristics... and have been converted to the cleaner and more modern method of firing, namely that of fuel oil... Both bread bakehouses keep in motion the "Pioneer" bread wrapping machine... on which in large degree – by its commendation to the public taste – the bread side has increased considerably during recent years. This machine is situated in a special department, and with huge spools of waxed papers placed in the brackets attached, wraps thousands of loaves every hour. So great has become the demand for, and so large has been the increased trade from wrapped bread, that the firm wrap also every cake before it leaves the building, either in waxed papers or "Cellaphane"[sic]. Even the trays of fancies for distribution to numerous agents are daintily covered with this transparent material. Indeed, in sponge fingers alone 10,000 are wrapped every week.

Fronting the new bakery building is one of the splendidly appointed shops of Messrs. Stevens, and over this is the wedding reception hall, whilst directly behind are the offices, the decorating room, and the cake wrapping department, but little does the passer-by know of the huge output of goods that is carried on in the rear of the spotlessly clean building and wonderfully modern plant that is engaged in the interests of quality and service to the large clientele. As much as £40 worth of real, fresh, country cream is bought every week. A huge refrigerating plant is also utilised for preserving freshness, and all the jams are made on the premises, as well as Xmas puddings and mincemeat. A special jam preserving pan with a unique gas flame spreader, supplied by the South Metropolitan Gas Company, and a special steam press facilitate this work.

The bakery, we are informed, is to be thrown open to public inspection. We would add that those who avail themselves of such an opportunity will not only have a very pleasant visit but also a much greater relish for the goods of the baker and confectioner. These, in this instance, are delivered to hundreds of agents by a specially equipped fleet of motor vehicles comprising Fords, Overland and Morris types of delivery vans.

THE NATIONAL BAKER, 5 March, 1927.
Both this and the preceding article are in the possession of
Samuel Stevens' great-granddaughter, Mrs Christine Coppen

The Tunesi family, Italian in origin, arrived in Clapham in 1854. They ran a business in Old Town and in the 1990s **Arthur Tunesi** *wrote a memoir in which he described life in the 1920s.*

AS A BOY I LIVED IN DOWNERS COTTAGES, OLD TOWN. My father and grandfather were in business together as ice merchants and sawdust contractors. They used stables at the end of the Terrace. Before ice was made artificially, natural ice blocks were imported from Scandinavia, so an ice well was constructed 20 feet deep to house them, lowered and raised by chains and pulleys and then delivered by my parents. In severe winter ice was also taken from the ponds on Clapham Common.

Fishmongers and butchers were our regular customers; confectioners in the summer made ice cream, themselves using ice and freezing salt. Butchers had delivered hindquarters and forequarters of beef and carcasses of pork and lamb which were hung up on rails. As they thawed out, blood would drip away, and so sawdust was used to soak this up. Oak sawdust was used by fishmongers to smoke kippers, haddock and other fish. Both these shops had ice rooms, where their goods were stored overnight and weekends surrounded by ice. With the manufacture of ice my parents use of the ice well was unnecessary and it was filled in. The ice was made in blocks of 3 cwt. An ice pick and dog irons were necessary to manipulate these blocks, to cut them to size and to draw them from the van. The dog irons were akin to large sugar tongs. The ice was covered with wet sacks to save thawing.

On the other side of the Terrace "Harris and Others" had a factory. They made high class car bodywork and repairs, and during the 1st World War did a large amount of munition work. My mother machined hundreds of ammunition holders on a treadle sewing machine at home. I cut and stacked them. We cottagers were all familiar with the bosses and workmen of this firm. Sadly they, together with the cottages and stables, were bombed out in the 2nd World War with a land mine, but fortunately with no loss of life.

I attended Wirtemburg Street elementary school (renamed Stonhouse Street after the First War) [now Clapham Manor School]. Misdeeds were punished with 6 handers of the cane. Across the palms were bearable but across the tips of fingers was agonising. The deed was entered into a ledger. My name adorns many pages. My brother and cousins also attended the school and were good and clever scholars. I was the rebel, my consolation being that I won the school's swimming championship, having learnt to swim in the Mount Pond on Clapham Common during the summer holiday. I then took part in the South London Championships at Nine Elms Baths, finishing 3rd to a boy from Aristotle Road.

During my periods of leisure I helped my parents in stable feeding, mucking out the horse beds and filling sawdust into sacks for delivery to customers on weekly rounds. My father was contracted to supply donkeys to pull the bakers' vans (made by Stanford in North Street) for Stevens Bakers on The Pavement. These were very unsatisfactory as the farrier was averse to shoeing them. A twitch was used on their lips, twisted to stop them rearing up during shoeing. I dreaded the walk to Park Crescent to Woodisons the Farrier.

These donkeys were replaced by 3 Shetland ponies who were perfect. Each day they were collected by the roundsman, but would not pass my mother's door (she waited for them with carrots and tit bits) until they had been treated. They returned around 4.30pm, and later on Saturdays. After a rainy day the harness was dried and oiled for the next day. Sunday mornings all harnesses were cleaned for the 3 ponies, 3 horses and 1 mule.

Annually the 3 ponies were entered in Regents Park Horse Show and our hard work was rewarded by being awarded 8 merit medals which I possess. 5 are brass and 3 are in aluminium to commemorate the Silver Jubilee (1935). These ponies were named Bob, Peter and Call Boy (bought from the winnings when Lord Derby's horse "Call Boy" won the Derby). I took them to the Balham Hippodrome to draw the coach in a Cinderella Pantomime, and enjoyed cleaning them with a dandy brush and curry comb. They were very much a part of the family.

We also had a nanny goat. I went to feed the horses one evening and found

Nan giving birth to a kid. The horses never moved whilst this took place. In an amazingly short time after the kid was licked clean, it was prancing around! An unforgettable experience. Afterwards Nan expressed milk which was used to our and our neighbours' delight!

We also had a goose which at one time waddled to the Cock pond and would not leave. I swam in after her and following a struggle, capture brought her to shore!

In those days dense fogs, hot summers and cold winters were the norm. In the summer holidays, all boys had some type of job to earn their pocket money. I carried out paper rounds, made ice cream, did milk rounds, was a baker's boy, a laundry boy, sold manure, and was even a doctor's delivery boy. Clapham Common tube station was situated on the corner of Clapham Park Road, and a lift brought the passengers up to road level. We awaited the exodus, and offered to carry cases to their destination. How we managed to carry luggage as big as us so far was a miracle. We were rewarded by a generous or mean tip. If we could endure it we returned again for the next lift emptyings.

Another promise of riches was the repair of Clapham High Street. It was composed of wooden tarred blocks which were taken up and replaced by asphalt. Boys appeared with bags and barrows, and depleted the stocks removed that day. Some were used for home consumption for the grate and the surplus bundled for sale around the street – the result of sales being spent on saveloys and meat pies at the coffee stall. In Clapham High Street there were four. Each had his favourite mecca for this meal, after which some would rinse their hands in a nearby horses drinking trough!

Clapham High Street was outstanding for the Penny Bazaar, and for the Plough Inn which had a cobbled passage leading to a stable for horse buses. A Clapham notable was Mr Pullen the licensee – an immaculate man with a coloured bowler hat and always a buttonhole at his lapel (purchased from the flower lady with her large basket, stationed permanently outside the inn). Woollands the gentlemans outfitters was the choice of the Clapham Beau Brummels!

During horse-racing hours, having prior placed their bets/wagers illegally, punters congregated around the Clock Tower at Clapham Cross, where newsboys hawked the newspapers. Each race result was obtained by the public phone adjacent to the tube station, stamped in the Stop Press and when bought and perused by the waiting gamblers, glee or dismay was registered by the information. Each race result was eagerly purchased but alas few after the final race were in profit, except the vendors who earned 8d a quire (27), so wealth was, as usual, elusive to the punters who hoped that the next day fortune would smile upon them and scowl on the bookmakers! Periodically bookmakers were arrested for illegal gaming and fined. Each time the fine was increased, so a deputy was substituted, when informed of impending arrest, to appear in court and charged a small fine as first offender.

Whites Square was notable for its 2 street bookmakers (illegal) and every Sunday for gathering a crowd playing "Pieman". This consisted of two coins on a stick tossed in the air. When they landed 2 heads or 2 tails you gambled on each. There were two schools, one for large bets and, my choice, small amounts. It was risky for a stranger to venture into their domain. People were locally close knit and prior to the last war were mainly related. An argument with one incurred the wrath of many.

On Guy Fawkes night a huge bonfire was ignited in the square. In the past soot and flour were liberally showered on interlopers! All household surplus was collected for this beforehand.

Each holiday, (Christmas excepted), a fair was held in Rookery Road (joining South Side and Long Road). I took a saddled horse to hire at 3d or 6d per ride. Each stall was represented by pig skin balloons which were used as a means of warfare. Tattooed men swallowed razor blades and burning torches. All types of chestnuts, baked potatoes, sweets, ice cream, and monkey nuts were for sale. Girls wearing "kiss me" hats were chased! Coconut shies, dart boards, playing cards and hoop-la, together with sledge hammers swung to ring bells, were all in force. Many a courtship began amid the hustle and bustle! People danced around the band stand and quenched their thirst and rested their feet in the cafe alongside.

Each Sunday political meetings were held, and famous cricket elevens played on the Big Field. Tennis courts were hired and boys were engaged for each game to retrieve over-hit balls and anything the player requested.

The four ponds caused much pleasure: Mount Pond – swimming and then paddle boats; Long Pond – sailing boats; Windmill Pond – fishing rods; Cock Pond – dragging for fish using a sack. The Windmill Inn was a famous stopping place for horse drawn traffic, the busiest time being Derby Day. The route from Epsom was lined with children shouting "Throw out your mouldies!" If a punter had been lucky he would accede to the request, otherwise a flick of the whip would ensue! The forelegs of the horse often had a pair of ladies bloomers fastened to them. The coaches and traps would remain for an hour or so, and then trot away to the next inn, prewarned by the shrill hoots of trumpets – an annual event looked forward to with zest and relish!

Prior to the bus terminus in the Old Town, a market was started. Stalls of all kinds were in use. My father rented these stalls out when they were not in use at the market, but unfortunately this met with little success. One of my father's tenants (a coffee stall) moved into The Polygon and opened a cafe. That is now a betting shop [now The Polygon Bar and Grill].

In his youth, my grandfather opened a shop in the Old Town. Home-made ginger beer ice cream was sold there and also from tents on Clapham Common. He had a large family comprising 7 sons and 2 daughters, so as the shop was not able to support them all the ice and sawdust business was started. The rounds extended to Wimbledon, where a tow shire horse was engaged to help pull the loads up Wimbledon Hill.

Three of my uncles had stables – in the Triangle (Clapham Park Road) in Macaulay Road and in Bowyers Passage (joining Manor Street and Stonhouse). Another uncle felled trees to clear building sites and several cousins set up various businesses. Two cousins were greengrocers in Acre Lane and Manor Street, another a canary breeder and landlord, and one a sheet-metal worker. All in all hard work led them to success.

There was racial discrimination in those days, against the three ethnic groups, the Irish, Jews and Italians. This often resulted in fights, and black eyes were shared by those involved! These three groups were very hardworking however and were an asset to Britain. My family unfortunately did not keep together and differences were thus enlarged – otherwise we could have been a powerful business unit.

In my youth hawkers were numerous, the following being but a few: cats' meat on skewers; bakers' barrows; milk carts; greengrocers; muffins on a flat board, perched on the head and accompanied by a ringing bell; and the sale of winkles, whelks and shrimps. The rag and bone man usually gave you a balloon for your offerings. Also delivered were firewood and logs, ice cream and hokey-pokey, baked chestnuts, baked potatoes, jellied eels and garden manure. Horses' droppings were quickly swept up! Everyone strived to be a Rockefeller!

Christmas gifts had to last a year. A girl's wooden hoop which was bowled along with the hand or stick was frequently repaired with string. Five Stones was a popular game with boys. This entailed a variation of placing and catching a stone, which carried on until dropped, and then your rival continued where you had failed. At last the winner emerged. Each stage was more difficult. Team games were organised. Hop-Scotch played on a chalk-marked pavement and skipping were girls' pastimes. Boys played Leap-Frog and Jump Jimmy Knacker, Robbers and Coppers, etc. No article was necessary.

The kitchen usually had an open fire and the toasting fork was in much demand. Later some had a Larbard stove installed; this was closed in with an oven on the side, with the kettle permanently singing over the fire. The sinks were York Stone in the scullery, and were very shallow with a bowl used for washing. That and a mangle completed the contents for domestic chores. Outside lavatories were normal.

All thoroughfares were illuminated by lamp posts approx 12' overall. Just below the lantern, an iron bar was fixed horizontally, which was used for resting a ladder for cleaning. Morning and night a lamp-lighter with a pole turned it on or off. Boys used to climb the lamp post and turn a somersault on the bar.

Arthur Tunesi

As very few boys owned a cycle, they hired one @ 6d an hour! Half the time was spent pumping up tyres, adjusting brakes and replacing the chain. But it was a pleasant hour, if fine! If it was raining, the wheels splashed through puddles, backs became soaked and mud guards worked loose, if not missing.

There were no parking problems in those days. Horse traffic was housed in stables, so all roads were uncongested. Policemen patrolled regular beats every night, ensuring buildings were secure. Crime was rare in comparison with today. When a carman had his respite, he pulled in outside a dining room, and having removed the horse's bit, then placed a nose-bag over its head, filled with chaff and a sprinkling of oats. Sadly some carmen failed to remove the bit and the horse was unable to eat properly. I have removed the bit when I noticed a horse in difficulty due to the driver's indifference.

The dustman's horse-drawn cart was filled ascending a ladder hooked onto the side. The men carried the dustbins, which smelled vile, and emptied them. A scotch was placed under the wheel to stop the horse from moving. As remains of fishbones and bones were normal contents, maggots thrived and these were collected by anglers!

The building trade has changed. To name but a few instances: a colourman was employed to tint white lead to the colours needed, and scaffolding comprised of tree boles fastened with rope, later changed to wire bonds. Ceilings were rendered with lime and hair and finished with Keens' cement, adhering to laths nailed to joists. Plumbing was all lead piping and solder joints and sheet zinc and lead for weathering roofs. Carpenters then made doors, sashes and mouldings. With the introduction of electricity, gas lighting became obsolete. Mechanical tools have replaced gangs of men using shovels for digging and swinging in unison with sledge-hammers, hitting a chisel to break concrete. Horse and 2-wheel jipcarts were used for the transport of excavated earth and material.

Stale bread was sold cheaply and collected in bags each morning. Part-rotten fruit was also obtained, cleaned and boiled for tarts and puddings. Poverty took advantage of cheap food and apparel, as social benefits did not exist. Shopkeepers used carrier cycles to deliver their orders. Also, boxed tricycles were used for bulky goods.

Horse flesh cooked and skewered for cats food, delivered by hawker in pony and trap, was eagerly awaited by cat owners. Butchers were open in the evenings for the sale of pease pudding, faggots, saveloys and cooked meats. Likewise fish and chip shops. The price of a piece of fish was 3d (1¼ pence now!), salt and vinegar on the counter to be used before wrapping up. Toffee apples on sticks were also in demand.

French onion hawkers came annually with their cycles carrying strings of onions, sometimes also garlic, hanging from the crossbars of cycles. They remained for a month usually selling their stored crop to eager buyers.

Round bundles of chopped firewood were sold to fire stoves and paraffin oil was used for heaters. Baked chestnuts and potatoes were sold in winter months. Sausages, mashed potatoes and onion shops were a Mecca after leaving the cinemas and theatres.

People's attire has changed. Waistcoats were included in men's suits; they possessed four pockets, the lower two were used for a pocket watch and chain, the upper two for a fountain pen and pencil. Boots were usual – now unusual. Stiff collars were worn with a necktie. Scarves and mufflers were replaced by collar and tie by many. Top hats, bowler, trilby, pork pie, berets and caps were used to warm the head. Woollen long pants and vests protected the body and legs and clean dickies were buttoned onto the front of the chest. Capes, over-coats and mackintoshes completed the wardrobe.

Looking back, although life was hard, at least people were free to roam without being mugged or molested. Police were friendly, and often a bobby was invited to join a family party in the early hours. Young offenders were often cuffed and warned not to repeat the misdemeanour. Neighbours were helpful in times of stress and child birth. The tempo was slower.

ARTHUR TUNESI, *unpublished memoir*, c1995

In an address to master printers in 1938
John R Battley *(1880-1952), founder of*
Battley Brothers Printers, outlined some of the principles
behind his successful printing business.
This address was later reprinted as a small booklet
and illustrated with amusing drawings by the in-house artist,
some of which are reproduced below

…I LEARNED EARLY THAT I MUST TRY to make the name of my firm a household one. I, therefore, coined our slogan "If it's in the Rainbow Battley Brothers can put it on paper." Many and many a time have customers and friends said to me in jesting earnestness: "Damn your slogan, I can never look now on a rainbow, nor can I think of a rainbow without think-ing of Battley Brothers."

In conjunction with the slogan, I found it was necessary to design an imprint or emblem. In collaboration with our artist, we designed an emblem which, I think, is expressive not only of our particular ambitions, but also of the locality in which our office is situated. Our Press is named "The Queensgate Press." It is in Clapham Park.

By symbolising a leaping stag – an animal of surpassing grace, symmetry and beauty and, as you know, a frequenter of Royal Parks – and superimposing this over a tree, we were able to combine our ideals with our geographical position.

He was an enlightened employer who introduced holidays
and rest breaks in excess of the legal requirements

...I initiated a week's holiday in our firm as far back as 1904, when I commenced business as a master printer, and ever since the week's holiday became a rule of the trade, our employees' holiday was increased to a fortnight, and even now all our senior employees have a fortnight and the juniors are eligible for the same.

We make a lunch break in the middle of the morning and one for tea in the afternoon. All the motors and machines are shut down for this purpose. This has been in operation since about 1912, and is greatly valued and appreciated by the staff...

...A small matter which I found influenced very considerably the standard of our work is this, I arranged for our employees to wear overalls, and the firm went 50/50 with them in paying the bill, and 50/50 with the weekly cost of washing...

...When I remember that in my boyhood days the hours were 54 per week, and the minimum wage £1.16s. 0d., it does not need much imagination to see that the 45-hour week for a minimum wage of £4. 9s. 0d. has placed our employees in an enviable position compared with many other trades. It has placed us as employers in that happy position where we can with pride think of the improving conditions of labour in our several businesses – a

 state of things I feel sure all of us without exception desire and encourage.

JOHN R BATTLEY,
Address to the
South-West London
Master Printers
Association,
March 1938

Ted Didcock *joined the local printers, Battley Brothers,
in 1920 as a messenger boy. He stayed with the company
all his working life. When he retired, in 1970, he wrote a memoir
of his early working days.*

I SAW A NOTICE UP IN THE FRONT WINDOW of Battley Bros. which was in Queens Road [now Queenstown Road] in those days: "Messenger Boy wanted". I saw the notice on a Friday evening and at 7.30 am on Saturday morning I was round there waiting for the shop to open and asked to see the Governor... I saw Mr John Battley, – "Please can I have that messenger boy job". He said: "How old are you? – I said: "Fourteen", "Left school?" "Yes" "Right". So I showed him my school reference, they called it a character in those days. He said "Very well" and asked me where I lived and a few other particulars. "Right, come into the office" and there I filled up a form, signed my name and he said: "One thing we haven't discussed is how much wages to pay you". I didn't know, I didn't really worry about money, I was thinking about getting a job. I said "I leave that to you Sir." He said: "You trust me?" "Yes Sir," "Right, I will pay you 16/6d a week, that's more than I have paid any other boy." I said "Thank you very much, can I start now?" "Oh no, you'd better go home and tell your Mother and Father what you are going to do and come and start here on Monday morning at 8 o'clock."

So Monday morning I was there sharp at 8 o'clock. I had on a brand new cap, which my Mother had bought me, a clean shirt and shoes cleaned and polished. My first job every morning was to sweep the front of the three shops and dust all the ledges and clean the windows as far as I could reach, and by jingo, I had to clean them right. Why I remember one morning Mr Battley coming to me and saying "This is the way to clean windows my boy, like this, across and down, across and down, that's the way."

...Then of course I would take the parcels all over the place...I had many deliveries up into the City, I used to go by tram car from the top of Queenstown Road, the fare was then 2d all the way, this was after 10 o'clock in the morning...One of the times I went up the City I had so many deliveries, delivering calendars, picking up stuff, it was 2d all the way again, but when I got back to Blackfriars after waiting so long at Spicers [one of the suppliers from whom he had collected], the last 2d all the way had gone and it was 3d – and a 3d fare would take you to Queenstown Road, but I only had 2d. I did have a ¹/2d of my own so that only made it 2 $^1/_2$d. so I had to walk along the Embankment and as I was walking along a tramp came up to me "Have you got an odd $^1/_2$d you don't want" – what a coincidence, that was all I wanted myself was an odd $^1/_2$d and I could have rode all the way. Anyhow I couldn't help the poor old chap so I carried on. I walked until I got to Lambeth Bridge, from there that 2d would take me to Wandsworth Road Station. So I got on at Lambeth Bridge and thought "Oh I'll stay on this tram car till we get to Queenstown Road" but Oh no, the conductor, he was watching me like a hawk and as soon as we got to Wandsworth Road Station he didn't kick me off but he said"Get off! You have had your tuppence worth".

When I got back to the firm of course there was a hue and cry – where had I been! Of course I explained I was waiting for ages for the material I was fetching back and showed them my book stamped with the time I left Spicers; this showed why I missed the 2d all the way tram back, so the Governor gave instructions that in future when I went out I was always to carry extra money in my pocket so I would never be in that position again…

…I used to get the men their morning and afternoon tea. I used to have a long pole and collect their billycans and hang them on the pole and go across to the Dining Shop, which was almost opposite in Queenstown Road, and get maybe a pennyworth or twopennyworth of tea in a can for them and their cakes. Because in those days we had no canteen or anything like that the boys would do this and I loved that little job…

…I used to clean up the shavings and waste paper where they did the cutting on the guillotine and sweep the Machine Room… my next move was to the Composing Room as a copyholder… I used to help Mr Payne who was our Reader and our poster setter. You have no idea how many posters we used to do…about 20 to 30 on a Saturday morning.

Next I found myself working in the Machine Room, on the platens. There was only one motor to govern all the platen machines and every time one stopped and restarted it slowed all the others down. These were all hand fed – there were no automatic machines in those days. Every sheet of paper had to be handled and handled right so as not to crack it. When you started on the platen machines you didn't start on the power machines, you used to have to treadle them and your old leg would be going up and down and you tended to race the power machines. I suppose you could do a thousand an hour! Now that takes some doing and your leg used to get very tired.

My next move was to the Finishing Department, where everything was folded by hand – 32 pages on a sheet. A full sheet of 32 pages and very thin super calendered [glazed] paper which we folded with our bone folders and then inserted into sections, to be hand-stitched. In the next room was a hand guillotine, where my first job was to turn the handle for whoever was doing the trimming...

...I must mention too, another side of the firm, the social side. One time an outing had been arranged to go to Worthing. We went by motor coach and had a lovely day. It was the first time I had ever seen the sea. Nowadays you would never dream that any lad of 14 had not seen the sea, but I hadn't...

...About 1923, I think it was, we moved from Queenstown Road to new premises in Clapham Park Road, and the warehouse was the first department to be moved, so that made me the first person to go into the new factory... and I was able to organise my stores exactly as I wanted them...

...I must mention that Battley Bros. was one of the first firms to give extra holidays to the workers – an extra day for each year of service up to a maximum

A coach outing in the early 1930s

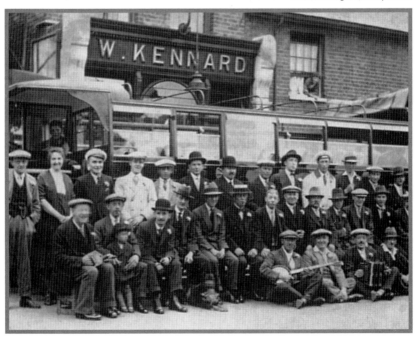

of two weeks. This was a wonderful thing and gave a great incentive for people to want to work at the firm.

In 1926, that was the year of the General Strike, when everybody was out on strike except for the apprentices and learners who were the only ones left in the firm. We younger ones had a great responsibility and we thought we kept the firm going. We used to do quite a lot of work, but oh how pleased we really were when the strike was over and all the men came back...

...At Clapham Park Road we had a canteen where we had hot coffee and rolls and cakes. The rolls were delivered each morning from the bakeries and the delivery man used to come with a huge basket full of rolls and they were buttered and filled with cheese in the morning and in the afternoon we had tea and home made cakes. This was grand – I loved those buttered rolls...

...One of the fine art jobs we printed in those days was for Sir Philip Sassoon. It was an illustrated catalogue on the finest art paper we could possibly get and very good blocks – I think we used 130 or 150 screen blocks and it had a very special suede cover which came from France. The women had to work all Saturday afternoon – this was quite a thing in those days – sewing up this job, getting it ready for delivery for the exhibition on Monday morning. Battley Bros. never failed, the goods were delivered on time.

TED DIDCOCK, *unpublished manuscript*, 1970
in the possession of Bernard Battley

5

THE SECOND WORLD WAR

*John Lamb (see Chapter 3) was twelve
when the Second World War broke out in 1939.*

AS A FAMILY WE LISTENED TO Neville Chamberlain's broadcast on 3 September 1939 stating that we were now at war with Germany. Suddenly the newly installed air raid sirens were set off bringing the curious minded householders on to the streets. This was not what the police and authorities had in mind! We then had the spectacle of policemen riding round on bicycles asking everyone to go back indoors.

Apart from the unfortunate people of Poland the next few months were known to some as the 'Phoney War' at least on land.

Everywhere there was a great sense of determination, the blackout was enforced, air raid wardens and fire-watchers recruited, barrage balloons sent up, anti-aircraft guns set up on the Common complete with an army camp and canteen. The lady in charge of the canteen was of the Lamont Clan from Scotland. Many years later I had a long chat with this lady at a Clan Lamont gathering.

Gas masks and ration books were issued, everyone had to register with a retailer for foods covered by the ration books, and the evacuation of school children from London was put in hand. Our family moved to 20 Manchuria Road off the west side of the Common near the tennis courts. In 1940 the war was not going well and the evacuation of children continued. David and I found ourselves in the Cornish town of Launceston where we were billeted with a family who had a fishmonger's business. The family treated us kindly and even took us in the bus to Plymouth to ride on the open top trams and visit relations. While we were there we had our first experience of an air raid, sheltering in the main Post Office building until the "all clear".

Early in the New Year the bombing seemed to have subsided and mother came down to take us back to London. This proved to be only a lull and soon after we returned regular bombing raids resumed, Clapham Junction being the main local target. The enemy did not get to London without a fight, and sometimes in their haste to get back home unloaded their bombs anywhere. It was just our luck, or lack of it, that a stick of these bombs fell in roads off West Side. New replacement houses can be seen today in Kyrle Road and Broxash Road.

When it came to Manchuria Road things became more personal. Like many families we took a pragmatic view of life – in our case a Christian one. We did not go into air raid shelters (goodness knows what germs one could catch, especially in the damp ones!) and if anything happened we would all go together. The Edwardian houses were built with a back extension with a concrete path and narrow strip of garden leading to the kitchen and middle room with its French doors. Our personal bomb missed the concrete path and went deep into the flower bed before it exploded taking down the side wall of the extension where our elderly landlord and his daughter had their bedrooms. Fortunately they both got out on the right side of their beds! Like us they were unhurt and my parents comforted them as best they could; shortly afterwards there was a knocking on the front door. My father answered the door to

Sleeping quaters in one of the huts of the anti-aircraft defences on Clapham Common

be confronted by the indignant foreman of the rescue party complete with a set of vehicles to dig us out. My father was a man of few words!

Next morning a party of workmen was sent to put up tarpaulin sheets, etc. One of the workmen asked my mother to go out into the kitchen and pointed out the saucepan fixed to the ceiling. Sadly, mother said this was stew she had prepared for the family but now she could not give it to them. The workmen asked if they could have it. After brushing off the dirt their verdict was that it was a jolly good stew!

The school situation had been considerably interrupted, but David and I later got scholarships to Battersea Central School going on to Hammersmith School of Building at Lime Grove, Shepherd's Bush opposite the BBC studios.

We had to move house and for a short time ended up in an upstairs flat in Devereux Road off Broomwood Road, and eventually to 49 Manchuria Road. Later a flying bomb destroyed the house in Devereux Road together with a number of others, inevitably with loss of life.

David and I had bikes and started paper rounds operating from a shop in Bellevue Road near Wandsworth Common Station. This was about a mile from our home before we went on to deliver the papers in roads off the south side of Wandsworth Common. I went to 108 houses while David delivered to 120 houses on weekdays and 140 on Sundays in all weathers. It had to be a very swift operation since mother insisted that we had a good breakfast before we started. All papers had to be put in letterboxes and finally we had to get our bikes back home before going off to school. We earned more than our friends with our wages of 12 shillings and six pence – 62.5 p in today's money – quite a lot when many adults' wages were £4–£5 per week.

Fortunately, the area we covered was spared most of the bombing but one morning we did find a land mine swinging from the trees near the station bridge and had to go to collect our papers from a second shop in Trinity Road.

Quite early in the war the Channel Islands had come under German occupation. In Battersea an ex-serviceman from the Great War, George Vibert, had founded the Wellington Boys Club in Gideon Road at the foot of the hill dominated by the large red brick Church of the Ascension in Lavender Hill. George Vibert, a Jersey man, was held in high esteem for his work amongst young people. The club was closed and the premises converted into "Ma Cabine", a war time home for Channel Island servicemen, with help from the Rotary Club and Red Cross. My mother was put in charge of the domestic side whilst

George Vibert managed the business side, and wrote many hundreds of letters to servicemen, while still holding down a full time job. It was amazing how news of "Ma Cabine" got around and this small figure of my mother became 'mother' to 800 Channel Island servicemen. It was not an easy task. She had to walk 1¼ miles down to "Ma Cabine" from home seven days a week with most of the journey home up hill. David and I were still at school and tried to do our bit at home, with David taking charge of food supplies with a book which noted quantities and prices. Both of us, together with my father, did our best to keep up mother's high standards in the home.

To try and get mother home in reasonable time I would often call in to "Ma Cabine" to help out. On quite a number of occasions we had our coats on ready to depart when there would be a knock on the door to reveal a group of servicemen with the cry "We are home mother!" The coats would come off, a warm welcoming smile and perhaps a hug, the kettle would be put on and a hot meal prepared while I would do my part by checking on beds and towels.

Later on, from June 1944 we had to contend with the V1 'Doodlebugs' or flying bombs. We had already got used to standing in house porches when the guns on the Common fired, to avoid the shrapnel which rained down after each firing! Fired from ramps in France the V1s came over Kent and were set to run

WAAFS (Women's Auxiliary Air Force) relaxing in a hut of the anti-aircraft defences on Clapham Common

out of fuel over South London. As many as four or five could be seen coming across the sky in quick succession. When the engine stopped they came down, but they did not penetrate the ground in the same way as an aerial bomb and consequently the damage was much more widespread. However, we just carried on as before when this menace came in our direction.

There was a small group of shops adjoining "Ma Cabine" where we did our weekly shopping. Everyone had to register with a grocer and the weekly rations could only be bought at that shop. David and I would take it in turns to haul the shopping on our bikes back to our home off West Side. One day, when it was my turn, I had just come out of Sisters Avenue off North Side and had reached the bend in the Avenue where it crosses the Common, to be confronted by a low flying "Doodlebug". I did not worry about smashing eggs, but threw myself flat on the ground as the engine cut out. This one glided straight into Sisters Avenue with an enormous explosion which demolished about a dozen houses on each side of the road.

News got around very quickly so I went back to "Ma Cabine" to assure my mother that I was alright and mentioned that the blast had also affected Sugden Road where our friends, May and Maurice, lived. Mother immediately started to make plans to put them up, which we did until their home was sorted out. This was part of everyday life.

Anti-aircrft gunners on Clapham Common cooking lunch

David had a similar experience in August 1944. He was cycling along West Side when the air raid sirens sounded, almost immediately followed by the hard note of an approaching V1's engine. There was a very low cloud and David saw the V1 emerge from the cloud and pass directly over him at about 500 ft. The engine cut out and the V1 fell on the Pavilion Cinema on Lavender Hill, sadly killing a number of people.

Up to this time we had had little contact with foreigners, but in Clapham we became familiar with the Free French sailors with their hats complete with red pompons, who were billeted at the vacant Convent of Notre Dame on South Side.

After the war the London County Council made considerable efforts to restore the Common as a public open space. The trench air raid shelters were filled in or covered over with tarmac; the gun emplacements and army camp were removed together with the prefab houses that had lined Long Road. Restoring the grass areas after the closing of the allotments was a major exercise which the Council endeavoured to speed up by the generous use of pig manure giving Clapham, for a short time, a country atmosphere which was not appreciated by those with delicate noses!

A vast mound of earth which had been excavated from the war time deep tunnel shelters at Clapham Common and Clapham South tube stations had been deposited on the field next to Nightingale Lane. There seemed to be no money available to move this mound and it was still there five years after the end of the war. Fortunately a large sum of money was made available for the Festival of Britain in 1951 and some of this was used to clear the mound in order to make a temporary car park for visitors. We then felt that the years of war had been, for the most part, erased from the Common.

JOHN LAMB, *unpublished manuscript*, 2002

During the Second World War, the Rector of Holy Trinity Church, **Canon JCV Durell**, wrote frequently to one of his Churchwardens, Samuel Hicks, who for most of the war was in Harrogate.

6TH OCTOBER, 1939: WHEN THE WAR BROKE OUT, I suggested turning the drawing room of the rectory into a chapel, should the necessity arise. Since then, I have had a better idea of forming a small temporary chapel at the east end of the south aisle, screening off the corner near the Lady Chapel [now the Wilberforce Centre] with curtains from St Anne's Hall and borrowing an altar from the Chapel at St Saviour's, which has not been used for many years. I trust that you will like these arrangements, which allow Early Celebrations to take place as usual in the dark mornings...

In the autumn of 1940, Holy Trinity was damaged...

by the blast from a nearby bomb, which shattered the windows,
brought down the chandelier and some roof beams
and ruined the Lady Chapel

12TH MAY, 1941: ... If you feel that you are able to allocate a sum of £25 to effect an insurance on the Organ for £1500 and on other Church goods for £250, the knowledge that you had done this would be very welcome to me....

16TH JUNE, 1941: With regard to an appeal to the Diocesan War Damage Committee for the temporary assistance of a loan, it would be well to include in this the cost of the repairs to the ceiling now being carried out by Messrs J. Garrett on Newell's instructions [Mr Newell was the other Church-warden], as this is likely to be a heavy item owing to the expense of scaffolding.

Before Sully's account is paid, his attention should be directed to the very rough character of the work of his carpenter, who has left gaps along the top of the opening into the chancel, owing to the bad fit of the timbers. As presumably it will not be possible to re-roof the Lady Chapel till after the war, it will be necessary to make these openings draught-tight before the winter. Perhaps you will consider whether the gaps should be filled in with plaster or whether the openings should be backed by some kind of felt...

...It is interesting to note the difference in cost of tuning the organ at St Peter's, Harrogate, and in this Church. Our instrument however is a particularly large one – probably, after the Cathedral, the largest in South London – which, though possibly justified in the palmy days of Clapham, is now a heavy burden...

1ST AUGUST, 1941: The erection of a barrier to keep the water out of the Church seems of doubtful expediency, as it would result in the accumulation of water on the floor of the chapel. My suggestion is that openings should be made in the boards where the level of the floor is lowest, to allow the water to drain off. I will delay communication with the architect, both as to the treatment of the chapel and the transfer of pews till I hear further from you or Newell.

19TH SEPTEMBER, 1941: I am glad that you have been able to send in your account to Canon Anderson and hope that the Government will be fairly expeditious in dealing with the [war damage] claim....

...It was, as you state, decided by the Church Council to accept Sidney Upton's offer to arrange for shaded lights in the chancel, which you say is done so successfully at Christ Church, Harrogate. A scheme of lighting was accordingly planned, in consultation with Mr Brundritt [the curate]; and this was tested after dark on Tuesday evening. Although the lights were screened in black bakelite shades, the reflections from the ground shone up through the windows of the nave, so that the regulations would not have been complied with. Sidney Upton then undertook to obtain blue coloured lamps for a trial, and these were tested on Friday night, but this scheme also proved unworkable...

...Somewhat surprisingly, as I learn indirectly from Deaconess, there are some people who still want the temporary chapel re-installed in the south aisle. This, however, is impracticable, as, when the chapel was perforce dismantled after the bombing, the curtains were sent by me to the laundry. The old crimson fabric was however so badly torn by the blast of the bomb that a great part fell to pieces...

...Mr Brundritt and I have been considering an alternative plan and have reached the conclusion that it will be practicable to arrange a chapel in the ambulatory behind the organ... The lighting of a chapel so arranged will present no difficulty, as the windows of the south gallery, through which alone the light could shine will be impervious to subdued rays, being $2/3$ blocked by mill-board and $1/3$ filled with opaque linen....

27TH JANUARY, 1942:...a representative of the Ecclesiastical Insurance Office has informed me over the telephone that a public liability exists in the case of an accident occurring through neglect, e.g. through the fall of a slate. It would therefore seem advisable to renew the insurance. If that is done, the office will require an assurance that all reasonable precautions have been taken. They should be informed that all parts of the building considered by the Borough Council to be dangerous have been demolished...

...With reference to your suggestion that the history of the Parish Church might be written, it is to be remembered that the Church on the Common only dates from 1775 and that the early history of Clapham is bound up with the old church. At first sight, there does not seem to be a great deal to write about Holy Trinity, but this shall be kept in mind...

24TH DECEMBER, 1942: The Dickens sale was a very gratifying success both socially and financially and Brundritt is to be congratulated on... his efforts....

...The political situation is now far brighter than seemed possible a short time ago and if General Smuts' prophecy of a sudden collapse of Germany is realised the war may be over in the coming year.

But a year and half later ...

...there is a remarkable absence of panic; and there seems every hope that the new menace will quickly be mastered. In the meantime the Germans are facing one disaster after another. I am thankful to say that the damage to Church and rectory is only of a minor character.

2ND JULY, 1944: You will be distressed to learn that the Church suffered heavy damage last night, catching the blast from a bomb which fell on Downers Cottages. The three East windows were completely destroyed, the windows in the vestries were blown in, the doors were burst and more plaster fell from the ceiling. We were able to clear a portion of the Church at the West End to enable services to be held today. Mr Newell will give the necessary notification of the damage to the [War Damage] Commission.

23RD NOVEMBER, 1944: I am thankful to say that we have had no further trouble here from the bombs, but two nights ago one fell on Battersea at the junction of Falcon Road and Battersea Park Road, causing a number of fatalities, including the death of the Vicar of Christ Church and his wife. This is the Church at the point where the tramlines turn at right angles from the Princes Head and it was this vicarage which I tried to secure for Mr Brundritt, at his request, when it fell vacant a year & a half ago. Had I succeeded, it may be presumed that he and Mrs Brundritt would have been the victims.

At the beginning of 1945, an immense landmine fell on the Common. Its blast was felt all over Clapham

11TH JANUARY, 1945: Many thanks for your considerate letter of yesterday's date and your expression of sympathy. The catastrophe is indeed a disaster, but we have to be thankful that it was not far worse, as the bomb fell on soft ground and expended a large part of its energy in creating a huge crater on the Common by the side of the Cock Pond [now the paddling pool]. The blast was terrific and the Church took the full force of it. Deaconess was in the vestry but mercifully was uninjured. The architect, Mr Humphrey, inspected the Church this afternoon and at once said that the public must be excluded, as the heavy ceiling is unsafe. We hope however to recondition the lower vestry for use for services. We do not yet know whether the Ministry will grant a licence to enable the windows, etc. to be filled in. If not, it is to be feared that the effect of the weather on the organ will be disastrous. I will write to you again later, when we can get a clearer idea of what work can be done. The blast was far-reaching extending as far as Miss Lawrence's house in The Chase and Klea Avenue on the South Side. The shops on The Pavement have been devastated. At the Rectory, the doors were blown in and a few windows smashed.

24TH JANUARY, 1945: The architect inspected the Church yesterday with the District Surveyor and Mr Dearle, of Garretts, and you will be sorry to learn that the damage is more serious and extensive than we had thought. The south wall is dangerous and will have to be shored up. The roof timbers have been badly smashed. The ceiling is dangerous and must be taken down. To carry out this work and make the Church temporarily weatherproof will cost about £900. Efforts are being made to obtain a licence to spend this sum. The architect, Mr Humphrey, and the district surveyor are both writing to the appropriate authorities to try to secure a licence but it is extremely difficult as priority is given to work on dwelling houses. It is hoped that, as the Church is scheduled as an historic monument, this will help a decision in our favour....

24TH MARCH, 1945: I have already replied to the Town Clerk, stating that no pensions are paid out of the funds of the charities administered by the Parish Church but that seven old people are pensioned in the Hibbert Almshouses...

We are still unable to obtain licence for further repairs to be carried out at the Parish Church. We are however arranging for security work on the organ.

The Tram Depot in Clapham High Street (where Sainsbury's now is) after air raid damage in April 1941

*The Rectory was at that time a very large building
in Macaulay Road, lived in by the Rector and his curate,
but also a convenient place to dump things*

9TH JUNE, 1945: Whether or no the moths are particularly prevalent this late spring I do not know. But I do know that there were hundreds of them in my drawing room until I was forced to set about clearing out some of the soft furnishing and fabrics, which various people have dumped there during the war years. This belated spring clean resulted in my being able to forward to Mrs Derham a cheque for £10 arising from the sale of cassocks, surplices, etc., which were the property of St Saviour's. This sum has been banked in the St Saviour's account, but most probably it will in due course find its way to the Holy Trinity account, as of course we know that the former church [in Cedars Road] will not be rebuilt, whereas everything is being done to hasten the restoration of the Parish Church. It is a great pity this stuff was not disposed of at about the same time that we gave St Saviour's vestments, etc., to St John's, Clapham Rise…

…Torn and patched surplices, a few split and moth-eaten cassocks, together with some cloths have been taken up by me to the S.P.G.[Society for the Propagation of the Gospel] House; so you see that I am managing to get things tidied up. But there still remains a terrific amount to be done, but that will be more easily tackled when the Bishop of Kingston manages to arrange for the collection of his furniture, at present stored in the drawing room…

*This was more of a burden on Canon Durell than he made it sound,
since he was at the same time receiving treatment for cancer. A year
later, in part of a long letter of 11th May 1946, he looked back*

…. While on the subject of the accounts, doubtless you can look up the entries of £6 paid to yourself and £10 paid to Mrs Derham about a year ago. So far as can be recollected, there were several of the clergy interested in procuring second-hand robes for clerics and choirs and, as my drawing room was crammed with the Bishop's furniture, other people's furniture and church furnishings, and as my housekeeper informed me that the Hagerty boys [Mr Hagerty was the curate] had dragged to the attic a valuable rug, on which they reclined for their smoking parties, it seemed to me that the sooner some of the stuff was cleared, the safer it would be. My hot endeavours to get this accomplished (at the time of my short-wave diathermy treatment and my daily visits to Guy's to obtain relief from chronic nasal catarrh) will ever be a painful memory…

…The S.P.G. accepted the offer of some iron-moulded surplices but turned down the offer of worn cassocks, although they had been laundered and extra matching material was supplied for renovating. Incidentally, they suggested that voluntary needlewomen, connected with our church, should undertake the repairs!…But the remaining vestments were placed in very needy hands indeed and may by this time be on their way to the Far East.

10TH JULY, 1945: Please accept my very grateful thanks for the generous donation of five guineas from yourself and Claudia [Mr Hicks' daughter] to the funds of the Summer Social Sale. I read the latter part of your letter at the opening ceremony. It all went off very well and realised £44.10.0 for the Church Fund and £8.10.0 for the West Indies Distress Fund. Captain Lowndes spoke very nicely and made himself very pleasant in conversation with the people. There seems to be an impression that he has been returned to Parliament by a narrow majority.

The election results were delayed while the votes of the servicemen and women were returned and counted. They were overwhelmingly Labour, and brought about the election of the Attlee Government. Captain Lowndes was defeated by John Battley, who became Clapham's first Labour MP. Towards the end of 1945, Canon Durell announced his retirement. Infirm and ill he went to live with friends in Teddington

8TH JANUARY, 1946: To me, too, it was sad that my last Christmas in office should be spent away from the Parish Church. Believe me, nothing but sheer physical weakness could have prevented it. There was so much to have said, so many faces to have seen, so many hands to have shaken, but, alas! the words were only thoughts, the faces only pictures and the handshakes not felt.…

6TH MARCH, 1946: … it is my fixed intention that every penny [of Canon Durell's farewell gift] is presented to the Restoration Fund of Clapham Parish Church.

… members of my family should be given the opportunity of forwarding a contribution…; and it is suggested that you, as Rector's Warden, might be willing to write a personal letter to each, inviting a cheque. But it cannot be too strongly emphasised that no member of my family must receive a copy of the circular letter owing to its allusion to my health and that your letter must make no mention whatsoever of my illness. My sister-in-law lost her son in the war; my nephew has just lost his father (my brother); and other members of my family have more than enough, about which to mourn, without being told that I have cancer of the bladder.

18TH MAY, 1946: Accept my appreciative interest in your vivid account of the Annual Church Meeting. Always there will be more than a corner of my heart filled with concern for the Clapham Parish Church. How vastly differently affairs are conducted today! When Colonel Bowyer [as Lord of the Manor] saw fit to appoint me to the living of Holy Trinity, Prebendary and Mrs Dalton gave me tea in the rectory drawing room and then suggested a saunter round the parish, for the purpose of introducing me to prominent members of the congregation... The Daltons' departure was carried out in luxurious leisure, whereas my leaving was made with painful haste. We are all fully aware that one cannot put back the clock; nevertheless it will need most forceful argument to convince me that the present time is an improvement on the old time.

With kind regards, Very sincerely yours, J.C.V. Durell.

Extracted from letters in the archive of
Holy Trinity Church, Clapham Common

Canon Durell died in August 1946, a month or so after the Revd. Niel Nye had been installed as his successor as the Rector of Clapham

Opened in 1916, the **South London Hospital for Women and Children** *had greatly expanded in the years between the wars. Its impressive new building faced the Common near Clapham South Underground Station.* **Margaret Louden** *described how, during the war, the hospital found itself in the front line.*

HISTORY WAS MADE EARLY IN THE WAR when by a special Act of Parliament, the South London Hospital was empowered to admit male patients of any age. The hospital was designated as a Casualty Hospital, and was protected by sandbags and other relatively inadequate measures. The Medical Staff was reduced in numbers as the Forces and other hospitals claimed some of them. During the first year male Service Sick were our only change but in September 1940, we entered the Front Line. The out-patient hall was our Casualty Reception Ward and the surrounding rooms were used as wards and theatres. After the night's "blitz", convoys of patients were arranged for evacuation to Base Hospitals and there was little time for rest for any of the staff.

While the medical women on the staff continued to do the casualty and routine hospital work, they were greatly helped by their male colleagues from other hospitals who visited to give advice on special problems such as eye, chest and brain injuries. The hospital was also assisted in a very useful way by a troop of Rover Scouts who acted as stretcher bearers, theatre porters, first-aid orderlies, messengers, fire-watchers, and who in many other unrecorded deeds contributed to the difficult organisation of those days.

One of the Scouts was **Gerald Rowe**. *In 1983, he wrote to the hospital to ask to have his time there certified as part of his war service. The correspondence survives in the hospital archives*

AT THE OUTBREAK OF WAR as a scout, Mr Robert Morrison (Scoutmaster of the 5th Balham Group) offered our services to the hospital to act in any capacity we were capable of until we were called up.

In two teams we slept at the hospital in "the dugout" (under the ramp) throughout the air raids, on duty in readiness of the event of air-raids, and throughout the same acted as stretcher-bearers. We also acted as fire wardens dealing with incendiaries. Even when the air-raids were not in process we did any job called upon to do (unloading air raid injured, moving them into theatre and to wards etc.). We became a part of the hospital and the "emergency hospital scheme", wearing the badge of 'stretcher bearer' 'SB' and on duty an armband.

Mr Morrison sat on the board with Miss Louden who was on the medical staff then.

During this period the hospital was open to male casualties of course and at one period I was one – also as a service battle casualty later, my after care wounds were treated under the direction of Miss Louden.

As each of us became of age for military service, so we left – tho' retaining social ties – and whilst on leave put ourselves on duty at the hospital along with the remaining scouts. Several of the hospital scouts were killed in action, mostly in the airforce, and they left behind broken-hearted nurses. Others later married nurses at the hospital while on leave.

I served at the hospital from the outbreak of the war until I joined the army in March/April 1942. Recently I applied for "the Defence Medal" (tho' it is of little importance as a medal) and was sent the enclosed. My service at the hospital combined with my home service in the army whilst in England amounts to the required 3 years – the qualifying period for the medal.

Mr Robert Morrison died several years ago, as did Mr Hanna, so they cannot signature my application, and I doubt if the hospital has records of my service (or that of the venture itself – tho' recently an item relating to it was mentioned in the local press) – but perhaps you will take my word for it. The medal is of no monetary value whatsoever and due to the large quantity distributed it never will be but I want it to go with my army medals for family posterity. When issued with my service medals following the war the medal office was not aware of my civil war service at the SLH.

[Postscript] During our duty we were awake all night – night after night during the raids – gaining no sleep, yet having to go to our place of employment the following day. Those off duty had to report to the hospital if a raid was in progress.

From a letter in the London Metropolitan Archives,
reproduced by permission of the St George's Hospital Health Authority

Miss Louden confirmed the facts and the hospital administrator signed Mr Rowe's certificate, adding: "Miss Louden asked me to give her best wishes and to tell you that she well remembers the excellent work undertaken by the Scouts during the war." Miss Louden's account continues

THE CLIMAX OF THE LONDON BLITZ was the night of April 6th/7th, 1941, when it seemed as if the hospital was the target for the night and the casualties were very heavy. Thereafter the air raids diminished in intensity and ordinary hospital work again became possible.

Once more we were in the Front Line in June, 1944, with the flying bomb attack. This time casualties were more serious and there was no respite throughout the day, so that the evacuation of convoys was fraught with great difficulty. The hospital itself had a miraculous escape from serious damage, although bombs dropped in the garden, on the Common, in neighbouring roads, the New Nurses Home was the only part to suffer a direct hit.

MISS MARGARET LOUDEN, *The South London Hospital*
for Women and Children, 1958

*Margaret Louden did pioneering work in the treatment
of bomb victims with crush injuries.
Her obituary acknowledged her achievements:*

...Had Margaret Louden chosen to publish an account of her work on crush syndrome she might have won considerable renown...

...During the war she dealt not only with victims of the crush syndrome, but also with wounded soldiers and pilots... After air raids, victims would be lying on stretchers and improvised beds in the corridors, and on at least one occasion Margaret Louden worked three nights and two days without a break.

One of those she treated was Sir James Martin, the inventor of the ejector seat, who had been injured in an encounter with gypsies. They became fast friends, and after the war Margaret Louden advised Martin on the effects of ejection on the human skeleton.

For thirty years from the end of the Second World War she continued to devote herself to the South London Hospital for Women and Children...

THE DAILY TELEGRAPH, 19 February 1999

Minnie Sullivan *lived in Leppoc Road during
the Second World War. In 1985 she talked about her experiences
for a season of events, held at a local church, about memories
of bringing up young families in wartime.*

I WAS EVACUATED ON THE 3RD SEPTEMBER 1939 with a friend of mine. [Cissy, who was also her lodger, living in the top of the house] I took Ruth [her daughter] with me and she took her little girl, [Anne] and we were sent to Henfield in Sussex. My friend had a bad billet, a mouse used to run round the cot. But I was sent to a very nice place, to a gardener to the local squire. They had their own vegetables. I was very lucky.

John wasn't born yet. I had to be evacuated because I was having him. Ruth was nearly three. I was sent to a nursing home in October before I had John in the November. The people at Henfield wanted to adopt Ruth – can you imagine me? I wouldn't have let Ruth be adopted. Any rate they were ever so good, and they looked after her while I was in the nursing home. They were very fond of her. I was back at the billet for Christmas, and my husband came down, and we all had Christmas together. John was christened down there, and I came back on 10th February 1940. I came back in thick snow – it was a terrible winter.

I didn't want to stay away. I had to go to have John, but I wouldn't have gone away but for that. When I did come back a neighbour of mine said "It's a good thing you've come home Mrs. Sullivan because I don't think you'd have had a husband to come home to soon. He's been living on beer and sandwiches". He hated me being away.

When the raids did start, we all come down to my living room and slept on the floor – the whole household. We had cushions. The old gentleman [who lodged with Cissy and her family upstairs] lay on my settee, and Anne and Ruth lay in the corner. After a while we got fed up with that, so we went to our own beds, raids or no raids. The Ack-Ack guns used to go off on the Common. You couldn't sleep through the guns.

There was a bomb in the middle of Leppoc Road. We were all supposed to be evacuated from the houses, because the bomb had not exploded. But you see, me having a small baby I had nowhere to go. So, they told us we must stay at the back of the house. We used to have to go to the top of the road to collect milk. They came to get the bomb out after about a week.

After that the people next door to me decided they would have to go away. They couldn't stand it any more. And she had a lot of damsons, so she gave them to me. I managed to get enough sugar, and I made jam on my open fire because I had no gas (when the bomb came down, the gas went off) Cissy and I made it, and we had damson jam between us. When we were without gas, we used a little round electric stove – portable – to cook the vegetables. I used to do a pot roast on the fire. It ruined all your saucepans of course.

I was registered to Mr. Nicholls [the grocer] on Clapham Park Road and I used to go down and get my rations once a week. And do you know it cost 10 shillings, and you'd get all your groceries and a piece of bacon and all with that. Then I was registered at the butchers. We had a ration book and you were allowed so much a week. They used to take the coupons out and they never used to allow you any more either. I don't know but I managed all right.

I didn't work till the children were both at school. There was a bomb one day on the way to school, and that made John ill that bomb. A nurse used to come in. He and his father were both ill. One time we never had any water. That was due to bombs. We used to go to St Alphonsus Road for the water. Dad used to go when he got home from work, and also before he went to work. He was fire-watching.

We never had a shelter until the doodlebugs came [in 1944], and then we had a Morrison shelter [a steel cage with a hard top and mesh side specially designed for use inside the house]. A bomb fell on the Common and my husband was coming out of the underground, and of course, he was blown back again. That was a shock. He was ill after that. He stopped and had a drink after in St Alphonsus Road. Of course he knew the bomb had dropped. Ruth and John were sitting in the living room – they were supposed to be in bed but they hadn't gone to bed. I said "Well, we'll go through and see if there's any more ceiling down, shall we?" We went along to see about the ceilings, but we didn't look in the front room, and the windows were out. It was a good job the children hadn't been put to bed, because the glass would have been all over them. So when Dad [her husband] came home he told us about the windows, and we had to go and clean up, and board them up for the night. I can't remember when we had any glass put in.

Leppoc Road VJ (Victory in Japan) party, August 1945

After that the children and I used to sleep in the Morrison shelter, and Dad had a single bed by the side. That bomb made him ill. He had a very high temperature. There was snow on the ground and the doctor suggested I went out and collected snow and put it on him in a cloth to bring his temperature down. While he was ill there was another bomb in Rodenhurst Road, and when I got back from shopping, all the windows were blown open – not blown in – blown open. And, of course, Dad was not supposed to be in a draught. He had bronchitis after that. The war ruined his health. On Friday afternoon my neighbour and I were waiting to go shopping, and a bomb dropped in Elms Road – a doodlebug – they used to just come over and cut-out and drop. No-one knew where they would drop. One night I was alone in the house, Dad was at the Stock Exchange where he worked fire-watching and I was really frightened. I had the responsibility for the two children, you see. I was sitting on Ruth's bed. I never picked her up if I could help it because I didn't want her to get out of routine. I used to sit on the bed if anything was wrong - all guns going and everything. She said to me: " Do you know, you're shaking my bed, Mum." I said: "Well you know, I'm so cold, Ruth". And she said, "Well, what are you sitting there for if you're so cold?"

You know, when you look back on it it wasn't funny at the time! Of course it affected the children's routine, however hard you tried. John was a baby, and no sooner did I have him out in the garden in his pram, than the alert would go, and I'd have to bring him in again. Ruth was at school, of course, but she seems to have spent more time under the table than anywhere.

I seemed to manage in spite of the food shortages. We had dried egg of course. I cooked quite well with dried egg. Although I did get ill at one time, and the doctor said I was neglecting myself – you know, I'd cook a dinner for the others, and have bread and butter myself. I thought it was important for the children to be nourished. I'd been well nourished as a child, and I got through it. In the end we kept chickens, and dug up the garden for a few vegetables – carrots, lettuce, beetroot and a few beans in season. We had a cock who made so much noise in the mornings that the neighbours complained. I had to put it down the cellar. We fattened it up there, and had it for Christmas dinner. At the end of the war they had a big children's party in Leppoc Road. We decorated the street and everyone was dressed in their best clothes, and wore paper hats and so on. Of course, that was the same in all the streets round here.

MINNIE SULLIVAN, 1985

*For London children, school still went on even in the midst of air raids and their consequences. In 1942, **Anna Jefferson Smith** started at Clapham Parochial School. In 2001 she recalled her family's experiences during the war years.*

BOMB DAMAGE IN THE SECOND WORLD WAR to the schools in Macaulay Road and Rectory Grove meant that Clapham Parochial School had to find alternative accommodation. As a result I began my schooling in St. Paul's Hall in Heath Road. We lived on the corner of Larkhall Rise and Gauden Road so this meant a total distance of around three miles to walk each day since pupils were expected to go home for lunch. Very few families had cars and possession of one would have been well beyond the reach of our family.

In spite of the war my memories of my primary school were very happy. Of course the sound of air raid warnings and the awaited "all clear" were part of our lives, but to a child the drills which included the donning of a Mickey Mouse gas mask or the walk to the air raid shelter often seemed an adventure. I remember trying out the "rude words" inscribed in the shelter on my parents with dramatic results.

During the war my father worked as a butcher in Victoria. One of his customers who had a much loved parrot thought for some unknown reason that the bird would be safer in Clapham. Hence the scraggy, somewhat ill tempered African Grey was installed in his cage in the corner of our kitchen. My father was fond of the bird, unoriginally called Polly, and would talk to him and be allowed to "scratch his poll?" My mother was not so keen, although the fact that Polly would often greet her entry into the room with "silly old fool" probably did not help.

The bird's owner was wrong about the safety of Clapham. We were close to such enemy attractions as Clapham Junction, Battersea Power Station, Battersea Gas Works and the Projectile armaments factory so air raids were not uncommon and our house badly shaken as a result. One morning when my parents came down to the kitchen it was to find that yet again plaster had come down from the ceiling with a plentiful quantity having landed on the cloth which covered Polly's cage. My father anxiously raised the cloth to be greeted by the bird hopping from claw to claw and squawking "Bloody Nazis, bloody Nazis". My mother, unimpressed, enquired "Who taught him to say that William?"

It was the small things which could cause most childish displeasure. Pupils were given a third of a pint of milk to drink at playtime every morning. The milk came in chubby glass bottles which were left on top of the large solid fuel burning stoves that warmed the classrooms for some time "to take the chill off". It was no doubt meant to be a kindness but to me it tasted very unappetising.

Many wartime stories were told where escapes or disasters were attributed to luck, good or bad. My father had a good luck story.

He had served in the First World War where his regiment, with its horses, had crossed to France. Like so many veterans of that war he shut away memories that were too bitter to share, even with his family. One of the few things we learnt was of his deep affection for the horses, especially one called Mickey for whom my father would save his issue of custard creams.

In 1944 his custom was to begin his half day with a leisurely pint, or two, at the Gauden Hotel in Gauden Road. One week in June a film co-starring a horse was being shown locally, and, breaking his usual routine, he went to see it. That sunny afternoon one of the pilotless planes, or "doodlebugs", hit the hotel causing ten deaths and a number of other casualties.

The "doodlebugs" in this last phase of the war were particularly frightening. Once having heard the sound of one approaching there was the wait to hear when the engine would cut out. Where would it fall? In our household we suffered more than most since we also had the excellent imitations by a certain parrot.

Now into my seventh decade, I have lived in Clapham nearly all my life and have never considered that the grass might be greener elsewhere.

ANNA JEFFERSON SMITH, 2001

*Other families were not so fortunate, losing their homes
and seeing neighbours killed.* **Mary Mallison** *lived in Batten Street,
just near the target area of Clapham Junction.
Aged ten at the outbreak of the war, she was interviewed by*
Luke Vivian-Neal, *aged ten in 2002.*

THE TENTH OF JUNE, 1944 will forever be ingrained in Mary's memory. It was 10.00 on a sunny Sunday morning in London as the grim warning of the air-raid siren shattered the peace. Mrs Mallison screamed for her children to run to their shelter in the yard. The sound of the aircraft overhead was deafening and the family threw themselves through the doorway of the shelter just as the whistle and screech of the first bombs rained down on them. The little family cowered together on the shelter floor as the dull *crump* of bombs landing met their ears. Suddenly, there was an almighty *thud*, a tremendous crash and a blast of hot air swirled around them from a huge explosion. Their home had suffered a direct hit.

As the siren sounded the all clear, Mary crawled through the shelter doorway and recoiled aghast at the sight that met her eyes. Her house was just a pile of rubble with pieces of furniture sticking out. Half out of her mind with shock, she picked her way through the debris and out of what was once her front door but was now a heap of splintered wood, into the street.

A terrible sight met her eyes. Batten Street was a wreck. Women were weeping over heaps of rubble that, a few minutes before, had once been houses. As the dust settled over the wreckage of a particular house, the figure of a man appeared, carrying a dreadful limp object. It was the body of his dear wife.

One woman who had fourteen children, escaped to the street shelter with eleven of her family, but three of her boys, who were in the army and on home leave, had been having a lie-in and were killed when a bomb hit their house.

Somehow, Mary and her family managed to walk to the local converted school where people who had had houses destroyed by bombing could find somewhere to sleep. For the next month, Mrs Mallison walked the streets of Clapham and Battersea, looking for an abandoned house. Mary began work aged fourteen in Clapham Old Town as an office junior with the National Union of Seamen and used her weekly wage of thirty-two shillings and sixpence to help make ends meet.

Eventually, just as Mary's mother had given up for the day, she spotted a derelict looking house in Battersea Park Road; she rushed over to it and pushed at the door, there was no one living there. Flushed with triumph she ran to the converted school to tell her children the news that she had found a deserted home. It took a month to get the house, during which time all of Mary's savings were used up. Eventually they moved in. Their furniture was utility, horribly drab, but better than nothing. They remained there until the end of the war when they returned to Batten Street. To this day Mary feels very sad when she recounts memories of the war, but her face brightens when she recalls the singular kindness of the British people to their friends and neighbours and how they were able to comfort each other during that terrible time.

MARY MALLINSON *interviewed by Luke Vivian-Neal*, 2002

The novelist **Graham Greene** *(1904-1991) lived in Clapham for a while in the 1930s and set his novel,* The End of the Affair, *published in 1951, in Clapham during the Second World War.*

WHAT A SUMMER IT WAS. I am not going to try and name the month exactly – I should have to go back to it through so much pain, but I remember leaving the hot and crowded room, after drinking too much bad sherry, and walking on the Common with Henry. The sun was falling flat across the Common and the grass was pale with it. In the distance the houses were the houses in a Victorian print, small and precisely drawn and quiet: only one child cried a long way off. The eighteenth-century church stood like a toy in an island of grass – the toy could be left outside in the dark, in the dry unbreakable weather. It was the hour when you make confidences to a stranger...

....It was a worse night than the one when I met Henry a month before. This time it was sleet instead of rain: it was half-way to snow and the edged drops seemed to slash their way in through the buttonholes of one's raincoat: they obscured the lamps on the Common, so that it was impossible to run, and I can't run fast anyway because of my leg. I wished I had brought my war-time torch with me, for it must have taken eight minutes for me to reach the house on North Side. I was just stepping off the pavement to cross when the door opened and Sarah came out. I thought with happiness, I have her now. I knew with absolute certainty that before the night was out we should have slept together again. And once that had been renewed, anything might happen. I had never known her before and I had never loved her so much. The more we know the more we love, I thought. I was back in the territory of trust.

She was in too much of a hurry to see me across the wide roadway through the sleet. She turned to the left and walked rapidly away. I thought, she will need somewhere to sit down and then I have her trapped. I followed twenty yards behind, but she never looked back. She skirted the Common, past the pond and the bombed bookshop, as though she were making for the tube. Well, if it were necessary, I was prepared to talk to her even in a crowded train. She went down the tube-stairs and up to the booking office, but she had no bag with her and when she felt in her pockets no loose money either – not even the three halfpence that would have enabled her to travel up and down till midnight. Up the stairs again, and across the road where the trams run. One earth had been stopped, but another had obviously come to mind. I was triumphant. She was afraid, but she wasn't afraid of me, she was afraid of herself and what was going to happen when we met. I felt I had won the game already, and I could afford to feel a certain pity for my victim. I wanted to say to her, Don't worry, there's nothing to fear, we'll both be happy soon, the nightmare's nearly over.

And then I lost her. I had been too confident and I had allowed her too big a start. She had crossed the road twenty yards ahead of me (I was delayed again by my bad leg coming up the stairs), a tram ran between, and she was gone. She might have turned left down the High Street or gone straight ahead down Park Road, but I couldn't see her. I wasn't very worried – if I didn't find her today, I would the next. Now I knew the whole absurd story of the vow, now I was certain of her love, I was assured of her. If two people loved, they slept together; it was a mathematical formula, tested and proved by human experience.

There was an A.B.C. [a chain of bakeries with cafés] in the High Street and I tried that. She wasn't there. Then I remembered the church at the corner of Park Road, [St Mary's Catholic Church, Clapham Park Road] and I knew at once that she had gone there. I followed, and sure enough there she was sitting in one of the side aisles close to a pillar and a hideous statue of the virgin. She wasn't praying. She was just sitting there with her eyes closed. I only saw her by the light of the candles before the statue, for the whole place was very dark. I sat down behind her like Mr Parkis and waited. I could have waited years now that I knew the end of the story. I was cold and wet and very happy. I could even look with charity towards the altar and the figure dangling there. She loves us both, I thought, but if there is to be a conflict between an image and a man, I know who will win. I could put my hand on her thigh or my mouth on her breast: he was imprisoned behind the altar and couldn't move to plead *his* cause.

GRAHAM GREENE, *The End of the Affair*, 1951

John Battley (1880-1952) *founder of a local printing firm, was closely involved in local affairs; a member of the London County Council and a Justice of the Peace. In 1945 he was elected the first Labour Member of Parliament for Clapham. He had been adopted as candidate for the 1939 election, which did not take place due to the outbreak of war.*

*In this address in 1941 he outlined his vision for Clapham
after the war. It is remarkable that relatively early in the war
such bold plans for post war reconstruction
should have been voiced.*

THE WHOLE OF WANDSWORTH ROAD and especially from Cedars Road to
Thessaly Road should be rebuilt on a bold plan, taking in the flats already built
in the general idea, confining the shops to a centre and not allowing them, ribbon-
like, to straggle along over the whole.

Clapham High Street should be dealt with in a general bold and artistic
scheme, embracing in its scope The Pavement and Clapham Park Road.
Included in the scheme should be the removal of the Tram Depot; [this was on
the site of Sainsbury's in Clapham High Street] and the camouflaging of the ugly
railway bridge at the junction of Clapham Road and the High Street. If such
bridges are to remain, and I do not suggest their removal, surely they can be
made less of an eyesore, and less unfairly used with competitive advertisements
of stores removed from Clapham. Underneath this bridge let each pavement be
lined with well lit shops. Surely we should not agree for ever to have ugliness
battened upon us?

The High Street (already town-planned as a 120 ft. road) being at the heart
of the constituency, it is here that a community centre should be established,
with its forum, where, among other things, our Member of Parliament, Members
of the London County Council, and our Borough Councillors, could be consulted
and questioned as to their work for our constituency. The hub of the amenities
of a community centre should be set and housed in a building which could be
used by all the worthy interests, associations and clubs, of Clapham. You can
readily see what a conspicuous place a Ratepayers' Association could and
should take in such a scheme.

Included in this community centre there should be a modern Cinema,
Repertoire Theatre, Library, Baths, and Public Hall with an efficient inquiry
and information Bureau and adequate car-parking facilities. These amenities
need not detract from its being a central shopping centre, nor should they
detract in any way from the moral purpose and the consequent right use of the
increased leisure of our people. In fact they should strengthen the moral
purpose and afford guidance in the right use of leisure…

…I suggest a well-constructed well-lit colonnade, built specially for the main shopping centre, enabling shoppers to make their purchases in comfort, a part of which to face the Common so that its beauties might be seen and appreciated by our women, even on a busy day. This colonnade should be surmounted by service flats with wide balconies, suitable for flowers or for having meals out of doors. The healthful air of Clapham is not nearly sufficiently appreciated…

…From a trading point of view we have to face the fact that many of our small traders have been squeezed out by the circumstances of the war. Possibly many more will follow.

But I want to say this, although after the war a less number of shops will be required, the neighbourhood will still need, although possibly not to so large a degree, the personal service of the imaginative and independent trader who sees in the mass-produced articles and automatic service of the multiple stores something to be deplored…

…I should like to see a Pensioners' Retreat on Clapham Common, where our old people could meet in pleasant and health-giving surroundings, to play, and to discuss, and to solve, the problems of this world and the next…

….Again, why should it be necessary for a war to teach us that tired working people enjoy music in the open air in their rest periods. A Band should play on Clapham Common every day while weather permits. A Swimming Pool should be built on the Common so that youth may squeeze the fullest benefit from our all too short summer. This would be a tremendous advance in a reconstructed health programme. There should be a Cafeteria similar to the one erected and opened in Battersea Park, with proper facilities for open air dancing.

The governmental restrictions and disciplines of the war period when lifted will result (if we simply seek abruptly to stop the natural swing of the pendulum) in extravagances which will both shock and repel. What we should do is to afford healthy scope for the physical exuberance of youth and the young men and women on demobilisation, as well as for their mental and spiritual development.

I should like to see well-designed centrally-heated groups of flats and labour-saving houses displacing the industrial slums of North Clapham. There is a good deal of misrepresentation about flats, and it is claimed that the ordinary person wants a small house and a garden. To me personally, the provision of houses with gardens is most desirable, and a programme I strongly endorse, but is it as common a desire as we imagine in our large cities? I feel sure if you were to ask the public men and women of Clapham what is the great and common demand, I am sure they will tell you that it is for flats, with proper amenities, rather than for houses and gardens.

It is undeniable that the flat, if its particular problems of design are sufficiently studied, can and does afford the pleasantest possible conditions of living for a very large proportion of the inhabitants of our large towns and cities. We have to face the changed attitude of girls and women to domestic duties and domestic service, and the fact that a large proportion of women are now entering the professional, commercial, and industrial fields at a pace which has been accelerated by the war; and, moreover, it is wise for us to note their changing views in relation to child-bearing and the providing of material for the high explosive and the incendiary to blast and to burn...

...If nursery schools, club rooms, restaurants, recreational facilities, reading rooms, craft rooms, lecture rooms, Institutes, Schools, and Churches are to be provided, they can best be provided with hopes of sustained success when they are near to or contiguous to groups of modern flats and well-planned estates of houses. And if public gardens and open spaces are interspersed, surely these will be a definite gain in external amenities, compared with ill-kept houses and gardens in various conditions of sprawled disorder and unkemptness. Again no group of flats should be erected without suitable playgrounds being provided for young children under the superintendence of games instructors.

Clapham had about 60,000 inhabitants before the war. It has now probably not more than between 25,000 to 30,000. In the County of London there are no more than 2,250,000 or about half the pre-war number. When the great influx occurs many strangers will be mixed with the throng; many who will expect, ready made, something more

John Battley

of Clapham than a peaceful super-respectable suburb...

...Why should we not have an open or covered market, say in the Old Town or perhaps a more convenient open spot, on a Friday or a Saturday, with its humanity relieving as it would, our drab asphalt and the stony desert of our streets by its colourful activity, beside adding to Clapham's trade and prosperity.

JOHN BATTLEY, *Address to Clapham Ratepayers' Association*, 30 September 1941

In the 1945 election **John Battley** *was elected Member of Parliament for Clapham. The local paper reported the first public meeting after his election.*

CHEERING AND SHOUTS OF "HE'S A JOLLY GOOD FELLOW" greeted Mr John Battley, the first Labour M.P. to be returned by Clapham, when he met his constituents on Friday evening at a social at Henry Thornton School and thanked them for their work during the recent election...

...He said that it was unusual in an election for an M.P. to be returned in the district where he had been born and lived all his life. The confidence which had been shown in him by the electors made him feel exceedingly proud, but at the same time very humble. The large majority he had secured filled him with the deepest emotion.

"I am among the people that I love, and I know that you love me.

Not many men could have faced through the last 6 or 7 weeks without realising the sacrifices that have been made on Labour's behalf.

You have done all this for the freedom of the common people, for which you have sacrificed yourselves not only for weeks, but for years.

Years ago it was not popular to be a Socialist. It was not even decent. I can remember the days when I attempted to stand on a platform on Clapham Common. My platform was pushed over, and I was threatened with immersion in the pond.

We have had a bloodless revolution, whereby the common people have at last come into their own and will have an opportunity of rebuilding this country. We shall erect an edifice that will bridge not only this country, but the whole world.

Clapham has set an example in this revolution. Nevermore will the light be dimmed that you have lighted in Clapham. Never again shall we live under the grey, gloomy and despicable regime that we have tolerated for so many years. Clapham's light will never be put out".

THE SOUTH LONDON PRESS, 31 July 1945

John Battley *carried out his many public duties with extraordinary conscientiousness, at the same time as running his business. He took a great interest in the history and traditions of Parliament, delighted in taking constituents on tours of the House and wrote a book about it. The penultimate sentence of this extract is particularly poignant, since he did not seek re-election in 1950 due to ill health and died two years later.*

MY NORMAL DAY STARTS AT 6 A.M.; I am at my office at 8 a.m., interviewing constituents until 10 a.m., when I leave for Committees, some of which I preside over as Chairman. After a sandwich lunch, at 2.30 I am again at the House of Commons, which, as is generally known, often sits until the early hours of the morning. During one exceptional week, I managed to obtain ten hours' sleep in four days! It is not surprising, therefore, that Members sitting for English constituencies are exempt from serving on juries.

The exceptionally long hours put in by Members during this Parliament are reflected in the prevalence of ill-health. A very apt remark was made recently when a Member said that if his Trade Union members were asked to do one half the work of their M.P. they would strike at once.

JOHN BATTLEY, A *Visit to the Houses of Parliament*, 1947

6

THE POST WAR YEARS

Pamela Hansford Johnson (1912-1981)
set her novel, An Impossible Marriage, in Clapham in the 1930s,
but towards the end of the story the narrator returns to Clapham after
the war. She recalls the area in her youth and remarks on the changes.

...I TOOK A CERTAIN PLEASURE IN SEEING THE NEIGHBOURHOOD AGAIN. I was
born near the Common. I had memories of crossing it on cold and frosty mornings
on my way to school; of walking there on blue and dusty summer evenings in
the exalted, painful insulation of first, childish love-affairs. I could see the island
on the pond, cone-shaped, thick with sunny trees, on which the little boys ran
naked, natural and Greek after swimming, until the borough council insisted on
bathing drawers. I could see the big field by North Side, the boys and girls
lounging in deck-chairs, playing ukuleles as the sun fell into ash and the new
moon hardened like steel in the lavender sky; the field behind the Parade, with
little low hawthorn hills, where less than innocent lovers lay locked by night.

I had not been there since the war.

Now, on that Sunday afternoon in October, I saw it changed, my world laid
waste. There were allotments in the big field; the scrawny, shabby cabbages

shrivelling on their knuckly stems; tangles of weed lying over the broken earth like travellers thirst-ridden in the desert crawling towards a water-hole. Here and there were tin huts, lopsided, peeling in the sun; and the row of high houses stretching from Sisters Avenue to Cedars Road had the shabby sadness of women too discouraged to paint their faces or get out of their dressing-gowns. And there were letting-boards. I could not remember anything being to let in my day.

The impression I had of it all was violent, too Gothic to be true – only true, perhaps, in relation to my romantic memories; but I felt depressed, a stranger there myself, and wished again that I had not yielded to Iris's importunities.

She was living on the second floor of a block of mansion flats, built of liver-coloured brick, and roofed in some approximation to château style. The turrets gleamed damply, like gun-metal, on the light-blue sky, and the glazed laurels flashed red and white below in the refracted light from the cars and buses. It was noisy on that corner, as I had remembered it; but far dustier – unless the dust were on the lens of my own memories. I went into the dankness of the tiled hallway, which was like the entrance to a municipal swimming baths, and in the aquarian gloom searched for her name on the Ins and Outs board, faintly hoping that by some accident I might find her proclaimed "Out" and so have an excuse for going away again.

PAMELA HANSFORD JOHNSON, *An Impossible Marriage*, 1954

George and Zette Cattermole (see Chapter 3)
returned to England after the war. Zette's widowed mother, Hélène, lived alone at 6 Northbourne Road. During the war she was required to divide the house into three flats to provide accommodation for bombed-out families. When these families were re-housed George and Zette moved in to look after Hélène as she got older. In 2001 they still live in the same house.

GEORGE: Clapham seemed rather dreary post-war with rationing and no jobs but Zette and I were happy in love. I remember when we got back Zette sent me down to the bakers at the end of the road for a loaf and they asked me 'Where's your ration book?' Of course, we had no idea about rationing coming from New Zealand, land of plenty. Mind you, for an extra 2/- slipped across the counter you could get ¹/₂ lb more lard at the butchers.

ZETTE: When we left, most of the houses in Northbourne Road were family houses, when we came back many had been turned into flats and boarding houses. Now it seems to be going back to family houses again. I like that. George had a difficult time finding a job but finally he was offered a post as a temporary civil servant at the Ministry of Health.

GEORGE: There was no work to do at the Ministry. I would sit at one desk and a beautifully spoken actor called Lowndes would sit at another. We read each other's newspapers and played 'Smash the Nazi Navy', a popular game played with paper and a pencil. Each person got one battleship, two cruisers, and a submarine. You had to beat the Nazi navy. Occasionally a woman would come around and apologise for the lack of work and say we would be busy soon but it never happened. I became great friends with Lowndes but sadly he killed himself out of frustration with post-war London.

*Meanwhile Zette commuted daily to the East End,
where she worked as an embroideress*

GEORGE: One of the biggest changes after the war was the opening of the first supermarket. I remember in about 1948 going to the opening of the first Tesco near Westminster. Zette and I shook hands with Mr. Jack Cohen. He said to me: 'Come in, take a basket, help yourself and we've people with machines who will add up your grocery bill as you come out. Don't forget today, this is just the first of many.' The store was named after Tessa, his wife (Tes) and Cohen (Co). Jack Cohen handed out £5 notes to the nine builders.

*This was a sociable time for George and Zette in Clapham. They loved
to give parties and dinners at 6 Northbourne Road. George had a fine
cellar and an interest in wines learned from his hotel days*

GEORGE: We used to get all the neighbours round and introduce them to each other. On one occasion we had 27 neighbours. I served them all sorts of cocktails to get the party going. We had brandy or gin based with Italian liqueurs and pink gins. I was addicted to parties.

Zette always did the food, she cooked beautifully. We had wonderful dinner parties, we could get 20 people seated at the table. I would lay out 56 glasses around the table if we had 10 guests and we would get through at least 4 different wines. In the 50's you had to go to Westminster or Pimlico to get decent wine, but now you can get it locally. Zette would cook soup with whatever was in season, then an entrée, followed by a main course and a light pudding. We had tremendous parties, at one stage I had 300 bottles of wine in my cellar.

Sue Lloyd, the actress in Crossroads lived at number 3, she was a very light-hearted lady, never miserable even when she could not get work. She was entertaining to have as a guest. We had 2 lawyers in the road and an ex-guardsman and we knew everyone. We had great fun in the 50's and 60's.

GEORGE AND ZETTE CATTERMOLE *interviewed by Annabel Allott*, 2001

Peter Skuse was born in Clapham in 1943 and lived in Abbeville Road for most of his childhood. Although he moved from the area long ago he retains an interest in Clapham and is still a member of the Clapham Society. His lively recollections of Clapham in the 1940s and 1950s highlight the changes not only in the area but also in the way we live fifty years later.

WHEN WE WENT BACK TO 138 ABBEVILLE ROAD in 1957, Eirlys [a tenant] had departed from the ground floor flat leaving her son's old busted pedal-car rusting in the back yard round by the kitchen window. Mum liked to call the kitchen the living room, for so it was, and the scullery she tried calling the kitchenette, but it never caught on. As a lad of fourteen I didn't fit into this five-year-old's car, but by bashing the boot with Dad's mallet I created a seat where, with bent-up knees, I could keep my balance and pedal furiously around the garden paths achieving maybe 3mph. That was one of the highlights of returning from our three-year sojourn in Streatham, necessitated by Grandad becoming a widower on the demise of Grandma Cocks, and our expectation of his coming to live with us. But he never did, in the end . . . I was Clapham born in 1943, and grew up in Clapham as they replaced route 45's open-stairs buses going round Parsons Corner [The junction of Clapham Park Road and Park Hill]. I always wanted to go upstairs on those buses because they reminded me of going on a helter-skelter when the Fair came to Clapham Common. We left in 1954 for three years, then returned.

Getting back to Clapham was a breath of fresh air: the brisk trot up Crescent Lane to the tube station, where we got the tube to Morden, where Auntie Mabs lived; the nip across the road to post letters in the box on the corner, close to Mrs Morley's sweet shop, where pocket money would be spent on 1d Trebor Chews, and a threepenny brick of ice cream from the freezer – often served by "My Pal Arry" who was a frequent visitor. There wasn't much room in the tiny shoplet that was round the corner in Crescent Lane and is now absorbed by the corner shop, which in the 1940s and 1950s was Mr Cropley's greengrocery.

When I was six, Mum and Dad bought me a dog and Clapham Common became even more important. My friends Bruce and Norm, whose gardens in Crescent Lane backed on to ours in Abbeville Road, were of a similar age, and as a trio we did loads of things together, all three up on the Common playing a three-person version of cricket, or football, or tennis against the big wall near the Mansions, as we called them [the large houses facing on to the Common in Windmill Drive]. Other outings included trips to Riddlesdown on the 115 bus, or an adventure to the woods at Streatham Common on the 137 that was a penny all the way from Parson's Corner. Then boxcart expeditions to Dulwich or Brockwell Parks, or to Streatham Common, when it was just two of us: one would push until he got tired, while the other sat in and steered, then we'd swop places. Parents just warned us not to take any inducement from strangers,

Crescent Lane in the early 1950s

and to stay in public areas. I'm certain it was no 'safer' then, but we weren't so restricted, and I'm talking here of age just into double figures.

No. 138 Abbeville Road had been Mum & Dad's home from 1938. I can remember being held up in the air with Mum standing on the front step, watching the searchlight beams moving about in the sky from an emplacement up on the Common by the AA [anti-aircraft] gun pits by the long pond. It was VE [Victory in Europe] day or something and is my earliest memory.

On a Saturday evening, Mum & Dad would settle down to the Saturday play on the wireless. We didn't get a TV until 1955 when ITV made an alternative to BBC, and weren't those adverts amazing! We'd not seen TV with adverts before. In fact, our family had only Auntie Elsie in Earlsfield with a telly, and there were sixteen in the family who bussed over there on June 2nd 1953 to watch the Coronation, in a curtains-closed hot room with a 12-inch TV screen in glorious shades of grey... The wireless was the chief source of news and entertainment, and on a Saturday I would be sent across the road with four shillings to Yardley's the Off Licence, and I'd come back with a pint of Guinness for Mum, a pint of Pale Ale for Dad, and a bottle of Tizer or Clayton's Cola for me. Only once was I not served, and couldn't understand why, though when I was really young my head only just showed above the counter. The man there knew who I was and could see where I took the bottles back to, and Mum or Dad would pop in from time to time to reassure the shop. Similarly, I would regularly get the Sunday paper from Mrs Parsons at Parsons Corner newsagent hut, together with ten Airman or Weights or Turf [brands of cigarette]. I was always served, despite being still of junior school age. There was a barber in the main building behind the hut, where I got a fortnightly haircut for 9d.

We knew just about everyone in Abbeville Road from the corner of Leppoc Road along to Briarwood Road on our side and a good number of folk across the road. We'd all be out in the front clipping hedges or watching for a coalman, who would deliver if you hailed him; men all down the road would be ready with a bucket and shovel at the top of the cellar steps, available within a minute or so if anyone saw a horse pause to drop valuable fertiliser in the street; it was better to scoop it up before it got flattened by vehicles. The Drain Out Cleaner would come around, always fun to watch, and the regular milkman with a hand cart would come down the road from Rowland's Dairy on the corner of Shandon [Road] or Hambalt [Road]. Mr Robinson, the insurance agent, came monthly to collect Mum's penny a week funeral insurance in case I didn't make it to my 21st, though I didn't know that at the time. I inherited this policy and cashed it in 1993 for £19.39. Another street regular was the street lamp cleaner, who would wind down the gas mantles in their glass bowls with a winch handle deployed into a socket inside a door on the lamp post, clean out the interior of moths and flies, then wind it up again until it snapped securely into the gas socket overhead. Sodium lamps and concrete lamp posts replaced the green ornate spluttery gas lamps during my childhood in Abbeville Road.

I didn't know of many people who owned their own houses. Most people paid a landlord rent, but we had the chance to buy our house in 1948 for £800 but Mum & Dad couldn't afford a mortgage for what they'd have had to borrow. They did get it in 1953 but it cost £1250 then, and Ivy & Len [tenants in the upstairs part of house] moved out a year or so later when Grandad Smith [Ivy's father] died.

Living there on the end of a terrace at 138 Abbeville Road, in the Borough of Wandsworth, I was the only boy to win a prize in the borough's road safety essay competition, entered by my school, Bonneville, whence I walked to and from daily, sometimes twice daily when I came home to dinner. Sort-of semi-

A gardening day with the neighbours, 1950s

detached, the house had a side entrance that enabled Dad to wheel the motor-bike through, after detaching it from the sidecar which he bought in the early spring of 1952. Dad was good with engines, having been a mechanic in the RAF during the war, and this engine (a 600cc BSA single) needed attention. We went on holiday and outings in it during the two years he kept it, before selling to a local plumber in 1954. It just fitted in the front garden; later Dad had the brick walls built at the front which are still there now from 1958. The coal-hole was regularly used, though it did mean my job of filling the scuttles during the winter - heating was coal fires in any room that needed to be warmed - required the carrying of filled scuttles up the cellar stairs, no mean feat when you're under ten years old!

The walk up to Parsons Corner to get the bus, maybe a 37 to Dulwich to walk round the park, or a 35 or 37 to Brixton shopping, or a 137 to Battersea Park or Crystal Palace, was short and easy. Across the big wide road, which was especially tricky to cross before the big brick-and-earth island was built, was a whole range of shops, starting with Stanley's bakery where one or two of the Saturday assistants still believed in baker's dozens, and would allow thirteen cakes for the price of twelve. A chemist and a dry cleaners called The Valet Service occupied premises close by, and there was a shoe shop on the bend. Round the corner were a timber yard, a DIY shop (Cooper & Hedges) and a general grocer (Rosam's) and a pet store. Further up Clapham Park Road on the King's Head side was a wet fish shop and Battley Brothers. Across from them was Matthews delicatessen which sold ham and that sort of product, and Isaacs the fish & chip shop which had on the wall painted in black on a green background an acrostic poem which read their name downwards, and finished: " 'S the best fish we have eaten!"

Walking to Bonneville School each day with maybe Isobel Bayly, the vicar's daughter at St James's, or with Clifford Cope from No.62, we'd pass by Walker's the sweet shop in what is now termed Abbeville Village. That was the only shop of any real interest, though there was a hardware store with amazing airguns and tools in the window...

...Bonneville School had tiered classrooms, and the bright children sat at the back – you literally moved up when you were good. Miss Rose was my teacher when I started in 1948, and Miss Standing was the infants' head-mistress, who publicly caned Stephen Kendidine within a term of my being there. He'd refused to cross his legs and put his hands on his knees during assembly when told, and then told Miss Standing that she was *a silly old cow*. School was fun, especially when Mr Furlong took you out of lessons for football practice for the Celts or the Danes (during my time there I somehow was in two houses), or Mr Lambert put you in charge of the class library... The desks all had inkwells and these were used by children who didn't have fountain pens; ball pens were strictly taboo since they frequently smudged. Desks were lift-up with a shelf or box beneath, and had a wooden tip-up seat.

The boys from Balham Central came and used woodworking facilities at one end of the playground and some would try to bully us juniors, but one day they picked on Harry Wake, who lived in one of the prefabs in Gaskarth Road. Harry was a fighter of renown, and despite being half the size of the *two* boys who set upon him, he whirlwinded his way out of the bundle doing much physical damage to the bullies, who quickly learned their lesson. This taught me always to fight back with as much vigour as can be mustered, if a fight was inevitable, and it stood me in good stead some eleven years later.

While I was at Bonneville I took part in the school's first-ever School Journey, which was to Wyke Regis in Dorset. The register for my class had 46 names in the year I left Bonneville; during the summer we had well over an hour for lunch, to allow boys and girls to walk home for dinner and walk back afterwards, since few mums went out to work - it wasn't the done thing for most families. My Mum felt guilty when family finances encouraged her to seek part-time work, but she always worked locally in Clapham or Brixton.

On Saturdays when I reached my teens, one of my jobs to earn my shilling pocket money was to walk up to Clapham High Street and do the shopping. About this time a supermarket opened: Jackson's, along past the Majestic cinema (where we went most weeks to see two films at "the pictures"). This was the first time Clapham residents self-selected their goods and took them to a checkout in a wire basket and was a novel experience at the time. I still had to go to Woolworths for biscuits, since they sold them loose and it was cheaper, and for 'real' bread you went to Stanley's in Clapham Park Road. There was usually a stop made at Bunty's the greengrocer near to the bus garage, later the Clapham Transport Museum [Sainsbury's is now on the site], for fruit and fresh vegetables. When rationing was still on, our coupons were collected by Rosam's Stores on the bend in Clapham Park Road – Mum never shopped along at the other end of Abbeville [Road] because these shops were all nearer.

As boys we used Clapham Common a lot. The bandstand was fun, whether there was a band playing or not, though we used to get told off every now and again for roller skating when people were trying to listen to the band. Occasionally we would watch the chess players, and there were always people sailing their model ships on the pond. We would hire a boat to row or paddle by turning the handles in the days when you were allowed to go all round the island, though not land on it. The jetty is still there but used only by anglers now. The children's playground had the really tall slide that lasted into the 1970s, before the authorities became more safety conscious, and the battering-ram swing and the witch's hat roundabout along with the traditional whirl-round jump-off type. I took my children there until it all became so bland that it was not exciting any more. We would explore the wooded area by the ash football pitches and named the trees so that we each had our own; we'd sometimes walk over to Clapham Junction station to count if there really were two trains a minute during the morning; but there was real danger in the AA gun pits, two of them, near to the Mansions, since they were not in any way fenced off and were frequently part-filled with rain water. In 1950 my dog attempted to leap across the width and failed to clear the gap, dropping heavily into water and disappearing beneath, though by the time I had run down the sloping part she had surfaced and was swimming until she came into her depth and could walk out, tail wagging!

The coronation in 1953 had pretty much every house displaying red, white

In the garden at 138 Abbeville Road

and blue banners in their front windows for all passers-by to see, and there was great celebration. When the King had died in February 1952 the school had had a solemn assembly with all of us being instructed in how to mourn, though we felt little ourselves it was apparent that the staff were being dutifully respectful. As schoolchildren we were walked up *en masse* to the Balham Odeon to see a colour film of the coronation...

...My end of Abbeville Road in the 1950s had people going to the Majestic weekly; travelling by 137 bus to the Festival Pleasure Gardens at Battersea and not owning a car; listening to the wireless and later the radio, maybe hired from the shop that amazingly is still there at the top corner of St Alphonsus Road across the road from the church; going to St Alphonsus telephone box to make a call with threepence, later fourpence. Shopping daily, locally, with a shopping basket; walking from Abbeville Road across the Common to Clapham Library, children and all; going for a special treat to the music hall at The Empress, Brixton; knowing most of the people living nearby, but using surnames with Mr or Mrs or Miss in nearly every case; eating dinner at 1pm and having tea at 5; asking upstairs down for a Christmas morning drink and entertaining special guests in the Front Room. Maybe it's just people who change, and Clapham hasn't changed that much?

PETER SKUSE, *unpublished memoir*, 2001

After the overwhelming Labour victory of 1945, the Conservatives struggled to re-establish themselves. **John Lamb** *(see Chapters 3 & 5) and his brother David, now in their late teens and early twenties, became keen members of the newly formed Young Conservatives.*

THE WAR TIME GOVERNMENT was a national coalition lead by Winston Churchill plus a very able deputy, Clement Attlee, with members from all the main political parties. However, after the war in Europe came to an end, cohesion began to come apart, deep divisions appeared in the way ahead and preparations were made for a fresh General Election. The Labour Party were quick off the mark in producing a new policy incorporating the forward thinking of the coalition government together with a socialist programme of nationalisation of basic industries such as coal, steel and transport. The Conservatives had no answer to this and entered the election with Winston Churchill as leader and the slogan; "Let him finish the job!"

Clapham, as part of the Borough of Wandsworth had produced some able Conservative leaders at local level such as solicitor, William Bonney, the wartime mayor, but their organisation had been run down and barely functioned locally from a tiny gas lit office over the Scotch Woolshop (now Bushells Estate Agents) on South Side. The Conservative candidate was a lively New Zealand ex-service-man, Roy Lowndes, with family links to the Lowndes family of Knightsbridge.

On the Labour side was John Battley, the head of a local printing company already well-known for his warm care and concern for local people. John Battley was backed by the finance and considerable organising power of the eight Trade Union headquarters which were located in Clapham. Another helpful factor for Labour was the Armed Services vote from folk who had had enough of being ordered about and wanted a fresh start in every way. John Battley became Clapham's MP and it is quite impossible to calculate how much time and effort he devoted to the welfare of the people of Clapham, sometimes seeing them in his office as early as 7 am before the work of business com-menced. Sadly he wore himself out through overwork and died much too soon – a great loss to the Clapham community.

More defeats followed for Conservatives with loss of county and borough coun-cil seats which resulted in much rethinking and rebuilding of the organisation. One of the brilliant new ideas taken up was the formation of the Young Conservative movement of which Clapham was one of the pioneer groups. A well attended 50th year reunion was held in Clapham in 1997. The Young Conservatives, whilst being part of the main party, had a considerable measure of independence with representation at all levels of the party and in its branches.

Besides the political talks, discussions and other political activities organ-ised by Clapham YCs there were dances with live bands (including a touring square dance team), tennis, badminton, swimming, rambles and other outings. A trip down the mine at Snowdown Colliery in Kent was organised by my brother, David, who for a time arranged the speakers for our weekly meetings. One of the speakers booked was a talented aeronautical engineer, Trevor Collins. Many years later he became the vicar of St Botolph's in Boston, Lincolnshire, the largest parish church in England, at a time when David was churchwarden.

Before the widespread ownership of a TV set in the home (in the late Thirties Dempseys the sports outfitters on South Side had shown a very small screen

TV in their shop window) most people went out for their entertainment. For Sunday afternoons Clapham had a small version of Hyde Park Speakers' Corner, adjoining The Avenue on the ground now used by travelling fairs etc. It was quite usual to have a dozen or so speakers from Labour and Liberal Parties, The Socialist Party of Great Britain (whose headquarters are still in the High Street) and even a member of the Pro-Fascist Union Movement (which only lasted a short time due to the hostile reception, and a half brick hitting their speaker!)

Much more entertaining was a well read humorous Communist who appeared without any party support, to poke fun at all and sundry as he finished up by walking round and round with a hat open for contributions. Not quite so entertaining were the other speakers making personal points and endeavouring to deal with the hecklers trying to score points against them. In this group was the Catholic Faith Society and a little gentleman trying to convince a sceptical audience that Britain was the lost tribe of Israel.

The meeting ground speakers stimulated David's and my interest in politics. What was this party (the Conservatives) which nothing good could be said about? David and I joined the founding of Clapham's Young Conservatives in 1945. To our surprise as teenagers, we were accepted by the older generation (perhaps with some reservations!) and put to work on the mundane task of delivering election literature.

One of our new recruits was very right wing and led a venture to form one of the rare Conservative Governments in Battersea Model Parliament, where many years before the famous John Burns MP (the champion on dockers' rights) had polished up his techniques. The production of bills for debate went far beyond the outer reaches of official party policies – curtailing the unions, increasing the working week and a very hard line in all sorts of areas, including law and order. This had an electrifying effect on the benches opposite, whose occupants rose as one to catch the Speaker's eye and promised public hangings to all and sundry! We learnt public speaking.

There followed a strong intake of ex-servicemen (membership was open to 15-35) fed up with the Labour Government with members who proclaimed "We are the masters now" and dubbed their opponents as "vermin" [a term once used by Aneurin Bevan, which caused a political storm]. These older members had considerable experience of organising with a lot of energy, to build up a highly effective political organisation which grew in numbers to over 200 in Clapham alone. Local and national issues were discussed and debated. David led a group which expressed concern about producing a sound policy on immigration, taking the case to area level and getting a motion for action passed, despite opposition from national leaders who fudged it.

The building up of strong canvassing teams played a major part in fighting the General Elections of 1950 and 1951 together with LCC and borough elections. At last we started to win back wards, starting with Clapham Town ward and going on to Clapham Park and Thornton wards.

Both David and I served as chairman with a "hands on" lead approach and a constant programme of building up records of support (i.e. marked up electoral roll) and taking our canvassing teams beyond Clapham for by-elections where extra support was needed, with a special relationship with Bermondsey YCs. Even in those days Clapham was a very mixed area. I remember canvassing in Albion Avenue off Larkhall Rise in the better class of council flats, when the door was opened by a maid in full uniform!

At national level, Clapham was looked upon as a tough area for Conservatives, with a well established Labour MP and massive support from Trade Union headquarters. In this sense it was an ideal place for budding parliamentary candidates to earn their spurs and see what impact they could make. One of the best was the late Sir William Van Straubenzee, who went on to become a Minister for Northern Ireland, and a Church Commissioner; a large rumbustious character full of fun and good stories of his many adventures. In canvassing Bill would always bring along some enthusiastic friends. I remember when canvassing in a road with pairs of close front doors, one of these friends, to speed things, rang both doors bells. The doors were each opened at the same time by a stern faced elderly lady. The call "Look Bill, two birds with one stone" did not earn any votes!

Bill Van Straubenzee lost the following General Election by less than 300 votes. The result might have been closer if our opponents had not spread the rumour that Bill's Dutch name was in fact German. In time Wandsworth Council became Conservative controlled and the much travelled Dr Alan Glyn became Conservative MP for Clapham in 1959.

Clapham remained a marginal seat, going with the Government of the day, until the constituency disappeared in a reorganisation of the early 1970s. In 1965, most of Clapham was transferred from the Borough of Wandsworth to the new London Borough of Lambeth.

JOHN LAMB, 2002

Marzenna Michalowska-Cummings *tells how her parents, both driven from Poland during the Second World War, met in England and came to form part of the strong Polish community established in Clapham after the war.*

ON 1 SEPTEMBER 1939, not expecting the Russians to invade from the East, my mother, Szczesna, then aged 14, and her family fled the oncoming German assault to Lwow in Eastern Poland. A few months later her family, like so many others, were forced at gunpoint by the Russians into cattle trucks to be "ethnically cleansed" in Russian labour camps deep behind the Ural mountains. Throughout the war years until 1947, they struggled for survival in the most primitive conditions, journeying on foot through Uzbekistan, Kazakhstan, Afghanistan and the furthest reaches of central Asia, eventually ending up in India from where they were initially, temporarily, brought to England.

In England my mother met my father, Stanislaw Michalowski. His route here had been different. As a young teenager he had had to hide from the Germans by joining the underground resistance movement in Poland. He ended up as an artillery officer in Poland's 2nd Carpathian Division under the command of General Anders. After fighting in Italy and the Middle East, he was eventually demobbed in the UK. Unable to return to Poland, because of the political situation there, he had to set about learning a new language, catching up on a lost education, and forging a future.

Although the military battle for Poland had ended, my parents 'fought' on for a free Poland. My father participated in the Polish Parliament in exile and in various political organisations that were established, such as the Ex-Combatants Association and the Federation of Poles in Great Britain. My mother devoted herself to keeping Polish culture and literature alive. She appeared on Radio Free Europe, set up the Polish Theatre Workshop, Pro-Arte, and was Vice-President of the Polish Artists Union. Ironically, on Christmas Eve 1994 Polish Television televised our 'South London' Polish Christmas Eve broadcasting from my mother's drawing room.

My parents' stories are not dissimilar to those of many Polish people who found themselves in Clapham after the war. Money was scarce and my parents wanted a house, which was big enough to also have tenants. Property was even scarcer. My father, his mortgage arranged, stood in a queue that had formed outside the door of one house all night in order to be the first one to see it. He ran all the way to the solicitor's office to be the first to put down the deposit, which secured the house.

What began as a trickle of Polish families into Clapham grew as friends moved into the area attracted by the property stock and the burgeoning community. The Polish Catholic mission arranged for a mass to be said in Polish in St Mary's Catholic Church in Clapham Park Road. The proximity of the church to the tube station meant it could serve a very dispersed community. The 12 o'clock mass on Sunday became, almost, the social high point of the week. Tomasz Arcziszewski, the last wartime Prime Minister of Poland, and his wife had also set up a centre to care for the many Polish orphans who had found themselves in the UK after the war. With funds raised predominantly in America, in 1947 they bought a substantial property on Nightingale Lane. This also housed a Polish school which continues to this day. The émigrés sent their children to Saturday Polish school to instil in them a love for a fatherland for which their parents had fought so hard and lost.

Honed by their wartime experiences and not afraid of hard work, the Polish community prospered. There were Polish delicatessens, chemists, doctors' surgeries and dentists. By the 1960s enough funds had been raised to buy Hamilton House on Balham High Street and establish this as a community centre, called the White Eagle Club. Mass was now said in Polish in the main hall there and, when enough funds had been gathered, in the newly acquired Church of Jesus Christ the King.

With the shift in the social and cultural epicentre of the community to Balham, Clapham became less of a focus. Nevertheless, the existing community and Polish infrastructure attracted, during the late 1970s and early 1980s, a new breed of Polish economic and political immigrant escaping the hard communist post-war regime. Rising house prices experienced in the early 1980s enabled many of the now older wartime generation to sell up and retire, some to the Polish run sheltered housing schemes in Balham. I bought my first house on Narbonne Avenue from a Polish family friend and coincidentally our next home had also been owned by a Polish family just after the war.

The Polish Parish is still very vibrant, although the most predominant group are now those families who came in the 1970s and 1980s. It is their children who are still going to Polish schools and learning Polish dancing and Polish culture, just like my generation did before them. As the first generation of Polish children born in the UK has grown up, married, had children, so the old post-war community has become much more integrated. My children, whilst expressing an interest in their mother's culture and language will not speak Polish as I do, they are English!

MARZENNA MICHALOWSKA-CUMMINGS, 2002

Stanislaus Pelc *(b 1923) also a member of the Polish underground army, came with them to England towards the end of the War. After living in London and the USA, he settled in Clapham in 1961.*

I WAS BORN IN LWOW IN POLAND and was sixteen years old when the Russians and the Germans divided my country between them. In 1942, when the Germans invaded Russia there were 700,000 people in Lwow. Half of us were Polish, about a third Ukrainians and the rest were Jewish. The Germans gave us Poles grey identity cards, the Ukrainians blue ones, while the Jews were put into ghettos. As a result of the war I had joined the Polish underground army of partisans known as the AK. By 1944 the Russians were advancing into Poland and I helped my mother and family to relocate to Gliwice in Southern Poland to get them out of harm's way. Things escalated and got too hot for the partisans who had survived the German action as the Russians were now liquidating them with their advance into our country. About 120 of us partisans, with the aid of the French resistance, were smuggled on a dangerous journey to an American Army camp in Czechoslovakia. We posed as Greeks as we spoke Russian which sounds a bit like Greek. However, finding out that the Russians were to take this camp over we had to move on again in small groups through Europe via Italy, and then eventually we moved with the remainder of the Polish underground army to England.

We were sent to an army camp near Liverpool and soon we were left to find jobs, anything we could. I started in a spinning factory, trying hard to learn English, word by word. In 1948 I was working in Tenby, Pembrokeshire. At first I was confused by the strange language which I later found out was Welsh. Later that year I got seasonal work in London, living in at the Junior United Services Club in Regent Street.

In that year I met Helena my future wife at the Polish Club in Knightsbridge. She had been born in Lodz, Poland, and when the Germans invaded she was sent to the ghetto, then in 1944 to Dachau and finally ended up in Bergen Belsen concentration camp as a slave labourer. Her entire line of family was exterminated in the camps. She was liberated by the British Army in Belsen and spent two years after that in the camp before arriving in England in late 1947.

We married in London in 1952. By this time I had become quite adept in the various club and restaurant jobs available at the time, making it my business to know how to mix drinks the way Americans liked them! We found lodgings in Swiss Cottage, then in 1957 with my wife pregnant and a small boy we decided to seek our fortunes in America. My second son was born in Chicago but we had a tough time in America and returned to England in 1959.

We found rooms in Earls Court which I could manage on the £4.10s. I earned a week plus generous tips, but with a growing family I needed a house. In 1961 I became head waiter at a club in Green Street, off Park Lane, and managed to buy a house in Kendoa Road, Clapham. I could not afford the £3,000, but managed with three separate loans. The house had 10 rooms, and we let most of them to help pay off the mortgage. In 1965 I became Club Manager of the Institute of Contemporary Arts (then in Green Street), under the direction of Sir Roland Penrose. This was one of the most enjoyable and demanding times of my life. I was organising receptions for Miro, Picasso and many other famous personalities in the art and film world as well as some members of the royal family. Unfortunately, this came to an abrupt end after a traffic accident which left me an invalid for a year. I later became head waiter at Simpsons in the Strand, a position I held for twelve years until my retirement.

We moved to Englewood Road in 1978, having already owned two properties in Clapham North, the second purchased from a good friend on generous terms. The lettings income helped us bring up our three sons. The first was brought up to speak Polish, but we found that this created difficulties at school, so our other children were encouraged to learn English as their first language, but were sent to a Polish school on Saturdays in Nightingale Lane to learn Polish.

Although my wife was Jewish and I was a Catholic, we found St Peter's Church in Clapham Manor Street very friendly, and our boys all joined the Scout Troop there. The curate at the time regularly called on us on his bicycle offering us help if we needed it. I keep my Polish connections, mainly through the Polish Clubs in Hammersmith and Balham, but feel integrated with Britain having lived here over 50 years. My sons all have English wives and I have delightful grandchildren all living locally.

Sadly, my wife died suddenly earlier this year. According to her wishes, she was given a Jewish burial and her body rests in the Liberal Jewish Cemetery in Streatham with full Jewish ceremony.

STANISLAUS PELC *interviewed by David Perkin*, 2002

In 1948 the first **West Indian immigrants** arrived
from Jamaica on the Empire Windrush.
*Those who did not have friends or relatives to go to
were brought by bus from Tilbury to Clapham and temporarily housed
in the deep shelters at Clapham South, which had been used
as air raid shelters during the Second World War.*

SOME OF THE 492 JAMAICAN EMIGRANTS who arrived in Britain yesterday in the Empire Windrush wore expensive suits.

There were even emigrants wearing zoot-style suits – very long-waisted jacket, big padded shoulders, slit pockets and peg-top trousers – costing 15 to 28 pounds. There were flash ties (from 10s 6d to one pound 1s) and white-and-tan shoes (75s). The explanation was given last night by one quietly dressed Jamaican, Oswald Denniston [sic], 35, sign-painter.

Mr Denniston told me: 'Most of us are job-seekers but others are here to finish their trades and education. The very poor can't leave Jamaica. They must have 28 pounds for their passage and another five pounds when they sail.

DAILY MIRROR
23 June 1948

THE BUS PULLED SLOWLY out of Tilbury Docks heading west towards London taking the new arrivals to an unknown destination.

The Windrushians were captivated but disappointed by their new surroundings. Everything was bleak. Colours merged as if a greyish-green rinse had been stroked across the landscape, and a damp misty cloud enveloped the atmosphere. The buoyant colours of the Caribbean were a distant memory.

Within the hour, as the vehicle neared central London, the long winding country stretches fringed with bushes were transformed into identical streets lined with shabby, run-down three-storey houses stacked side by side. The pace of the bus slowed as other vehicles took to the road.

A crowd of rather woeful-looking men with flat caps and women armed with baskets of shopping scurried along the narrow footpaths, skilfully dodging grubby carefree children playing hopscotch on the pavements. The Windrushians waved cheerily at the white passers-by. But soon became mystified by the perplexed, even horrified reactions.

Then all of a sudden the bus came to a halt.

"Here we are, Clapham Deep Shelter," shouted a voice from the front of the coach. "This is where you get off."

The deep shelter had been opened during the war as emergency housing in the event of a German bomb attack. The escort ushered the Windrushians to make their way through the tent-like opening, then slid open heavy wooden doors bearing a huge no smoking sign and beckoned them to step inside.

Nervously, the men piled in this cumbersome elevator and were transported one hundred and fifty feet below, deep into the bowels of the busy south London town. They curiously eyed the network of poorly lit, clammy, musty tunnels that had been offered to them as residence. It was primitive and unwelcoming, like a sparsely furnished rabbit's warren. But in a strange new land, there were few alternatives.

Each man was allocated a place at one of the endless rows of bunk beds and given coarse white linen and a grey blanket to sleep under. The weary Windrushians slept, dreaming of a prosperous future in this new land.

The chill that crept through the tunnels prematurely woke men who had been accustomed to rising to the warmth of the sunlight.

After being served with a cheery cup of traditional English tea and coarse

The canteen in the deep shelter at Clapham South

white bread with dripping - which they were warned to be grateful for as post-war Britain still had strict rationing - the men were strongly advised to try their luck and venture into the outside world.

VIVIENNE FRANCIS, *With Hope in their Eyes*, 1998

An interview with **Oswald Dennison***, who sailed from Jamaica on the* Empire Windrush *and, according to the press (see below), was one of the first immigrants to get a job.*

'WELL, WHEN WE ARRIVED AT TILBURY, a few people, political people, mostly Communists, you know, tried to befriend us. ...

....But all it needed at the time was who hadn't got any place to go to, wants somewhere to go, and that was uppermost in our minds. So I just went through the crowd and hear that to go into this place, Clapham South, I didn't know what the feeling was ashore, but I just followed the crowd, really. When we came to Clapham South, knowing that we were going to stay there temporary, everybody felt alright. The shelter was quite ordinary. It wasn't a family home, it was like a soldier's thing, as it was intended. Just like a camp, only it's down in the

New arrivals from the West Indies on Clapham Common, 1948

ground, small beds, well, the necessary convenience, apart from that it's only a place to sleep for a few nights. And when you got work, you had to leave. You had to go in by midnight, I think, I'm not quite sure, but you had to go in. You couldn't stay out all night. Paid two shillings a night for it, and that was cheap. But it was a good arrangement really, the hard up people coming, you know.

'I did not know how many people were there, but there was quite a few. But most of them didn't stay long at all. I, myself, I was only down there just over a week, call it two weeks, or something like that. Well, the truth is, I don't look for socialising. I was gambling on the ship from the time I left Jamaica, so if I can find people to play cards, I'm quite happy. ...The boys used to, you know, go outside and stand up by the Common there, congregate there and all that sort of thing. And gradually, some of them had friends to come and take them to the Labour Exchange and that sort of thing, 'cos you weren't restricted, you move about as you please. And very soon, the number was down to just a few.

'I remember a man came to me from the Ministry of Labour and asked me, "Can you get a few of the boys to go to the mines?" And I said, "Yes." It was the Ministry of Labour man asked me, because the fuss they were making of us and that, I thought I'd thank them, and they give me a job. I started working the same night, see that the fellows get food, because the WVS people provided food for us, 'cos everything was rationed in those days, so it wasn't easy to just get food like that.'

Under the headline 'Jamaica's Oswald Given Job', the *Daily Express* reported: 'Oswald M Denniston (sic) – the first of the 430 job-hunting Jamaicans to land at Tilbury yesterday morning from the trooper *Empire Windrush* – started a £4-a-week job last night.

Unpacking in the deep shelter at Clapham South

Wrapped in two warm blankets to keep warm, he settled in as night watchman of the meals marquee in Clapham Common, SW, where 240 of the Jamaicans are staying in deep wartime shelters. All of them sat down there to their first meal on English soil: roast beef, potatoes, vegetables, Yorkshire pudding, suet pudding with currants and custard. A bed and three hot meals will cost them 6s.6d. a day. Most of the Jamaicans have about £5 to last them until they find work. Oswald Denniston (sic) 35-year-old sign painter, got his job after making a speech of thanks to government officials. He called for three cheers for the Ministry of Labour and raised his Anthony Eden hat. Others clapped, Panamas, blue, pink, and biscuit trilbys, and one bowler were waved.'

(DAILY EXPRESS, 23 June 1948)
MIKE PHILLIPS & TREVOR PHILLIPS,
Windrush: The Irresistible Rise of Multi-Racial Britain, 1998

Pat Cox remembers the great 'smog' of December 1952.

IN 1952 I WAS LIVING IN HOLMSIDE ROAD, Clapham South, preparing for A level exams at the County Secondary School for Girls in Broomwood Road. It was a momentous year for me as in the December, I reached seventeen - and on that account I planned a birthday party.

I had invited several classmates and some boys whom I had met at dances. When the great day dawned, a thick fog enveloped London. When I walked to Clapham Junction in the morning the market traders in Northcote Road were burning flares to light their stalls. The fog or 'smog' was thick and yellow. No electric light could penetrate it, and it was impossible to drive either cars or buses. When I returned home I discovered that my mother was upbraiding my sister for having stained the bath with hair dye. My sister was rightly indignant and denied all knowledge of the bright yellow stains. We then realised that the fog itself was seeping into the house and that the sulphur it contained was dissolving out onto the water droplets on the bath! All windows were then shut tight. We peered out in some concern. I was afraid that no one would come to my party and that all our preparations would be wasted.

Luckily, everybody came, either on foot or by tube. Several boys came from Peckham armed with beer and 78 rpm records to play on the gramophone. The food was quite simple – sausage rolls, trifle, birthday cake – that sort of thing. There may have been a bottle of wine or cider to drink a toast, but no other alcohol. My parents tactfully went out for the evening, returning about 11 pm.

By then darkness had increased the problem of the fog, which had not lifted. The boys were becoming anxious about getting back to Peckham, where they lived in a residential boys' home. My father came to the rescue with an idea from his youth. He provided each boy with a household candle tightly wrapped in a rolled-up newspaper. The candles were then lit, so that the wax ran down into the paper. Armed with these torches the boys made for the tube station. When they got there they found the station closed. They had no option but to walk all the way home. As the fog was now so thick it was impossible to see the road, they hit upon the idea of following the tramlines which they were just able to pick out, glinting in the light of the home-made torches. By this means they were able to reach Peckham in the early hours of the morning.

Following that, the worst of the London 'smogs', the use of open coal fires in houses was banned and the Clean Air Acts came in. Many old people had died from the pollution carried in the fog.

PAT COX, 2001

More than 40 years after the Steinie Morrison case (Chapter 2), the Common was the scene of another murder which led to a contentious trial. **Michael John Davies** *was convicted of a stabbing after a series of fights which had started at the bandstand.* The Clapham Observer *described the first stages.*

CROWDS WAITED THREE HOURS outside the South-Western Court on Monday for a glimpse of the five youths charged with being concerned in the murder of 17-year-old John Ernest Beckley at Clapham Common on the previous Thursday. Among them were mothers with young children. A number of youths, who climbed on a wall for a better view, were turned away by the police....

Inspector John Davies, who took less than ten minutes to give evidence of arrest, applied for all five youths to be remanded to a prison because of their unruly dispositions, and the nature of the charge...

Three of the boys were without ties. Lawson, short and red-haired, Davies, tall and dark, and Power, a tall, slim youth, sat in the dock. Coleman, fair haired and dressed in sports coat and flannels, and Woodman, tall and wearing a brown suit, sat as juveniles in front of the dock...

THE CLAPHAM OBSERVER, 10 July 1953

Six people eventually stood trial for murder at the Old Bailey. Of these, Davies was convicted and sentenced to death. On legal issues, the case went to the House of Lords; and on 19 February 1954, Davies' appeal was rejected. In the dry legal judicial language of the **Lord Chancellor (Lord Simonds)**, *this is what had happened on the evening of 2 July 1953.*

FOUR YOUTHS, Beckley (the victim of the murder), Chandler, Ryan and Carter, were sitting on benches near a bandstand on Clapham Common. Two were on each of two benches facing each other, and each propped his feet on the bench opposite him, so that no one could pass between the benches towards the stand. Coleman came along and prepared to pass between the benches, but their occupants refused to give way and it would seem that one of them used, concerning Coleman, what he took to be an insulting expression. Coleman then went to a group of persons round the bandstand; and the four boys on the benches, fearing reprisals, withdrew to what has been called "the Fountain," some way off. The group whom Coleman joined and to whom he said something about the affront he had suffered consisted of a number of people including Davies. From this group about eight, including Davies, later moved off towards the fountain in pursuit of the four. But it is important to note that before this happened two persons by the bandstand, a man called Leaver and a Miss Pilkington (neither of whom could by any stretch be called accomplices of Davies) agree that Davies, after hearing Coleman's communication, drew out a green-handled knife from his pocket – a small knife with a "push" handle. Leaver further says he heard Davies say: "I shall be all right with this." A lad called Wood also saw a green-handled knife in Davies' possession just after Coleman had spoken to Davies.

Davies and his companions, including Lawson, then proceeded to the fountain, and a fight developed there between them and the four fugitives. Davies admits hitting Ryan, and Ryan later discovered a stab wound under his left arm-pit. Lawson was engaged in this fight. At some stage in it two of the fugitives alleged that someone shouted: "Get out the knives." There was no evidence that at this stage Lawson was still there or that he heard this cry. He swears he did not. Ryan and Carter seem to have moved off from the fountain in one direction while Beckley and Chandler fled in a different direction to a motor omnibus, which they boarded while it was held up by traffic lights [it was a 137, at the junction of North Side and Cedars Road]. When it reached its next stop [by Trinity Hospice] they were torn from its tailboard by Davies and his followers. Davies admits "doubling up" Chandler with a blow to the stomach, in which region, it appeared afterwards, he had been stabbed. Beckley was pursued to a point 113 yards beyond the bus stop. The evidence as to the precise succession of events at this stage is conflicting, but a Miss Frayling, sitting on the front right-hand bench on the top of the bus, testified that she saw Davies (whom she identified with the greatest confidence) "shake" someone, who could only have been Beckley, and who fell to the ground. She then saw Davies cross the road in front of the bus, and as he did so put a green-handled knife into his right-hand inside jacket pocket. In the same pocket later were found bloodstains. Beckley had eight or nine knife wounds, and died shortly after. There was further evidence of threats by Davies later on to two witnesses who said that, if necessary, they would say who was really responsible for Beckley's death. ...

Lawson's evidence was, briefly, that some time after the affray, and after he had heard of Beckley's death, he met Davies at a coffee stall in Venn Street, and that Davies said to him that all he tried to do was to "run a knife up and down", and illustrated by a gesture the difference between this and stabbing.

HOUSE OF LORDS RECORDS OFFICE, 1954

Davies was reprieved, and imprisoned until 1960.
He had always protested his innocence, and on his release,
Lord Longford took up his case. The Home Office was not persuaded,
but a legal commentator has written:

"HAVING READ THE EVIDENCE and discussed the case with Davies I hardly think that his guilt was established 'beyond all reasonable doubt'."

RUPERT FURNEAUX, *Michael John Davies*, 1962

ALL CHANGE
LIFE IN THE 60s AND 70s

Brian Luff *recalls growing up on an estate
in Clapham Park in the 1950s and 1960s, schooldays at
Henry Thornton School and early married life in St Luke's Avenue.*

I WAS BORN ON CHRISTMAS EVE 1950, the illegitimate son of a fifteen year old girl from a small village in Berkshire.

My mother left the wagging tongues and spiteful air of the country to come to London where I was born in St James' Hospital in Balham. Two years later she met my step-father and they were married. We lived in one room in West Kensington for two years before being offered a council flat in Clapham. My mother was pregnant again and somehow managed to get on the LCC [London County Council] housing list. We were given a 3-bedroom flat at 253, Poynders Gardens on the Poynders Road. Even at my very tender age I remember the space, all the rooms, a bathroom and toilet of our own. The estate had been built before the war but to us it was all brand new. My formative years were spent there, from the age of four in 1954 to the age of eighteen when I got married.

I visited the old estate in 1999 on a nostalgia trip and found to my delight, carved into the brickwork of the ground floor entrance...

...carved with love to my wife in 1966 when we were teenagers.

I loved living on the estate, my very own place, it was my life, my world, all my friends lived there, we went to the same school, Bonneville, just off the now fashionable Abbeville Road.

A fatalist might say that I was never meant to be a country boy and that Clapham was always going to be my destination. After all, I moved to Poynders as a four year old, there I met my best friend, Andy O'Keefe, twelve years later he met a girl called Christine who worked with a girl also called Christine as a hairdresser in Brixton Hill. The two Christines eventually came to Poynders. I was introduced to the Brixton Christine, I fell in love and we were married in June 1969.

"Community spirit" is a phrase we hear so often these days, mainly from politicians. It seems meaningless to me and to others who lived when there really was such a thing. People these days can live in a street of terraced houses as I do, and not know more than half a dozen people in the street. Growing up in the fifties and sixties in Poynders Gardens was so different to our new millennium lifestyle. All those clichés about leaving your front doors open to welcome neighbours, trusting people, expecting the best from people, are all true. Of course we had occasional problems but they were as nothing compared to today. People are now careful, cynical, fearful. We have burglar alarms, car immobilisers, big dogs, we all know someone who has been burgled or mugged but we still have no idea when or why it all went wrong.

The "community spirit" in Poynders was epitomised by the social club on the estate. Every Saturday night there would be bingo at 8 o'clock followed by music, dancing and cabaret, a small bar catered for drinkers and there were sandwiches etc. The entertainment was provided by a local trio who played all the old favourites, there were occasional performances from magicians and stand-up comics. There was one night in the middle 1960s I think, an old man came on to entertain us. He told lots of gags about being old and decrepit, he was terrific. At the end of his act as he took our applause he removed his wig and make-up to reveal a very young man. We didn't know him then but we do now, it was "Del Boy" himself David Jason – you may recall him doing his 'old man' gag in an episode of "Porridge" with Ronnie Barker.

The Poynders social club also ran a youth night when we played table tennis, darts and all kind of mad games invented by the youth leader. I enjoyed it so much that some years later I became youth leader myself, about 1965 that was.

During the summer the social club organised trips to the coast, charabanc trips down to Margate, Hastings, Eastbourne etc., wonderful trips, many of the younger ones had never seen the sea, me included. The two hours or so that we spent travelling to the seaside, we would sing all the old cockney songs, "Roll out the Barrel", "Maybe It's Because I'm a Londoner", and even a song which a social club member had written called "We are the Poynders Gang". On the trip back, our favourite was "Show Me the Way to Go Home". We would arrive back at the estate having had a thoroughly good day out, exhausted but looking forward to the next grand day out.

I only wish that I could help to instil the spirit in my friends, neighbours, and children. This has nothing to do with nostalgia but everything to do with a desire for something a little better for new generations. I am afraid that we may never enjoy that spirit again, the friendship, the trust, the joy of watching someone on the estate stepping out in their wedding finery, or the genuine sadness of watching someone stepping out in their mourning clothes for a funeral. Life passing us by, with respect…

…In 1955 I was taken to my first school by my mother, Bonneville Infants. The school was already fifty years old then, so goodness knows how many Clapham kids had passed through its door before me.

I remember doing some tests during the first week after which we were assigned to our classes. I was in 1A with Mr McMahon, a six foot Australian with hands like shovels, as the backs of my legs can testify. The head was a lady called Mrs Lovelace and I can also recall a Mrs Valentine – funny how you can forget the names of people that you met last week at a party yet still remember teachers from 45 years ago. And who can forget the smells of a polished parquet floor, chalk in the classroom, or something cooking in the school kitchen. School dinners then were a shilling. My favourite was a pudding of semolina with a blob of jam which we would stir in until it was a rather nice pink, we would scoff it quick and then run to try and get seconds.

Discipline at Bonneville was fairly strict when you consider that we were aged only five to eleven years. Slaps on the legs and arms were common, parents never complained and in fact expected us to be punished for our misdeeds.

Schooldays of course were for us kids fairly humdrum, not much excitement. However, every year we would get a visit from the local police of

Cavendish Road station. They would send a few motorcycle officers to demonstrate road safety and we would be thrilled by their daring exploits, pretending to be knocked down or riding three on a bike like circus performers. Nowadays of course the police visit schools to explain about the dangers of drugs, knives or about being lured into cars by strangers – how innocent it all seemed in those days.

I went on from Bonneville Infants to the Junior school which luckily is next door. My mother stopped taking me at the age of nine and I made my own way from Poynders Gardens through the Oaklands Estate to Bonneville Gardens in less than ten minutes. There was no such thing as the 'school run' in those days, very few working-class people had cars and anyway it was considered perfectly safe for young children to walk to school.

I remember marvellous teachers, Mr Furlong, Mr Lambert, Mr Champion, who encouraged me with my sporting abilities and the headmaster WH Gibson, a wonderful man who taught me how to play chess at the age of nine (having never even seen a chess piece before), an appreciation of music and most important a lifelong love of books.

Crowning the May Queen, Poynders Gardens, c1960

In 1960 I was fortunate enough to pass my eleven plus exam and get a place at Henry Thornton Grammar on Clapham Common South Side. My parents had to struggle to find the money to kit me out with the school uniform, trousers, shirt, pullover, tie, cap and blazer with the Henry Thornton badge (three trees). They had to buy them from the official supplier, a shop opposite Clapham Common Station, Wakelings – I believe it was next to the Bellevue public house.

Henry Thornton was run like a public school, our teachers were all referred to as masters who wore black capes. They frightened the life out of me, swishing down the corridors like vampires in some Hammer horror film. I still remember their names but only surnames, we never realised that they may have had first names as well. From 1962 to 1968 I recall Messrs Willerton, Davies, Read, Allott, Taylor and the headmaster BJF Dorrington. Mr Dorrington had an unusual statue outside his office, a modern art figure. I visited the school recently and it is still standing there, looking as strange now as it did then. I particularly remember the statue because I had to look at it through the head-master's window while he caned me, six of the best for uttering profanity at lunch. A better memory of the school was the aroma which invaded our class-rooms from the Batgers sweet factory next door to the school.

Henry Thornton is now Lambeth College. Sadly the original mansion facing the common was demolished; in my school days it housed the school dining rooms, the music room and the sixth form common rooms. I believe the original building was called South Lodge and was at one time the home to the Gorringes of department store fame. I still have some of my school reports from Henry Thornton, a constant reminder of what a great school it was and how I squandered so much of my time there. As some of my reports say "could have done better".

In 1972 the family moved to St Luke's Avenue

I had been living in Saxby Road in Brixton Hill with my wife and baby son, along with my wife's parents and their other five children. It was a bit crowded. My wife's uncle had financial problems and had to give up his room in St Luke's Avenue. In fact he did a moonlight flit leaving behind all his debts including 3 months rent arrears.

We moved into the house in 1972 – 30 St Luke's Avenue – a three storey Victorian terrace. If nothing else it was quieter than our previous situation. We had a front room facing the street, a back room facing the yard, a dining room and a scullery. There was no bathroom, we had our baths in a five foot tin receptacle which was a relic from pre-war days I'm sure, but we had nothing else so just made do. We had an outside toilet which I suppose in these days of en-suite, jacuzzis etc. must seem Dickensian, but it was fairly common then. While my wife and baby and I occupied the street level flat we had people on the first floor and even more people on the top floor so there was no privacy and there were many embarrassing moments.

Anyway, further into our residence the landlord realised that we were different people from the wife's uncle whose name was on the rent book. We persuaded him that we would be good tenants and continued to pay our weekly rent of £2.00. The rent was collected weekly in cash by an old woman, can you imagine such a thing today?

We soon realised that there were public baths in Clapham Manor Street and we would treat ourselves once a week to a glorious proper bath and forsake the tin bath hanging on the wall in the back yard. Even though this sounds like a take from "Oliver Twist", it was in fact fairly recent, only thirty years ago.

Six years after we had taken up residence in St Luke's Avenue the landlord offered to buy us out because he wanted to redevelop the property. We took £1,000 and a maisonette in Wingford Road, Brixton Hill. Houses in St Luke's Avenue these days can fetch anything up to £300,000, seems like a long time since my £2.00 per week, I only hope that the new owners have bathroom and toilets indoors.

My best memory of St Luke's Avenue is the genuine community of people living in the semi-poverty. We had plenty of parties and social evenings with neighbours who welcomed us with warmth and understanding.

Those years of relative hardship, when we would sometimes hide when the rent collector knocked, taught me and my family a great deal about friends, neighbours and community and how we miss it these days.

BRIAN S LUFF, 2001

Derrick McRobert came from Yorkshire to London *as a student in the 1960s. Writing in 2002, he recalls his student days in Clapham and how he came to buy his first house in the area.*

I FIRST EXPLORED CLAPHAM when I was a student (1964-68) at the London College of Printing at the Elephant and Castle. Students had to arrange their own accommodation and the Welfare Officer at the College told me about a flat that was available quite close by, in Clapham. My interview for admission to the college had been my first ever visit to London, but I could see from the A-Z that I had bought on that trip that Clapham was very conveniently positioned. There were three of us from Ermysted's Grammar School at Skipton to share the flat in Rusham Road, off Nightingale Lane. Roger, who was studying at the Architectural Association and Joe, who was also at the LCP. He came from a farming family near Yockenthwaite in Upper Wharfedale and standing at Clapham South station on our arrival in Clapham, with a typical dales-farmer's thought of stock and money; said; 'By heck, you could get a lot of sheep on here!'

Clapham seemed to be all student accommodation then. Other lads from Ermysted's were at Halliday Hall and The Windmill was a regular meeting place. It was an awful pub then, extremely tatty and dirty, but it had a piano and live music. The pianist seeming oblivious to the rickety state of his seat, which was held together with string. Coming from a village where the nearest pub was still a working farm with a bar attached, I took me quite a long time to figure out that in many pubs in London the difference between public bar and lounge bar was mainly one of price!

In that first year in London, Clapham and south London seemed to be an extension of my northern life. Tom Eckersley, who ran the graphic design course never lost his Lancashire accent and at my first History of Art tutorial, I was greeted by the Head of Department — and William Morris expert — Ray Watkinson, with 'Sit thissen dahn, Lad!' and the whole tutorial was held in Yorkshire dialect. He told me that he already knew quite a lot about me as his sister lived in the next hamlet and his three nephews had been at school with me. I met my headmistress from the village infants school in a shop in Nightingale Lane, and discovered that I was living opposite her sister.

I didn't like sharing, I seemed to end up doing all the washing-up, so I went to live on my own after the first year and for the rest of my course I lived in the top room of 92 Englewood Road. I had a small gas ring and grill – no running water but there was a bathroom on the floor below, and I paid £2.10/- a week for the three years I was there. I could leave boxes of belongings in the attic when I wasn't there – at no charge – and my landlady, Mrs Pomykala would let out my room during the summer holidays (once to a man who was wanted for questioning by The Garda in Ireland, suspected of murder!). It was a good room for a design student as the room contained a very large table on which I could work and a comfortable dining chair. It also had a gas fire! This was a new experience, there being no gas supply where I spent my childhood, (we still had a fireside oven), and I immediately fell in love with the instant heat and friendly flickering flame of gas. Even toasted bread on it!

I often felt that I was not alone in this room, perhaps there was a ghost, it was certainly never malevolent. However one morning I realised that indeed I was not alone, but my 'visitor' was my landlady raiding the gas meter for school-dinner money for her daughter. She said I had never woken up before!

Fellow students at LCP who had started in 'digs' in Bayswater and Kensington soon moved to the much cheaper accommodation in Balham and North Side and though our social life mostly revolved around the Elephant or the National Film Theatre we would also meet at the cinema in Balham Hill. The Beaufoy Arms in Wandsworth Road was also a favourite venue. It had a wonderful jazzband – a band of very cheerful grey-haired West Indians who could play any tune, harmonising together it seemed by telepathy. I still harboured the thought that I would become a famous trumpet player then but lack of practice space, and new interests resulted in the loss of my 'lip'.

Most of my meals during the week were taken at the college canteen but shopping for weekends, etc, was done at a small shop on the corner of Englewood Road and South Side. I think it was just called *The Dairy*. The two ladies in the shop 'mothered' me and made sure that I got bargains and good value, and didn't overbuy! Their care certainly worked as in the four years I was at college I survived on my maintenance grant from the West Riding County Council – supported by work in the holidays. As my father earned very little as a head gardener, I had the luxury of a full award from the WRCC and when he died during my last term at college the grant kept me until I got my first job with the Central Office of Information at Bankside.

Cleanliness, always portrayed as a permanent student problem, was in fact no problem at all. Mrs Pomykala changed and washed my bed linen and Sunday morning marked the regular trip to the launderette in Balham Hill. Collecting on the way *The Observer* and a bar of hazel nut chocolate which constituted breakfast. All colours went into the one wash, so white items soon became grey, and all items had to experience the very fierce driers so they went straight back into the wardrobe without the need for airing. Luckily 'fashion' among the male design students at LCP consisted of corduroy trousers with Indian Madras cotton striped shirts, so nothing really needed ironing. Suede desert boots with crepe soles, not well suited to wet and slippery Clapham pavements, were the standard footwear. Ties were my speciality, hand-made from material bought from market stalls and 'run-up' whenever I had access to a sewing machine.

After getting married in 1968 we lived in Bayswater and Fitzrovia before we bought our first home in Bonneville Gardens in 1971. Clapham was still 'cheap' and we moved back to the area because it was well served by public transport and convenient for work. Eleanor was working at the National Central Library in Store Street and I was in Victoria. 'Cheap' was £5,750 for a three-bedroom, ground floor maisonette and the monthly repayments took most of our income. Being back in Clapham also meant a return to my 'mothers' at *The Dairy* and a thorough interrogation about what I had been up to in the intervening three years.

I have never found London to be an unfriendly environment. The village I left when I was eighteen was surrounded by fields, but my city life has been a reversal with the various 'villages' of Clapham surrounding one big field – the Common. And I still wonder just how many sheep could graze on it?

DERRICK McROBERT, 2002

The journalist John Walsh (b1953) moved to a house in Battersea Rise at the age of ten, when his father became the local general practitioner. In his autobiography he vividly recalls the life of an Irish immigrant family in the area in the 1960s.

FROM THE AGE OF TEN OR SO, on Sunday mornings before lunch, I would go for walks with my Dad and my sister across Clapham Common leaving Mother to cook a leg of lamb for lunch. We would take a scooter, a bicycle, a football, a tennis ball, a cricket bat and stumps. Arrayed with an arsenal of non-Irish sporting implements, we would make our way through the small mini-common, cross the Avenue ('Don't hop the ball where there are cars,' he'd always say on the pedestrian crossing) and trek through the main common with the grand early-nineteenth century houses on the left and the mild suburban forest of spiky bushes and long grass on the right. There were rumours that horrible people lurked in there by night, and you could occasionally find fragments of noisome evidence: brown paper bags with murder victim's shoes inside (though you didn't actually look), fluttering leaves of lavatory paper ... My father tended to bustle us past the wooded bits, and out onto the sunlit uplands, where we'd plunge the stumps into the soft ground and play cricket for an hour...

...It was a big house, but hardly a Big House. It stood at the crest of a hill and it resembled the prow of a ship. Where Battersea Rise and Lavender Sweep met at a sharply acute angle, our back garden formed a thin V-shape, with a black wrought-iron lamp at its apex, the figure-head of the SS *Walsh*. Seen from the road, the house had a certain naval quality, with its big forecastle of rooms sticking out at odd angles, and its dramatic air of forging ahead, as if it were surging through the waves of Battersea and pulling the neighbouring shops along with it.

When we first moved there in 1963, I was ecstatic to find an air-raid shelter at the end of the garden, even though it was dank and evil-smelling and the steps down to its murky interior were spongy with mildew and home to a thousand weevils. From the garden you could see the edge of Clapham Common. The war had left its scars there in the form of two great ugly blisters of concrete, where anti-aircraft batteries had once stood during the Blitz, and had been subsequently turfed over.

It was a very English sort of place. It had been a haven of middle-class luxury. In the nineteenth century, home to well-heeled merchants and City gents who rode up to town each morning in gigs and stove-pipe hats. E. M. Forster's paternal cousins lived in a mansion called 'Battersea Rise' on the west side of the Common. ...He regrets that the name of the house will mean 'nothing to the post-war generation' and deplores the way the loveliness of the place, its historical glow, its connection with tradition and the Clapham sect of evangelicals – its *Howards-End*iness – inevitably vanished under the creeping spread of London. 'Clapham,' he sniffily concludes, 'once infested by highwaymen, turned first into a pleasant and then into an unpleasant suburb.'

He would have done more than wrinkle his nose had he seen what became of the place by the time we got there. The Battersea end of Clapham Common was a dump, a service area for Clapham Junction: the busiest, noisiest and dirtiest railway junction in the country. It was a stridently working-class and immigrant neighbourhood then; a tough, coarse-grained part of inner suburbia. The skinhead phenomenon of the late sixties started around the Junction, where gangs of forty or fifty bald adolescents with braces and Doc Marten boots would congregate before marauding across the Common in search of homosexuals, hippies and (later on) Asian youths to bash up. The pedestrian walkway that led to the station featured in the movie *Up the Junction*, giving my backyard a sudden, dodgy gleam of trendy squalour. In the film, a smart Chelsea girl (played by

Suzy Kendall) leaves her parents' posh SW3 residence every morning to cross Battersea Bridge and go to work in a horrible factory in Clapham. Her intentions in doing so are inscrutable – something to do with working-class life and conveyor-belt banter being more 'real' than hanging out among the well-bred but bloodless rich folk – as are her reasons for going out with a local biker and van-driver's assistant (played by [Clapham reared] Dennis Waterman). But it put Clapham Junction on the map as the essence of 'Sarf Lunnen' – a place of gormless, listless, violent, Philistine, charmless non-endeavour – occasionally enlivened by shrieks of laughter from big girls with ragged stockings and white lipstick, who all looked like Adrienne Posta [another actress in the film].

That, at any rate, was one perspective of Battersea – my home town. But, between the ages of ten and seventeen, I had a different view. I knew it as a tripartite ghetto, shared among the blacks, the Irish and the Poles.

The Polish community in London SW11 kept themselves to themselves, were invariably bilingual and modest, and were mostly refugees from the war. You only knew of their existence because of the special Polish Mass they attended at the Catholic church in Clapham Common on Sundays. They all wore discreet dark-grey coats and black hats, and moved in a kind of mono-chrome filter, as though still dazed by what had happened to their families just twenty years earlier. I struck up a friendship round at our local church with a handsome Polish father of two called Danny, with whom I used to alternate the reading of Bidding Prayers on the altar, but we fell out over some absurd misunderstanding about whose turn it was. He simply melted away and I never saw him in the church again.

The blacks and the Irish, by contrast, were noisily competitive about whose place it was. I remember a day when my mother and I (aged twelve) were return-ing home from church, when she stopped dead in the middle of the pavement.

'Will you look at the cheek o'that,' she said. I looked and saw a man parking his beaten-up Austin 1100 outside the back door of our house, precisely in the spot overlooked by a printed sign that announced: ' DOCTOR'S HOUSE. NO PARKING HERE PLEASE.'

'Leave it, mum,' I said. 'He isn't doing any harm.'

'Isn't he indeed?' she said, her mouth setting in a grimace like a mantrap. She strode over to the Austin, where the driver was yanking on the brake, and rapped sharply on the window. A black face looked out. 'Would you mind offaly,' said Mother in her most piercingly polite voice, 'not parkin' here? Because you see, the doctor needs to park his car here, where he can get to it easily if he has to go out on an urgent call. Otherwise, he might have to park half a mile away and by the time he'd found his car the patient'd be dead, d'you see?' Having sketched this tragic scenario, she subsided. We both waited for a reply.

'Lady,' said the man in the car, equably. 'Why don't you go back where ya came from?'

She flinched as if she'd been hit in the face. 'Lookit,' she said. 'I was livin' in London a long time before *you* fellers came near the place.'

'That so?' said the man, unimpressed. 'Time ya went back.'

'Mum ....' I said, worried that we might have an interracial war on our doorstep if this went much further.

'Park this thing somewhere else,' she said, rapping a finger on the roof of his invasive vehicle, 'and don't be so disrespectful. There'll come a time when you'll be needin' a doctor and God help you then.'

'God save us *ahlll*,' said the man, 'from people like you.' But he drove off anyway, to park in some less contentious territory. A small victory, but Mother marched home in triumph...

...Every Saturday, the Northcote Road market would move in and transform the bottom of our road into a multi-coloured souk of vegetables, meat, fish, groceries, American comics, old-style weighing scales, sheets of the *Daily Sketch* and the *People* to wrap your carrots in, and brawny men calling out, like so many Stanley Holloways playing Eliza Doolittle's dad, 'Gitcha lovely spuds 'ere, ahnly two bob a pahnd'; the Irish matrons would gaze suspiciously at the yams and sweet potatoes and plantains on display, and my mother would look away disgustedly from the sight of a woman emptying her nose into the gutter...

...Battersea wasn't the kind of place that encouraged you to linger when you visited, or made you feel like getting to know it when you lived there. It was a boring, dusty, Junction-serving corridor between the smart end of Clapham and the newly proliferating suburban sprawl of Wandsworth. And our road, Battersea Rise, a name that had once caused E. M. Forster such a thrill of excitement, had become subsumed under a later name: the South Circular Road.

It would have been pleasant to grow up in a town, or to feel oneself becoming part of a town; but we weren't a town. We weren't a village. We were barely a district. We were just an artery, a migratory conduit, just as England had mutated into 'Airstrip One' in Orwell's *Nineteen Eighty-Four*. Huge, coughing trucks, immense Italian juggernauts, transporters carrying cages of new and reconstituted cars from Dagenham and Cowley to London dealers came wheezing and crashing up the Rise each night, their headlights sending long bars of light marching across my bedroom ceiling, making my whole bed shake. For years, on holidays and school trips, I couldn't get to sleep if things were too quiet outside. Silence unnerved me. I was used to the sound of machines going places, grindingly, relentlessly, effortfully. I could only sleep to the rhythm of things in transit.

We didn't know our neighbours. Our house was at the end of a row of shops. There was nobody on one side, and a nondescript terraced house, in three flats, on the other. The inhabitants of Number 10 changed from time to time, but nobody ever dreamed of coming round to say hello when they moved in. For years the ground floor was occupied by a hard-faced thirtysomething tough guy, a typical sixties figure with his Jeff Beck haircut, his tinted shades, his nasty green Ford Capri and his amazing blonde girlfriend. She had once been beautiful, but her looks had hardened into a permanent heat-sealed sulk. Her hair, though, was cut like Julie Christie's and, at thirteen, I thought she was a goddess. I schemed about rescuing her from the clutches of her nasty beau, as I watched them leaving the house together, he steering her with a claw-like grip on her elbow, as if half-expecting her to run away...

...St Vincent's was, and is, a bleak little church in Altenburg Gardens, one street away from Lavender Gardens. As churches go, it was modest to the point of invisibility. It had a lady chapel, a choir loft with an organ, and a hellfire-preacher pulpit, but there was nothing about it that would occupy more than a tiny paragraph in Pevsner's *Great English Churches*. It always needed a new coat of paint, a new heating system and some new unchipped statues. An air of mystery or solemnity or wonder would have been nice too, but instead it radiated a crouched atmosphere of dogged survivalism, embodied in the faces, the stance and the horrible clothes of the elderly ladies who made up the bulk of the congregation. My parents attended church all the time and my sister and I had to accompany them. Neither of us ever felt we fitted in. From being an altar server I rose through the ranks to become 'MC' – the top job, the dizzying senior posting of the serving fraternity, the seraphic panjandrum who stands by the priest's right hand at High Mass, turning the pages of the giant missal with its illuminated text, its singing passages marked in square black crochets and minims, its little leather tabs on the side of key pages to alleviate the wear and tear on the sacred paper when we were about to embark on the Offertory or the final Blessing...

...For I was a wild revolutionary outlaw. I performed shocking acts of civil disobedience, like walking up the stairs at Clapham Common tube station when the sign at the top clearly stated, 'other side up'. (Sadly, there was nobody around to see.) I adopted the look and swagger and pose of a rebel, only occasionally frustrated by my mother's counter-revolutionary tactics. I tried to grow my hair over the collar of my school blazer, and was sent off to the barber's on Lavender Hill on a Friday morning, to have it pruned to convict proportions. I tried to coax some rudimentary bumfluff on my check into sideburns, but it was a doomed enterprise. I tried to smoke my father's Guards cigarettes (disgusting), his pipe and Holland House tobacco (too fiddly) and his Henri Wintermans cigars (too pungent). I concealed stolen cigarettes in ingenious hiding places (two of them down the hollow legs of a plastic Airfix model of Napoleon), smoked them on the train from school to Clapham Junction, craftily applied a breath-renewing potion called Gold Spot to my tongue (it tasted like earwax) and went home, where my mother immediately, and angrily demanded: 'Have you been smoking?'...

...On Saturday evenings, my family used to go to St Mary's Church, a handsomely Gothic monstrosity near Clapham Common, in order to attend the Novena, a glum half-hour parade of prayers and sermons which, if you attended it nine times in a row, qualified you for special blessings or a couple of weeks off your sentence in Purgatory. The only real interest I took in going near the place was the road where my father parked the car. There was a big movie poster site on the corner. It changed every week, but seemed to specialise in shockers. *Maniac* was illustrated by a pair of huge staring eyes and the legend. 'Don't go alone – take a brave, nerveless friend with you!'

JOHN WALSH, *The Falling Angels*, 1999

Patrick Kelly *has observed the changes in Clapham over the forty years he has been drinking at The Windmill.*

MY LOVE AFFAIR WITH THE WINDMILL started in 1967. My mother and I had moved to Lynette Avenue, Clapham from Ireland to join my father who had been here since the war. He was in the building trade like all of my family, he was a plasterer. There was a lot of building work then and my family covered all of the building trades.

I went to St Gerard's Catholic School for Boys, which was in a beautiful Georgian building just across from The Windmill. It was torn down and they put in St Gerard's Close; that was a sin.

My very first drink was in 1967 in The Windmill and I came in with a teacher and a couple of mates. Paul Davison, a Mancunian gym teacher with one lung, I will never forget him. He bought me my first pint of Brown and Bitter. We had two pints each that first visit and left the pub staggering. I was 15 then and I have been a regular ever since. I used to be in here five days a week, but now it is less often – more like three. There are plenty of us regulars, some who have been coming longer than me.

The Windmill was a lot more formal in the 60's – the décor was like a club with Queen Anne-style black and green marble topped tables and House of Commons green leather club chairs. It was full of City types reading the FT, smoking a pipe and drinking brandy. It was a bit intimidating for us builders – but then you get over that with time. Word is that a departing manager stripped the place bare. The bit we are in used to be a stable with cobbles but it got covered over before my time. There were five different bars then, including a small one at the front which was like Coronation Street with old ladies sipping port and lemon.

A busy day at The Windmill, 1980

Clapham and the Common were buzzing and beautiful in the 1960s. I'll tell you what though, people used to say you were more likely to get a **** than ever see a taxi in Clapham with its light on. They never wanted to come to Clapham then. The end of the 1960s I remember some of the first Asians arriving. Sharif had a shop called Westburys at Clapham South. I think he was one of the first Asians. He worked hard. It is a Costcutters now.

There used to be gangs in those days – five or more lads who walked the streets, drank coffee and listened to music. There was no violence then and no dress code but we tried to wear the same sort of gear. We played football on the Common and then repaired to The Windmill for a few pints.

By the mid 1970s this place was heaving five nights a week with five deep at the bar. It was all go then. We had some fun I can tell you. In 1979 The Windmill built a £100,000 extension to provide 13 bedrooms. Mr Patrick Read, MD of Youngs Brewery at the time said: "We believe that the new facilities at the Windmill will be a great asset to the community. There is a shortage of hotel accommodation in the areas and, in addition, we feel that some overseas visitors may like to experience a real pub and The Windmill is certainly that, for it sells nearly a million pints of beer a year".

I don't remember why exactly, but in the 80's The Windmill was a bit boring and dull. I went and drank elsewhere. It became less busy and business slacked. Since the 90's this place has been full every night with young people. They are more serious about the food here now but they still pour a good pint. Cheers!

PATRICK KELLY *interviewed by Annabel Allott*, 2001

In a series of nineteen articles
for The Times *from 1972 to 1975*
the journalist **Halldora Blair** *followed*
the fierce battle fought by local residents
against the proposed compulsory
purchase, demolition and redevelopment of an area of Clapham
around St Paul's Church.
Property and land in Wandsworth Road
and Iveley Road were at issue.

*Lambeth Borough Council
had passed resolutions to compulsorily purchase
parts of these roads in October 1971.*

23 SEPTEMBER 1972: CLAPHAM SAGA OF THE COUNCIL CPO [Compulsory Purchase Order]... in 1968... the Blackwells decided their Battersea flat could no longer cope as both a home and the centre of Mrs Blackwell's activities as Pamela Price, a cordon bleu cook ... the Blackwells had to find a house large enough to provide a home for them and room for expansion of her culinary enterprise. Numbers 33 Iveley Road, and 623 Wandsworth Road, Clapham, supplied the required potential. These two addresses combine to form a Victorianly solid, large detached house...

*Pamela and
John Blackwell*

The Blackwells bought the house. Some time was spent securing alternative accommodation for the "controlled tenant" who lived there. Early in 1972 they had the house to themselves and started plans to adapt it. Then forms arrived from the council

Everyone in the proscribed area was being requested to state his interest in the property he occupied; the council were ascertaining who were the actual owners of the land... Although they then knew next to nothing about compulsory purchase procedures, [the Blackwells] swiftly discovered that the council's resolution ... was but a declaration of intent. The order would have to be approved by the Secretary of State for the Environment before it could become effective and, in the meantime, a public enquiry would be held.

So the Blackwells suffered and recovered from the shock; they stopped their planning and started campaigning. Together with some neighbours who became immediately active, they hastily sounded out local opinion "We were afraid initially that people wouldn't care – but they do" says Pamela. She was swiftly elected secretary of Clapham Action, St Paul's Area. (CASPA)

30 SEPTEMBER 1972: RESIDENTS MOBILIZE AGAINST THE CPO. The owner occupiers... were the first to "Say no to CPO"...CASPA could not assume, however, that all tenants in the area would have the same views as the home owners. Many of the tenants' houses are without bathrooms or inside lavatories and need substantial modernization; for some, rehousing might well be the realization of a dream. Its first task, therefore, was to discover the views of all the residents and whether they would welcome action in their name. An initial count indicated a substantial majority in favour of opposition to the compulsory purchase scheme and a public meeting on April 24 elected a committee...

A survey then conducted by the committee revealed interesting evidence of the existence of a stable community...

The relatively small numbers living in the five acres concerned may well have influenced the council in its decision to compulsorily purchase it; ...but the explanation for the present low density is important. A large part of the area is taken up by open space consisting of the lower churchyard, the allotments which are all worked by people within the area and a green... The other explanation ... is that there are business premises on the area...

As a result of the survey, a petition was drawn up... it was delivered to one of the area's councillors for presentation to the council. Signed by over 170 people, it deplored the lack of consultation between council and residents and asked for withdrawal of the present proposals for compulsory purchase.

21 OCTOBER 1972: COUNCIL'S REASONS FOR THE CPO. CASPA has now met the council. In St Paul's Community Centre last Monday evening, three youthful councillors took on the local residents. As one of the representatives for the area, Councillor Bing was given the nicely neutral position of Chairman. He was flanked by Councillors Noble and Livingstone... [In 2000 elected Mayor for London]...The council faced about 130 guests... The Vicar of St Paul's and Mr William Shelton, Tory MP for Clapham, Wandsworth attended and members of other local residents' associations...

Councillor Noble outlined the compulsory purchase procedure and time-table and he explained the council's choice of this area for redevelopment. Although most of the area is not "unfit" within Part 3 of the Housing Act, 1967, the council wished to acquire the rest of it because, redeveloped as a whole, the area could provide a housing gain of 200 per cent. With over 12,000 people on the waiting list for homes and a council aim of 2,000 new homes a year he argued that one could not ignore the potential of the area...

The residents' chief concern is for the existing community, so the subsequent questions which drew loudest cheers and applause were those which reflected a desire for its preservation... Council ownership would obliterate the wide range of ownership and tenancy now present. There was a complaint too, that there was as yet no plan for redevelopment.

Councillor Bing concluded the meeting by hoping that it has been informative and in some senses it was. Apart from the facts and figures and reassurances, the council has been seen to be composed not just of "faceless them", but more probably of sincere individuals.

9 DECEMBER 1972: ENERGETIC FIGHT TO DISPEL AIR OF GLOOM. ...CASPA knows that its only chance for saving even the best of the area lies in proposing a viable alternative. It is, therefore, taking seriously the council's invitation to put forward ideas.

In the meantime, a very much more detailed social survey is being undertaken...The belief that the council is all-powerful is not quickly dispelled. This attitude is easily labelled apathetic but most of the people I have met are not indifferent nor uninterested. Even though they appear to do very little about it, they do care about being moved from their homes or the area....

The enquiry is now scheduled for the middle of next year...even allowing for the determination of the various members of the (CASPA) committee it must be difficult to maintain momentum month after month.

Ted Hollamby, Lambeth's Director of Development and
Tony Collinson, Director of Housing discuss Lambeth's housing problem
and their programme to deal with it

7 APRIL 1973: REDEVELOPING: A COUNCIL PERSPECTIVE. Mr Hollamby is emphatic "We do not want to drive a bulldozer through the borough. We think we are in marked contrast to our neighbours. We want to keep a balance"... "Traditionally in the past we have tried to latch compulsory purchase areas on to a nucleus of unfit housing but now we are moving on and looking for areas, which though not unfit within the definition of the Housing Acts, are running down and are capable of giving us a housing gain... The council's planning has... been blighted by the slow progress of the Greater London development plan... but Mr Hollamby hopes that some form of go-ahead will soon be given.

"We feel we need a balance of owner occupation in redevelopments and we must do our best to get the reason behind this across," said Mr Collinson... Sometimes they admit to finding the residents unrealistic... Iveley Road is by no means an isolated instance; Lambeth Council has some 39 more compulsory purchase orders awaiting submission or confirmation by the Secretary of State, within its seven-year programme.

5 MAY 1973: CASPA'S FIGHT MOVES TO COUNCIL CHAMBER. CASPA's... request to be heard as a deputation was duly made by not less than 20 rate-payers or electors and the Town Clerk determined that the Housing Committee had to face the group... Anna Jefferson Smith was the deputation's spokesman. Clapham born and bred... she repeated many of the by now familiar arguments against the proposal. She also complained of the delays... She suggested a re-examination of Lambeth's entire housing programme. She referred to a statistical analysis of the borough's housing figures, prepared by Dil Husain, who accompanied her... Mrs Jefferson Smith summed up: "We would like to work with you, not against you."

Yesterday CASPA received its answer from the Housing Committee... the proposed order should stand.

12 MAY 1973: FIRST ÉMIGRÉS' OF THE CPO. Mr and Mrs Arthur Theobald were founder members of CASPA; Mr Theobald was elected its first chairman... They owned and lived in 605 Wandsworth Road, a Victorian terrace house on which they had spent incalculable hours and pounds... Today CASPA has no chairman and the Theobalds live in a modern council house on a Surrey hillside... Weeks after the news of the compulsory purchase order, Arthur was...offered an immediate transfer to Aldershot [by Boots, his employers, who were closing their London premises where he worked as a driver]; the alternative was a probable redundancy... To go or not to go boiled down to a question of security for the family... But, "If the house had not been threatened with compulsory purchase, I'd have put the house before the job", says Arthur.

16 JUNE 1973: CPO: SOMETHING HAPPENING AT LAST. The order... should now be on its way to... the Secretary of State... This order affects some 18 houses and a piece of land. Eleven houses are deemed to be "unfit"... the rest are adjoining lands required for satisfactory development of the area to be

cleared... CASPA's latest public meeting took place... CASPA had invited along two speakers experienced in compulsory purchase.

But there were now long delays. CASPA sent a humorous card to the housing committee's chairman. But some feared that delay would benefit the Council

27 OCTOBER 1973: LAMBETH COUNCIL'S CPO AND THE SYMBOL OF A SNAIL. There are only 57 houses in the area and it is known that at least five belong to the council already. There may in fact be more in its possession and if one of the landlords who owns a number of houses were to sell his interest, the council could quickly become a major owner in the area. Such a situation would... be brought out at the public enquiry and could easily have a telling effect.

17 NOVEMBER 1973: CPO SAGA: THE VICAR'S VIEW. St Paul's Clapham stands in a parish of compulsory purchase... half an acre of its graveyard and grass lie within the confines of that scheme and on three sides the church is bounded by its area... Peter Southwell-Sander [Vicar of St Paul's] claims that "it is no exaggeration to say that the hanging around and uncertainty create social problems, both physical and mental. People are frustrated at their inability to make any long-term plans...".

An important reason behind the parochial council's recent decision not to sell the lower churchyard to the council ahead of the actual compulsory purchase, was the feeling that thereby it would prejudice CASPA's case...

23 MARCH 1974: BUILDING UP TO CPO PUBLIC INQUIRY. The public inquiry is fixed for July 9 and, despite hopes and hints of some change in council policy on compulsory purchase, it seems clearer than ever that nothing short of ministerial decision or a miracle will reprieve the area. This depressing fact received confirmation at the last meeting of Lambeth council's housing committee.

In yet another attempt to convince committee members that wholesale compulsory purchase and redevelopment are not always the answer to housing shortages, CASPA had sought leave to address this meeting. "Given the difficulties your construction programme faces" said Mr Jefferson Smith, " you will forgive us for saying that any future gain from eventual redevelopment looks to us like pie in the sky. What is needed is a firm grip on the redevelopment plans to make sure that they are realistic and do not do more harm than good, we suggest that you should not resolve on a CPO unless you can carry it through quickly".

The answer CASPA received was that despite the slow progress, the hardship caused and the possible marginal advantage of redevelopment over rehabilitation, the scheme must go to an inquiry for decision

15 JUNE 1974: CPO INQUIRY AROUND CORNER. The public inquiry into the compulsory purchase order takes place next month… The invitation to "Save Old Clapham" has met with such an encouraging response that the appeal brochure has gone to a reprint and CASPA is now confident that it will have sufficient insurance against having to pay all the costs of the professional representation at the public enquiry…

An inquiry (held on Wednesday 17 July) into the compulsory purchase of houses in an adjoining area, Rectory Grove, took place at the same time. That CPO was opposed by another local group, Clapham Action Rectory Grove or CARG

3 AUGUST 1974: WAITING FOR THE VERDICT AFTER THE CPO INQUIRY. [Lambeth Council's] chief planning officer put in an impressively professional performance and was at pains to put the issues in a borough basis. Clearly he

The cover of the CASPA brochure

appreciated CASPA's and CARG's case but, in his view, local protectionism had to give way to the claims of the homeless...

[CASPA's consultant planner explained] his view... that the unfit houses could be rehabilitated instead of demolished... He suggested that [the council] had been over optimistic about the number of persons the redeveloped site could accommodate...

CASPA's treasurer... doubted whether [the council] was yet capable of proceeding with redevelopment at any reasonable speed... He also gave evidence from CASPA's survey of the cohesive nature of the existing community... Over half the... sample... had relatives living within walking distance.

The comparative costs of redevelopment and rehabilitation were emphasized not just by CASPA but by CARG's planner and a representative of a local squatters' organization.

The individual objectors provided more domestic detail. The wife of a disabled man who now has only to cross the road to reach his place of employment; the divorced woman who put all her savings and six years' effort into doing up a cottage... the Polish lady who provides furnished accommodation for three tenants...

Many objectors did not want to or could not attend but, in their absence, were assured that their letters would be taken into consideration, along with all the statements, maps, brochures and other papers submitted...

A substantial submission came from the Clapham Society and reflected its concern that "the structure and function" of Clapham as "a village centre" was in jeopardy as a result of piecemeal council development. The society pleaded for consultation and a wider co-ordinated plan for Clapham.

Submissions were also made by the London Association for Saving Homes, Esso Petroleum, who had a site on Wandsworth Road and the large local employer, Normand Electrical Holdings Ltd

The closing speeches were not lengthy: CARG and CASPA's mutual counsel sat down to his clients' applause. There was a general feeling that he had... done... a very good job.

14 JUNE 1975. A CLAPHAM TRIUMPH AGAINST THE CPO BULLDOZER. CASPA has won; Lambeth's bulldozer has been halted... [The Secretary of State for the Department of the Environment, Mr Anthony Crosland] "accepts that

[Lambeth] Council have an urgent need for additional housing but on the evidence at present before him he is not convinced that redevelopment... is the best method of achieving the Council's objective. He considers that a more satisfactory result might be achieved by retaining the existing buildings as far as it is reasonable to do so and that to this end the Council may wish to give further consideration to the possibility of repair, improvement, and in some cases, conversion of suitable houses, together with infill development where the latter is clearly necessary."

...the inspector acknowledged CASPA's influence... The presence of a strong action group was, he considered, a forcible demonstration of a "well integrated community living happily and neighbourly."...CASPA also owes much to its friends... Much of the Clapham Society's evidence impressed the inspector...

Anyone faced with a similar challenge should know that CASPA's protest demanded much expenditure of money, energy and time.

Extracted from articles by HALLDORA BLAIR *in* The Times
on the dates shown in the text, between September 1972 and June 1975

The novelist and essayist, **Angela Carter** *(1940-1992)*
*lived in Clapham at various times of her life and considered herself
a true South Londoner. In an essay for* New Society *in 1977
she reflected on the changes over the years.*

AFTER AN ABSENCE, I NOW LIVE IN SOUTH LONDON AGAIN. And the girls, I see, still do have a style all of their own. Last autumn, it was ankle-length, knife-edged pleated tartan skirts, with ankle socks and plastic sandals. This summer it seems to be decorous punk – tapered jeans, rouge, and a lot of chains every-where – as if to indicate that, however much things might seem to have changed, everything remains fundamentally the same.

In 1960, I went for a job on a glossy magazine and said, with typical south London sullen defiance: 'Balham', when the editor asked me where I lived. She drummed her enamelled fingertips on her leather desk for a long time, then inquired, almost solicitous: 'Do you find that perfectly convenient?' It was terribly convenient for the Northern Line, but she did not mean that. Where I live now is only two stops nearer the West End on the Northern Line; but these days she would be more likely to say: 'Clapham? Why, some friends of mine have just moved there.'...

...For us born-and-bred south Londoners, sun is always the herald of rain. Things are always less good than they were; or, we prophesy with relish, not as bad as they're going to be... We lugubriously enjoy the area's reputation for violence.

The lady in the newsagent's on the Wandsworth Road told me that every week, regular as clockwork, five of her customers – five little old ladies – get mugged. Always the same five? How little? How old? And was it mugging or dipping? Because to have your pockets non-violently picked is not the same thing at all as being hit over the head with a bottle. Well, she said, maybe dipping. Still, it's a rotten thing to do to a little old lady, isn't it? She had me there. I could only concur.

But the Teds used to enjoy waylaying little old ladies, and they used razors, too. I don't think it's got much worse. It's probably stayed the same. But more people notice. Fewer people regard it as simply one of the hazards of inner-city life. We had certain techniques of urban hygiene drummed into us from an early age: never cross the Common at night, unless accompanied by a responsible adult who has not offered you sweets. May marks the beginning of the open season for flashers on the Common. Lock all doors and windows. Lock all car doors, even if you are only gone for a moment. Do not leave your washing unattended in the machine at the launderette. Even so, they'll probably get you...

...At the crossroads, the Queenstown Road is dominated by the magnificent pile of Battersea power station, a monolithic backdrop like a still from a Soviet propaganda film of the 1930s. On the corner, on a wooden bench, at the foot of a hoarding, occasionally lie red-eyed men with bottles in paper bags. Nearby, an Italian ice-cream parlour does a roaring trade. A couple of Indian grocers, two bistros and a brace of antique shops – as if everything round here goes in pairs, like coppers traditionally do...

...Round Clapham Common, of course, it has always been more or less posh and always pleasant though never possessing that raffish chic the newcomers hanker for, or the seediness the alternatives relish. Here you may find Victorian and Edwardian residential Clapham with its interesting quality of unflashy, solid, unshakeable money and, somehow, also, of worth. The founder of the *Church Times*, G. J. Palmer, lived round here. Lots of evangelists and do-gooders. William Wilberforce, even Marianne Thornton, who organised ragged schools, boys' schools, girls' schools, Sunday schools, infants' schools, and one particularly offensive one – school for the daughters of tradesmen, 'my Middlings', she called them.

You get the picture? Piety and good works: plain living and high thinking. It must have been round here, in one of these substantial but discreet red-brick villas, that the man in the Clapham Omnibus lived, the solid, sensible, rational chap with his natural sense of justice and decency.

These houses are solid, decent, English, middle-class values, rendered in bricks and mortar. They are constantly leafleted by the Socialist Party of Great Britain, the International Marxist Group, the Workers Revolutionary Party and the Socialist Workers' Party, some of whom even live there. But I kind of hear Elgar playing when I look at these houses. I suspect it is from here the Afghan hounds come who are walked on the Common on summer Sunday afternoons, beneath the kites flown by clean children and laughing alternatives.

These houses were only briefly, if ever, down. They're now almost fully recovered from the indignity of multi-occupancy. You can't walk home from the tube these days without seeing somebody moving their Swiss-cheese plants into a white-painted room, probably with a chrome and glass coffee table and maybe spotlight fittings. The newcomers who've just moved into Clapham must all be the same kind of young professional couples. A health food shop has opened to sell them black beans. The book-shop has display cases of Picador Books, the publications of Pluto Press, Spare Rib, and God knows what else besides. The entire Rive Gauchy bit, in fact, from seedy bohemia to radical chic, to kids called Gareth and Emma playing with their Galt toys on the floor of the bank while – at the same time – down the road, an old lady in the pub removes her teeth in order to sing 'Some of these days' with passion and vibrancy, to tumultuous applause. Even the Rastas in the front bar applaud her.

It is all very confusing indeed, and hypocrite that I am, I've made it sound absolutely delicious, haven't I? Anyway, if you just stand still, social mobility will catch up with you anywhere, these days.

ANGELA CARTER, *from an essay in* New Society, 1977
Republished in *Shaking a leg, Journalism and Writings*, 1997

8

ALL CHANGE
AT WORK

In the late 1990s the main building of the former factory
of **Ross Ensign**, *optical glass manufacturers, on North Side,*
was converted for use by the software company **QAS**.
Thus, a place which had begun at the forefront of one technology
ended the century at the forefront of another. An article in a local
newspaper described the Ross factory in the 1960s.

UP-TO-DATE MACHINES INSTALLED at Ross Ensign Ltd's Clapham factory in
the glass polishing department only a few months ago are no different from old
machines which have been fitted with dual speed motors.

The firm was founded in 1829 by Mr. Andrew Ross who was himself a
craftsman. Recently Mr H.R. Price, the present managing director, discovered that
two microscopes made by Mr. Ross are still in use… In 1920 Sir Charles Parsons
joined the company. Up to this time they had concentrated on manufacturing
optical equipment, microscopes, binoculars, and photographic equipment. But a
man called Wenham invented the gas burner, and for a time Ross broke away
from their optical business to manufacture these burners until the demand for them
ceased. In 1949 British Photographic Industries took over the control of Ross.

At one time Ross cameras were famous, …but the company stopped manufacturing cameras in 1959 for economic reasons. Today their name is a household word so far as binoculars are concerned. But they also manufacture radar and naval equipment, periscopes, photographic enlarging lenses, spotting-scopes, epidiascopes, and special binoculars for people who wear glasses.

The firm does a great deal of work for Government departments, and makes telescopes, binoculars and scientific instruments to the highest standards of accuracy, functional performance and quality specified by naval and military services, several foreign governments, universities and scientific laboratories throughout the world.

The company pride themselves on being a family concern, even more so now than in the past. At one time there were at least 1,200 people working in the factory but now there are only about 400.

A few months ago it was decided to concentrate the works into a much smaller area. The whole staff helped to move their own machines and equipment, and more than 300 machines were moved between Thursday and Monday lunch time when they were in use again. When this happened there were several men of 83 or even older who had spent most of their working life with the company.

"All excellent workers right up to the last moment, they still keep up their interest and come along to see us," said Mr. Price. "In the optical industry as in no other industry the perfection of the glass is left entirely to the individual. There is no first, second or third quality. We do not have any 'not fit for export' quality, either it is perfect or we throw it away."

The staff includes men like 76-year-old York Garlike, [of] Christian Fields, Norbury, who has to work to a tolerance of one-hundredth of a millimetre when edging and setting up equipment in the lens polishing department. Mr. Garlike, who was presented with a gold watch for 50 years service some years ago, finds that experience and precision are still very important today.

It takes several years to train a skilled glass worker. "We try to do the train-ing in our own works so that we can safeguard the quality of Ross products," commented Mr. Price. "No machines have been made that will take away the skill of the individual worker in glass polishing. We do practically everything ourselves; we manufacture our own tools and thread gauges; we have our own pattern makers and at one time we even had our own foundry."

The senior shop steward in the glass polishing department, Mr. Wardlaw, thinks there is every chance for a keen youngster in the trade. "But you want a lot of patience – because you might work all day long and not get results." He agrees that there is a friendly atmosphere in the works, and there is a 100 per cent union membership.

After the lenses and prisms have been polished, they are bloomed and cemented together. First they are cleaned electronically in a partial vacuum, then the air is completely pumped out and a fine deposit forms on the surface of the glass.

In the past wine glasses had to be made by hand and it was a long, involved process. Recently, Ross, working with the English Glass Corporation, developed 24 prototype machines which will make glasses automatically. Ross optic cement, one of the company's inventions, is now specified by all Government departments. Every jar of cement which is sold has a small steel ball with it, and before it is used the viscosity of the cement is checked by seeing how long the ball takes to reach the bottom of the jar. Binoculars are the company's bread-and-butter line but they do not intend to concentrate on them alone. Increasing interest is being shown in a micro reader which was put on the market about 18 months ago, and inquiries have been received from libraries all over the country.

Everyone in the optical trade has to obtain slab glass to specification from one firm in this country. It is possible to import glass from France or Austria – but import duties mean that the cost is higher than in this country.

"We are the premier optical company in the United Kingdom at the moment but we want to be once again the premier company in the world." claims Mr. Price.

Mr. Price does not fear competition from the Continent, in fact he rather welcomes the advent of the Common Market.

"The Hong Kong manufacturers and the Japanese have got some really worthwhile stuff. Between the wars the Japanese would take up any British manufactured project and make a rather second rate, shoddy copy. But that is not so today."

GLORIA WALKER, The Clapham News and Observer, 19 October 1962

Despite Mr Price's brave words, Ross did not survive the lowering of world-wide tariffs and our entry into the European Economic Community. For some years after the firm closed, the building was used as a Lambeth training centre, and renamed **George West House** *after a former local councillor.*

Jenny Cain describes how *QAS* came into being,
and then moved into George West House.

AN ADVERT FOR A JOB WITHIN QAS was placed in Stockwell Job Centre where I worked in 1994. After numerous candidates were sent for an interview and no one had succeeded in getting through, a visit was arranged. Arriving at the offices in Old Town where 30 people worked on one of the hottest days of the year, a friendly atmosphere and a real buzz to the offices encouraged me to apply.

Five interviews and a very large glass of wine later I was told I could start in a new job as a Sales Co-ordinator providing admin support to the UK sales force. At 21, the IT industry was a big mystery but I was determined to learn and progress.

I was number thirty-seven on the payroll of QAS, the UK's leading provider of address management software. Two offices existed in London and Scotland and I had daily contact with eight sales staff. Now with offices around the world, over one hundred sales staff and more than 300 staff in total I have seen so many changes and developments in just over seven years. If I stop and think about them, it can be quite frightening but still very exciting.

QAS offices, George West House, Clapham Common North Side in 2000

The initial idea of address management was thought of by Tony Bickford, the QAS chairman. By entering a postcode, a fully postcoded Royal Mail address could be returned ensuring that companies who sent out a lot of mail or took details over the phone could capture accurate data. I had heard it being used so many times over the phone and now I was working for the company that made the software. From a simple idea, adaptations of the software including database cleaning, web based products, business-to-business data and now a worldwide solution have been developed.

The first sales of software were done from Tony's dining room and once established and running as a proper company, offices were found in Balham. QAS moved to Old Town, Clapham Common in January 1994 and since then has grown from strength to strength. Within the courtyard, office space owned by other companies was eventually leased to QAS and within four years, the problem of running out of space arose.

Most people think of software companies being based in the M4 corridor surrounded by companies of the same ilk. The QAS building is in the heart of Clapham Common and is surrounded by beautiful old (and new) residential houses and one of the biggest patches of Common in London. With the search on for new space, the board of directors were keen to remain in the area.

The old Lambeth Training Services Building (formerly Ross Optical) seemed the best option in the area. With a lot of work, the building would accommodate the current level of staff and leave room to grow as well for the future. After nearly two years of restoration and renovation, the removal of the scaffolding revealed the new headquarters of QAS.

The opening party for the building was attended by 300 guests consisting of family and friends of those who worked at QAS along with staff from local businesses. The link to the local community is important to QAS. Held on the roof of the building the party gave everyone the chance to see what a wonderful view of London we have from GWH [George West House]. It was also a chance for us to all show off and feel proud of the company and the environment we worked in. Derek West, the son of George West, was amongst those who attended and was pleased to see that a hi-tech company had managed to retain character and atmosphere in their working environment in the building named after his father, a local councillor for Lambeth.

My journey starts each day in Carshalton, Surrey and takes me through South London before parking outside the Windmill pub. Having parked there for many years, the seasons control the look and feel of the area. In the summer, locals drink and play games on the common, the autumn sees a colourful array of leaves falling and in winter a cosy look through the windows makes it look very welcoming.

My daily stroll across the Common gives me a chance to begin to think about my day ahead – will I have to go out anywhere, what meetings do I have, what are the priorities for the day? A lot of the people walking in the direction of the tube have the same look of concentration on their face. I often wonder where they end up on a daily basis.

Arriving at George West House, breakfast is first on the agenda. On Mondays, staff are given this free as a buffet. Stories are swapped about the weekend and the bustle of the week begins. As we settle down to work in GWH e-mails are checked and sent, meetings attended, events booked and organised and the world of marketing QuickAddress begins again for another week.

I am now Marketing Events Manager for QAS and it is my job to ensure the smooth running of trade shows and seminars within the UK and Europe. I also liaise with the other Marketing Executives we have in the USA, Australia and Europe on new images we can use and new ideas we have used for the stand. Work with my colleagues in the UK includes ensuring we have enough pre-show marketing coverage for each event including advertising, direct mail and a presence on our website.

Each lunchtime there is a multitude of places to go. Spoilt by pubs and restaurants, it is never hard to find something to eat from the greasy spoon to a pizza to just a sandwich. The odd bit of shopping for dinner or birthday presents means a trip to the High Street at least once week. Fridays is the weekly trip to the Pepper Tree where QAS pay for staff to have lunch. It allows staff from the two London based offices to meet up and socialise before the final afternoon of the week.

As well as using our surroundings for our own personal benefit, QAS have given back something to the community. Thousands of daffodils were planted on the Common, the local community hall was painted with the help of QAS staff and more recently a donation of books was made to the library. We are all very lucky to work within Clapham and this ensures that others also benefit.

QAS have a social committee for the staff and always include activities in Clapham. Subsidised trips to the cinema in the winter ensure we all get to see the latest blockbuster films. During the summer, football, softball and volleyball are amongst the favourite games played on the Common. The link to local charities is very strong with support given to a wide variety of causes. Each year the QAS summer ball is held within the Trinity Hospice grounds. It always follows a theme and provides a great excuse for us all to get dressed up and enjoy ourselves for a very worthy cause.

Life at QAS is based on a mini community. Although Sales are based in Old Town and the Technical and Business Support departments are based in GWH, there is a real sense of pride in the company that we work for and many social occasions are held in various locations in Clapham.

The Calf (formerly known as the Friesian and Firkin) has seen many end of Sales year parties on the last day of March. Talk of one drink and then going home seems to have been just talk so many times. The end of year party is one of the biggest nights of the social calendar and allows us all a chance to let our hair down after a very busy twelve months.

The majority of my twenties have been spent in Clapham. As Marketing Events Manager, my job has taken me abroad many times in the last eighteen months to the USA and Europe. The thousands of miles travelled are great but the 15 miles to work in the morning brings me to one of the nicest areas of London I know.

If someone had said to me just over seven years ago I was going to be an Events Manager and work for an international company I would have laughed. The mixture of QAS and Clapham have made my twenties an eventful decade. I wonder what my thirties will bring and which postal area I will spend most of my time in.

JENNY CAIN, 2001

Brian Vincent *joined Battley Brothers as General Manager in 1971. He became a director of the company and retired in 1995. His recollections of working at Battleys reflect some of the changes in the industry by the last quarter of the century.*

OVER THE YEARS Battley Brothers have always been very aware of the importance of good communications with our customers due to the immediacy of our work. We made good use of motorcycle messengers before many other companies did and with a good amount of success. The people operating the services were of mixed ability and could, for the most part, only be evaluated by experiencing their efficiency. You were not over impressed by the messenger who, when you handed him the envelope for delivery, stressing that the utmost urgency was required, tried to leave your premises by entering your broom cupboard. One company who for the most part provided a good service had one weak link whom we dubbed "Electric Man". His appearance which until he lifted his helmet's visor was a cross between John Surtees [motor-cycle champion] and Evel Knievel [stuntman], belied the fact that when he reached the car park he was going to leap upon a dilapidated moped. In addition to this he specialised in falling off his machine on reaching his destination in the hope that he would be plied with a cup of coffee (or better still scotch) and somewhere to sit down and recover!...

...As soon as we found that we could install two-way radios in our cars and vans we realised what a time saver it could be and had them fitted straight away. Ted Sawtell with his RAF background masterminded the procedures for call signs and use. There was to be none of your "Rubber Duck to Big Daddy" or references to "Bears and Smokies". Our system had a closer affinity to "The

Brian Vincent (centre) explaining a printing process to John Goodwin and Lyn Haill from the National Theatre, c 1980

Battle of Britain"; we were in the "Red Leader to Base" answered by "This is Base receiving you, come in Red Leader" mode.

The use of the radios was very successful with customers in the early days, bemused by how we could arrive on the scene just after they had put the phone down. It could be frustrating to find yourself recalled to the firm before you had got out of Clapham on your way home, or diverted a couple of times before you reached your original destination, but it far more often saved time and was a great boon... The plus points far outweighed the drawbacks and radios were in use until we updated with mobile phones.

The other improvement was the use of Fax machines, which enabled us to transmit proofs and receive corrected proofs and copy from customers and know they had been received and if they were satisfactory almost immediately. A great improvement on the days when a motorcycle messenger disappeared off the face of the earth with a large parcel of urgent proofs and copy. ...

...Another of the vast areas of change during the past twenty years is that Composing Departments including their ancillary departments of Monotype, Linotype and Reading have been replaced with Digitalised Graphic equipment. This has a certain Jekyll and Hyde factor about it, but its advantages far out-weigh its disadvantages and will even more so with its development at an ever increasing speed and covering an ever wider area. ...

...The disappearance from the trade generally of Readers is one downside. It is only now that you are seeing the deterioration in quality caused by their absence, that you can appreciate the high standards that they maintained. It was rather unfairly thought that the qualification for becoming a reader was to be a compositor with dodgy feet – not so! Spell checks on computers will quite hap-pily accept things like *someone writing out a check* or something *that costs two much*. The responsibility these days rests far more heavily with the customer, as in all fairness, the printers are often handed discs or tape that they have had no responsibility for setting and style has suffered. An origination department now consists of an office where the electronic equipment outnumbers the operatives and is no longer a factory workshop, with its attendant noise of machinery and proportionally large workforce...

...The period that I worked for the Clapham company got as close to twenty-five years as it could.... That period of twenty years plus was one of general change. I remember reading at the beginning of that time that you could walk quite a way through a printers without barking your shins on a computer. By the end of that period I would say it was down to yards. The trade was in a state of change and in an ever decreasing time scale. Some trades disappearing entirely, and others changing out of all recognition. In my early years with the company I think it would be fair to say that I could cover for just about any of the areas of the trade, but by the finish with the increases in the use of electronics, and the digitalisation of origination and source material, this was no longer the case.

Those same years were ones of continual fluctuation in the national economy and markets. Firstly there was raging inflation which was so bad that we once had to cancel the purchase of a machine due to the increase in its cost while we were waiting for delivery, which put it beyond our reach. It was a case of a couple of good years if you were lucky, followed by a couple of bad years. At the same time it was a period of change with legislation and trade unions. A considerable amount of time had to be spent negotiating with staff. Some of the negotiating got pretty acrimonious, with unions being reluctant to see changes brought about affecting their traditional methods of work. All understandable, but very difficult to get over to them, the fact that things were such that it was a case of "change or go under!".

In spite of all that, and the fact that the last few years were spent operating in what was a 'Buyers Market', (which meant you were under continuous pressure), it was for the most part an enjoyable and exciting way to earn a living. As for more than twenty of those years I was also on the Board of Directors, I also felt a certain amount of satisfaction that the company was still trading, after going through a time that put many companies out of business. We were also reasonably up to date with the technology, and for a medium sized independent company, that was an achievement. The capital required to keep up with such an ever changing technology was considerable.

BRIAN VINCENT, Recollections compiled on his retirement in 1995 and subsequently included in his autobiography, *Partial Recall*, 1996

Jagdish Rai Treohan and his family run a shop
in Abbeville Road, where you can buy anything
from a delicious organic loaf and a
state of-the-art toaster to toast it in,...

… to the finest Arabica coffee beans and a coffee machine in which to grind and percolate them, genuine Turkish Delight, Fentimans ginger beer, a new lock for your door and the tools with which to fit it.

I CAME TO CLAPHAM FROM INDIA IN 1973. In those days I was working as an accountant at the Indian High Commission in London. My family and I lived above what was then the Bon Bon, a good old-fashioned sweet shop in Abbeville Road. The children all went to Bonneville School and later to local secondary schools.

I opened the first shop in 1979 selling a standard range of products. Opposite Treohans, where the Abbeville Restaurant and Bar is now, was Derek Orme's wine bar. Orme's reputation attracted many new people to Clapham and to help provide for this clientele I decided to expand the business to include delicatessen foods. I attended many fine food fairs and exhibitions to learn about the kind of food my new customers would require and gradually we grew from a basic grocery shop into a specialist food store.

In 1987 I bought the shop next door. Everyone advised me to start an Indian restaurant, but I perceived that the real need of the neighbourhood was for a hardware shop. Clapham is an area which attracts many couples with young families and my decision has resulted in a shop which can meet the demands of the most avid DIY enthusiast and home-improver. A local estate agent sometimes shows his prospective buyers around Treohans as an incentive to them to move to Clapham.

It is a family business. My wife, Kamla, and I live above the shops. We run the business with our two sons, Kapil and Vijnish and our daughter, Vandana, and their partners. I believe a family business must be controlled by the family. If you go away for too long you come back and it won't be there any more.

When I came to Clapham local houses cost around £5,000. Now, as we know, they command up to and above £500,000. There have been many changes. Local village shops such as the butcher, fishmonger, chemist and greengrocer have given way to a proliferation of restaurants and estate agents but this area has given us our livelihood. We have worked very hard and I never want to go away from here, or change Treohans' use. I will retire here.

Our family 'service with a smile' has won us the prestigious *Evening Standard* award for the best corner shop in London.

JAGDISH RAI TREOHAN *interviewed by Virginia Lester*, 2001

Clement Baptiste has been the proprietor of the
Do-it-Yourself shop in Clapham Park Road for 25 years.
In 2002 he spoke about his arrival in England over 40 years ago
and his pleasure in running a family business.

I CAME TO ENGLAND FROM GUYANA – British Guiana as it was then – in 1956.
I went to live in Battersea because I had relatives who
were already in the area. I managed to get a job
as a welder with a firm in Wandsworth
called Duval Autos. I had worked as a
welder before I came to England, but I
was not qualified and while I was
working at Duval I went to night
school in Hammersmith and got
my City and Guilds qualification.

I moved to Clapham in the
1960s when I bought a house in
Elms Road. In the 1970s Duval
decided to scrap welding. I was
treated very well by the boss who
explained the situation and wanted
me to stay. They became Duval
Products, makers of Dexion shelving
and still exist today. I did stay on for a
while but I felt motivated to run my
own business and I was on the look-out
for something suitable.

Eventually in the late 1970s, I saw an

Clement Baptiste

advertisement for this shop in Clapham Park Road. The owner, Mr Robertson,
wanted to retire and his assistant could not afford to buy the business. So,
although my bank manager told me that I would make more money working for
someone else than running my own business, he agreed to lend me some money
and I went ahead and bought the business. One problem was that the lease was
from the GLC [Greater London Council] who refused to sell me the freehold.
When the GLC was disbanded by Margaret Thatcher [in 1986] they
approached me and offered me the freehold. There were still problems as I was

nearly gazumped, but I finally succeeded in buying it.

My wife is also from Guyana. Our four children were all born in Clapham. They went to Bonneville School and the three girls then went to Marianne Thornton [on West Side, demolished in 1997 and houses built on the site] and the boy to Henry Thornton [South Side, now Lambeth College]. We are members of the Church of the Holy Spirit and were involved years ago with the fund-raising for the Contact Centre [in Hambalt Road]. My wife used to run the Girl Guides.

Of course, Clapham has changed in the time I have been here. New people have moved in and a lot of the older ones have moved out. I would say about 90 per cent of the people who were here when I first came have moved. But I have very loyal and regular customers. Lots of people just pop in to say 'Hello' and to ask how I am. They don't only come when they want to buy something. And I really like that. I am happy to give advice too and I have been in the business so long that I can answer most of the questions I am asked. I have plenty of new younger customers, but I find that many older people are very independent and like to do things for themselves. They think they will do a good job themselves, and they don't trust someone else to do it properly.

I am seventy years old and I am gradually easing out of the business. My children are helping me now and will take over and run it between them. I have never employed anyone outside the family. This is my family business and I like it this way. I like the friends I have made and although it is hard work running your own business I don't really have anything to complain about.

CLEMENT BAPTISTE interviewed by Alyson Wilson, 2002

*The actress, **Leslie Ash**, star of the current television series 'Where the heart is' was brought up in Clapham, living over the decorating shop which her parents ran in Clapham High Street. When the business closed in the late 1990s Leslie and her ex-footballer husband, Lee Chapman, took over the lease and opened a bar, SO.UK.*

MY FATHER ORIGINALLY WORKED WITH HIS FAMILY FIRM of builders' merchants in Balham, but decided to sell out his share and start his own business with my mother. In the early 1970s they opened Unidec in Clapham High Street and my parents, my sister and I moved in to the flat over the shop. I was about ten at the time and my sister three and a half years older. We both started going to dancing lessons at the Italia Conti stage school on Saturdays to give us something to do while my mother was working. We really loved it and finished up going there full time. It was a good broad education in acting, dancing and singing, though not very academic. I left when I was 16 with only one 'O' level! My sister became a dancer and I started modelling for teenage magazines and eventually found myself an agent and got into acting and television.

I loved growing up right in the middle of Clapham, with the Common so close and plenty to occupy us. I remember many of the shops which have now gone – including Woolworths, which after a long absence came back again last year. There seemed to be a lot of pubs, each one of them with a totally different feeling. The Plough [now The Goose and Granite] was quite rough and we could almost guarantee that if we looked out of our window on a Saturday night we would see a fight going on, while The Windmill (on the Common) was very pleasant and almost sedate. My mother would always buy her flowers at Leslie's just along from us on South Side [still there]. But my favourite shop was Tracy Originals just further along South Side. I always wanted to be a skinhead girl as a teenager, though my

Lesley Ash with her mother, Ellie

mother did everything she could to restrain me. For years it seemed that Tracys had in the window the type of two-tone suit I really coveted.

The shop was a very sociable place. My mother, who was known to all her customers as Ellie, seemed to know everybody and she was a fund of useful information. Lots of people would come in to ask her advice about their decorating and all sorts of other subjects, or just to have a chat. I still meet people regularly who remember her fondly and tell me how kind and helpful she was, and a real friend to all her customers. She was very proud of my sister and me and told everyone all about us and eventually about our children. One of her good friends was the local policeman, Barry, and I remember him regularly calling in on his bicycle to see us.

I left Clapham and moved to Sheffield for a while when I married Lee Chapman, who was playing for Sheffield Wednesday at the time. We moved around to various places for a few years but came back to South London eventually when Lee left football and we went into the restaurant business. We opened our first restaurant, Teatro, in Shaftesbury Avenue.

At one stage my parents went to live in Spain briefly, leaving Unidec in the hands of a manager, but this was not a success. They came back again and ran the business for another 10 years or so, before they decided it was time to retire. They had to face the problem that they could not sell the business because by then, with the rise of chain stores like Homebase and B & Q, the shop could no longer thrive as it had in the past. In addition the rents on the High Street were going up and up. But if they gave up the lease on the shop they would lose their flat too. Lee and I had always thought we would like to open a bar out of Central London but in a local High Street and here was an opportunity in an area we knew and liked. So we bought my parents a flat in Streatham and renegotiated the lease, so that we took on the ground floor and the flat was let separately.

We had some difficulty getting the appropriate change of use and licence for a bar, and sadly, my mother died in April 1999, just a few days before it was all finalised. It was really tragic that she died so soon after her well-earned retirement and the number of people who came to her funeral at Holy Trinity Church reminded us of just what a popular local figure she had been.

We opened SO.UK just over a year later, in June 2000. I like seeing Clapham High Street buzzing with activity every evening, and I think it is exciting that there are so many young people around and new flats being built. It is sad that some smaller shops have gone from the centre of Clapham, but the High Street was becoming run down and dreary and it is good to see money being spent to bring it to life again. Times have changed and people live differently. I enjoyed growing up in Clapham in the 1970s, but I don't regret the changes we are seeing now. I am happy that I still live in the area with my family, and I am still involved with the property where I grew up. It is an irony that I recently made a television advertisement for Homebase, one of the companies responsible for the demise of the High Street decorating shop where I was brought up!

LESLIE ASH *interviewed by Alyson Wilson*, 2002

John Phillimore, *a local resident and experienced bookseller opened a second-hand book shop in Old Town in 1991. He talked about running the shop in an interview in 1995. The shop closed in 1998.*

FOR SOME TIME... I HAD BEEN THINKING that my part of Clapham would be a good area to open a book shop, in particular this little bit called Old Town. Of course I'm now told by the experts that the shop should be on the other side of the road. I could always have a sandwich board saying, 'Look over here, you bastards!'

There used to be a bookshop in Clapham Park Road before the War. The oldies are always referring to it wistfully – no doubt wishing I was it. Anyway Old Town Books opened in September 1991 and has managed to attract some good regular customers. For quite some time I had been salting away books, so that I did in fact start the shop without having to buy much stock. Of course a lot of the books were rather generously arranged sideways on the shelves and, at the last moment, I did panic and Angus O'Neill filled a stack which I sold on commission for him...

...When I first started, the rent here was £12,000 a year, which was far too much. I got it down by about £2,000 and have sublet shelf space to some guys who call themselves Pronk and deal in philosophy books. Part of the deal with the philosophers is that they do one day a week in the shop. I also have an absurdly over-qualified assistant called Andrew Railing who speaks Russian and Chinese, though he doesn't get much opportunity in the shop. And I've just gone into partnership with Simon Cobley, the archivist for Weidenfeld & Nicolson.

Running a shop is fine as long as I don't have to be in it all the time. On the whole I prefer buying books to selling them... Ideally I would have read every book in the shop and only have books that I enjoy. For example I always try to have at least one copy of Roger Longrigg's *Daughters of Mulberry*, which is the greatest book ever written in any language by anybody. Everyone who has read it agrees with me. Longrigg's a fascinating writer with several aliases including Rosalind Erskine who wrote *The Passion-Flower Hotel*. The cover has a picture of a rather unlikely looking woman facing the other way - presumably Roger in a wig.

I don't know what can be done to make people read more books – beating perhaps? It's obviously the fault of the schools. Most of the children who come into the shop are incredibly ignorant. There was one who used to come just to make a nuisance of himself. One day he said something very sad. I had been telling him that he ought to work hard, go to university, make friends and so on.

All he said was 'What do you want friends for? They'd only know when you done a burglary'.

Actually we get more lunatics in the shop than criminals. So-called 'care in the community' is becoming a real problem for everybody in the retail trade. People come in, looking quite normal and then suddenly break down in verbal diarrhoea. At least once a day someone walks quickly to the middle of the shop and then rushes out looking stunned. I want to shout after them 'What did you expect to find in a book shop?' Then there's the lonely man with the wrecked gut. I think I've heard more about it than his doctor.

At the moment I'm trying to learn about Japan and Japanese literature. During the summer our Oriental cousins come into the shop, mostly asking directions to the Soseki Museum. Natsume Soseki spent a few miserable years at the turn of the century living in a house round the corner in The Chase which is now a museum…

…I'm not disillusioned about bookselling as such, it's just so difficult to make enough money at it. Of course this may have something to do with my own incompetence. I don't think it's the recession. If anything, people probably buy more of my type of book – priced at a fiver or a tenner— during a recession when they can't afford perhaps to buy a three-figure book.

JOHN PHILLIMORE, *interviewed by Sheila Markham,*
published in The Bookdealer, January 1995

Throughout the century, Clapham residents commuted
to the centre of London to work. **Peter Jefferson Smith**
did so for 34 years, using the tube, buses and surface rail.

ONE SUNDAY AFTERNOON, IN THE AUTUMN OF 1960, I arrived at Liverpool Street station with a large trunk and two boxes. I had taken "digs" (a furnished bed-sit) with an elderly couple in Rodenhurst Road, and at the station got a taxi to take me and my luggage to Clapham. Once we left the main roads, I had to direct the driver down dark streets which I had only visited once before. These were days in which north London taxis did not go to Clapham if they could help it, and the driver behaved as if he was many miles from civilisation, first claiming that the journey was over the six mile limit covered by the meter, and then expecting an enormous tip. (Still, I managed better than my father did a few years later, when the taxi taking him from Liverpool Street to Clapham broke down just at the top of the ramp up from the station, leaving him, a frail man of nearly seventy, to struggle with his luggage to the Underground. He thought that the taxi had broken down at the mere thought of going to Clapham.) It was only many years later that I found that taxis willingly ventured south of the river.

On the Monday morning, I set off for my first day of work in the civil service, to an office near Bank. At the bottom of Park Hill, I bought my newspaper from the wooden kiosk at Parsons Corner, still run by the daughter of the Mr Parsons whose pre-war shop gave the place its name. At the tube station, the tickets were sold from two large wooden booths, which you walked past to get to the escalator; or there were two or three coin operated machines. I cannot remember the fare, beyond that a return ticket to Bank gave you change from two shillings. At platform level, it was much as now, though the much cruder train indicators just showed the destination and route of the first and second northbound trains – the signs showing how long you would wait came many years later. The platforms were much worse lit and usually had a very dusty atmosphere; and on the return journey, between Clapham North and Clapham Common, the trains would hit a wall of repellently stale air.

In 1968 I moved for three years to Whitehall; now living off the Wandsworth Road, it suited me best to go by bus. It was also a lot cheaper; the

Clapham Common Underground Station Ticket Office 1955

single fare was ninepence – old, pre-decimal pence – and I soon found that if I walked just one stop along the road, it was only sixpence. Compared with how it was at the end of the century, the roads were less congested, and there were more buses, but they were much better used. Coming back from Whitehall in the evening, it could be quite a struggle to get on, and it was sensible to wait for one which had started at the Horse Guards and was nearly empty. Among the crowds waiting to get on, I often saw a blind lady, probably a typist or telephonist in one of the Government offices, whose labrador would lead her onto the bus and sit at her feet.

On returning to my old department in the City, I went back to the tube. But this was getting more and more crowded, and the opening of the Victoria Line, by offering a new route to the West End, made our part of the Northern Line even worse. You were lucky to get a seat at Clapham Common in the morning, and the return journey between Bank and London Bridge was so bad that it was just as easy to walk to London Bridge and get the tube there. But living where I did, I had an alternative, which was to use British Rail, travelling from Wandsworth Road, on the line between Victoria and London Bridge. In those days (the mid 1970s), Wandsworth Road had its ticket office, manned alternately by Ron and Roy. The service ran every twenty minutes or so at the peak times, but was very neglected – we seemed to have the oldest of trains, which on a Monday often smelt of damp and decay – and it was poorly used. So it was quite untypical of London and more like a rural branch line: the regular passengers knew each other, and Ron and Roy knew us. There was the man with the housebound wife, living in an old flat on the Wandsworth Road, whose dearest wish was to retire to Wales while they both still had some health left to them. There was the young nurse who worked at one of the hospitals in Denmark Hill, taking her two small sons with her, and needing a hand to get the push chair up the steps. (Years later, she stopped me in the street to tell me proudly that one was now an architect.)

You might have thought the line could not decline further, but it did. Weekend services disappeared, and the weekday service was cut to cover only working travel times. The ticket office closed and Ron and Roy were posted to Peckham. The rumour was that British Rail wanted to close the service so that the tracks could be used for the link to the Channel Tunnel. When things were just about at their worst, a local group was formed (SoLLTA, South London Line Travellers' Association), which has acted as a very effective pressure group to get stations done up and services restored. Their ambition now is to get back to a service every quarter of an hour throughout the day.

In 1989 my office relocated to the South Bank, near Blackfriars Bridge, so my travel pattern changed again. As so often in our area, I had a choice; I could take the Underground to Waterloo, or a bus to Waterloo, or a train from Queenstown Road to Waterloo. Compared with the others, the Underground was reliable but more and more unpleasant. The Northern Line was now notorious as the worst in London, and the press called it the "Misery Line". The best, because it was fast and above ground, was the train from Queenstown Road: but cancellations and delays made it very erratic. One memory that remains is of standing there on a sunny morning in December 1988, getting increasingly impatient as one train after another failed to arrive. I eventually realised that it was not just my train, but all the trains in and out of Waterloo were no longer appearing and the normal roar was turning to a strange silence: there was no explanation, but it emerged later that further down the line, there had been the disastrous multiple train crash outside Clapham Junction.

At times of transport crisis, I could and very occasionally did walk to work. The occasions were very few, but one of them was the day after the Great Storm of October 1987. On a sunny autumn morning, I walked down Larkhall Rise, past fallen trees, to a city which the weather had brought to a halt.

All through this time, fares were rising, except when Ken Livingstone had his fare cutting experiment at the GLC. By the 1980s or 90s, we had the ticket zone system, with season tickets useable on tube, bus or surface rail. Instead of the fare of less than two shillings a day I had started with in 1960, I now had a Zone 1 and 2 annual ticket; in 1994, the last year I was in full time work, it cost me £520, and by 2001 it was up to £718.

I never tried a bicycle, though my wife did. In the late 1990s, she was working at the Chelsea and Westminster Hospital in the Fulham Road. The only way to get there by public transport was by bus, and the congestion, especially at Battersea Bridge, was now such that she could take well over an hour for a journey which could be walked in 50 minutes. So she took to a bicycle, mainly through Battersea Park and along the river front. By that time, I had retired, and any journeys I took in the rush hour served only to convince me that I was well out of it.

PETER JEFFERSON SMITH, 2002

9

THE LAST DECADES

The writer, **Angela Carter** *(1940-1992), lived in Clapham
and was a patient at the South London Hospital in 1983,
the year before it closed. She wrote about it in an essay
in* The New Statesman *in that year.*

I HAVEN'T BEEN IN HOSPITAL FOR THIRTY YEARS, so I can't comment on the decline in the standards of the NHS; the floors aren't polished until they turn into lethal ice-rinks any more, which is no bad thing. The food has certainly improved, in comparison with the early fifties. The sheer wonder of the NHS remains; that they will do the best they can for us, that we are not at the mercy of a free market economy, that the lovely nurses smile as if they meant it and hug you when you are sad.

Inevitably, this particular hospital is scheduled for the axe. No amount of special pleading on behalf of women whose religion specifies they be treated by doctors of the same sex seems likely to save it; it is due to close down next April, its various wards - it's a general hospital - distributed around other local hospitals. The staff seems scarcely able to believe that some miracle won't save the place. If the Minister of Health turns into a woman tomorrow, there might be a chance, especially if (s)he then converted to Islam. It is a rather elegant, red-brick building convenient for Clapham South tube station (the Northern line). It overlooks green and pleasant Clapham Common. It is, obviously, very well equipped; only needs a coat or two of paint and a few vases of plastic flowers to be fit for - who? The young woman in the bed next to me made a shrewd guess as to what would happen to the building once the NHS moved out. 'They'll sell it to bloody BUPA, won't they,' she opined.

ANGELA CARTER, *from an essay in* The New Statesman, 1983
Republished in *Shaking a leg, Journalism and Writings,* 1997

Dr Juliet Boyd *was a consultant anaesthetist at the hospital for 12 years and closely involved with the campaign to prevent the closure of the hospital. In 2002 she recalled the thriving and popular hospital she knew, and the long fight to prevent closure.*

THE HOSPITAL MOTTO WAS "ET DATO GAUDETIS" *In giving you rejoice* expressing a spirit of service appropriate for such an institution.

In 1972 I joined the staff as a consultant anaesthetist and I immediately recognised the special atmosphere in the hospital. Morale amongst the staff was noticeably high. The hospital was big enough (190 beds) to provide a full range of services but small enough for staff to know each other and develop a corporate spirit with the common goal of *putting patients first.* "Patient-focussed care" was being practised there long before the term was invented!

As an anaesthetist, I worked mostly in the operating theatres and those at the South London Hospital (SLH) were exceptional. Situated on the top floor, they were light, spacious and well-designed. There were two theatres each with its own anaesthetic room, various ancillary rooms and a recovery room which was a great advantage at a time when such an asset was not available in all hospitals. This operating theatre unit had been opened in 1936 in memory of Miss Eleanor Davies-Colley (1874-1934). She was one of the founders of the hospital and a surgeon there at the time of her death. In 1911 she became the first female Fellow of the Royal College of Surgeons and a lecture theatre in the college is about to be refurbished in her honour, with the bronze plaque from the SLH operating theatres on display.

The 12 years I spent working in those operating theatres were busy and happy ones. Built in 1936, they were still providing excellent facilities almost 50 years later when the hospital was closed. The hospital had a busy maternity department and one of the first projects I undertook was to set up a service for the provision for epidural analgesia. I worked with many skilled surgeons at SLH, one of them being Miss Margaret Louden (1910-1998). Her distinguished career covered the Second World War during which time she treated many wounded service personnel and civilians. Her pioneering treatment of people crushed by buildings in the Blitz went unrecognised until much later.

The main building designed by an eminent architect, Sir Edwin Cooper, was well built in 1926 and had been very well maintained. Cooper supervised further developments in the 1930s and by 1948, when it was nationalised as part of the NHS, there were 250 beds. There was a very popular staff dining room which provided a focus for fostering good staff relations. The garden was another of the advantages of SLH; it was large, very well-cared for and winner of numerous prizes.

A ward in the South London Hospital for Women in the 1970s

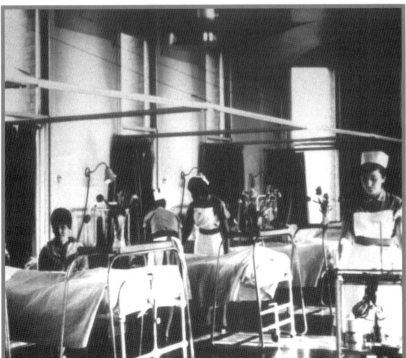

The hospital lies geographically in Lambeth but in the 1975 reorganisation it was incorporated into the Wandsworth Health Authority on the grounds that its maternity beds were necessary to the St George's midwifery school. This arrangement later proved to be detrimental to SLH.

During my time at SLH there were several notable years. One was 1977, the Queen's Silver Jubilee year. Her Majesty Queen Elizabeth the Queen Mother was Patron of the hospital and a great supporter. In 1924 one of her early official engagements as Her Royal Highness Duchess of York was the opening of a new wing. In 1948 as Her Majesty The Queen she opened another new wing. Every year she sent a small donation to the hospital and sometimes a birthday cake. She expressed her concern when we were threatened with closure and sent a letter expressing her sorrow when the final decision was announced. SLH had many royal links spanning its entire history so the Silver Jubilee celebrations included an exhibition of these royal occasions which began with the official opening of the hospital by Her Majesty Queen Mary in 1916.

SLH was one of only 10 hospitals to receive a special grant from the King's Fund in commemoration of the Queen's Silver Jubilee. This money was used for the up-grading of Queen Mary ward.

Responding to patients' needs was our aim, one example being a pioneering domiciliary physiotherapy service. Likewise in 1979 a new development was the opening of a day care unit, the only one in the district providing a particular focus for the termination and avoidance of unwanted pregnancies. It provided a comprehensive service with counselling and contraceptive advice.

In 1982 the 70th anniversary of the hospital's foundation was celebrated. It was a typically busy year during which there were 5,000 in-patients, 44,000 out-patients and 1,400 babies delivered. The Women's National Cancer Control Campaign parked their caravan outside the hospital to offer a walk-in cancer screening service. There was an appeal to purchase a laser for outpatient treatment of early cervical cancer. £25,000 was raised in 6 months enabling SLH to be one of the first hospitals to obtain such a laser. This treatment, which was more precise and less invasive, was a great advance. Other innovations included a Well Women Clinic, a clinic for women who wanted to give up smoking and modernisation of the outpatient clinics and the labour suite.

After 70 busy years all our plans for the future were to be thwarted the following year. In 1983 the Wandsworth Health Authority (WHA) proposed closure of SLH at their meeting on 27th January. Voting was 10-7 with 1 abstention.

The background to this proposal was given as follows. It had long been decided that St George's Hospital and Medical School should be re-built in Tooting on the site then occupied by the Grove Hospital and the Fountain Hospital. Phase 1 (Lanesborough Wing and the Medical School) had opened in 1980 but before work could commence on phase 2, the health authority had to demonstrate the source of funding. At first the WHA said that by closing SLH they would save £5 million (the annual running cost of SLH). This was soon revised to £4 million and later to £2 million. The costs of re-providing the services of SLH were under-estimated.

A SLH Staff Representatives Committee was set up to coordinate the fight against closure. Miss Margaret Louden, eminent retired surgeon, was the chairman and I was the vice-chairman. The proposal provoked an unprecedented level of opposition and developed into a national campaign. A wide range of national bodies, including every major women's organisation, pledged their support. West Lambeth Health Authority opposed the closure because it would lead to increased demand for their services. Ethnic minorities were also opposed on the grounds that Moslem women prefer to consult women doctors for religious reasons. The cause was taken up by local and national newspapers; also by magazines, radio and television. In the House of Commons, 101 MPs across the political spectrum signed an early day motion opposing the WHA's proposal to close the hospital.

Following the required period of consultation, the WHA voted again on 30th June, 1983 to close SLH (the vote was 11-7). The meeting was attended by over 200 members of hospital staff and supporters. On 13th July the South West Thames Regional Health Authority endorsed the WHA decision, but in view of the Wandsworth Community Health Council's opposition to the closure the matter was referred to the Secretary of State for Social Services for a final decision. A request was made for national funding of the hospital. Many patients became passionate campaigners. One of them was Christina Waller; she wrote to the Queen and presented a petition with 55,000 signatures to the Prime Minister in Downing Street. No banners were permitted so she knitted herself a white cardigan with "Save South London Hospital" stitched into the back in navy blue.

On 19th July there was an Adjournment debate in the House of Commons. For those of us in the Public Gallery, it was a long wait but our patience was rewarded just after 4 o'clock in the morning when we heard our two local MPs speak. William Shelton (Conservative) followed by Alf Dubs (Labour) each gave many valid and compelling reasons for saving the hospital from closure.

On 26th July there was a debate in the House of Lords, led by Baroness Macleod and supported by several of her colleagues. The hospital was visited by the Speaker of the House of Commons, Bernard Weatherill, three local MPs (William Shelton, Tom Cox and Alf Dubs), and three European MPs (Dame Shelagh Roberts, Richard Balfe and Derek Enwright). All those who visited the hospital were more than complimentary and it is ironic that many of those who voted for closure had never visited to see what they were condemning. On 26th September a delegation of staff representatives visited Kenneth Clarke, Secretary of State. On 10th October a Community Health Council delegation visited John Patten, Under-Secretary of State. Throughout this difficult time the staff were continuing to care for patients. The publicity we received led to a marked increase in demand for our services.

On 3rd November the Minister for Health announced his approval to the proposal by Wandsworth Health Authority to close the South London Hospital for Women. Once more there was an outpouring of support for the hospital. On 15th November questions were asked in the House of Commons. The Greater London Council Women's Committee launched a London-wide publicity campaign and organised an Emergency Public Meeting at County Hall. An all-night vigil was held outside the hospital. The case against closure of the hospital was referred to the European Parliament. All to no avail, and so provision for in-patients ceased at the end of July 1984. On 23rd July a Service of Thanksgiving was held. The Outpatients Hall was transformed into a chapel and was full of staff and ex-patients. The service was conducted by the Rt. Revd. Keith Sutton, Bishop of Kingston. It was a very moving occasion at the end of an era in the life of the hospital. Out-patient clinics continued until March 1985.

Peaceful protestors occupied the hospital from the end of July 1984 until they were evicted in a dawn raid by policewomen in March 1985. The hospital has been empty since then.

It had been managed by South West Thames Regional Health Authority until its closure, whereupon it became the property of the South East Thames RHA in whose area it was. The original deeds included a provision covering the situation of closure of the hospital. This resulted in a dispute between the University of London and SE Thames RHA. In 1994 a final agreement was reached whereby the site be sold and the proceeds be divided between the University of London and the Regional Health Authority. The London University money has been invested and the income is funding five Chadburn Lectureships, one at each of the medical schools. The purpose of these is to provide opportunities for doctors in training whose personal circumstances make it difficult to work full-time. It is good that the name of Miss Maud Chadburn is being perpetuated in this way.

Part of the land at the rear of the hospital grounds was finally used for the benefit of patients; the Minnie Kidd Nursing Home for frail elderly residents was built by the West Lambeth Health Authority and opened in 1993. The major part of the hospital was purchased by Tesco Stores Ltd whose first application in 1995 to build a supermarket was refused. Tesco submitted revised schemes which were also refused planning permission and then they submitted a scheme which included retention of the original Sir Edwin Cooper building. This was referred to the Secretary of State and the subject of a public enquiry in July 2000. Planning permission was granted in December 2001 but has been referred for a judicial review. The final chapter of The South London Hospital for Women remains unfinished.

Dr Juliet Boyd, 2002

Lee Seaman of Notre Dame Tenants and Residents Association
is actively involved in 2002 in an ambitious scheme to restore to use,
as part of a community development, the Orangery,
built in 1793 in the extensive gardens of one of the grand houses
on Clapham Common South Side.

I moved into the Notre Dame Estate in February 1994 living in Prestwich Terrace facing Crescent Lane. It was not long before I realised that an active Tenants Association existed and I wanted to belong to it. I quickly realised how vibrant and cohesive a community it was, and I soon became involved. Since then we have been working on a number of projects for the benefit of local people.

One major project is the development of the Clapham Orangery, now a Grade II listed Georgian structure; the plan is to develop the frontage (overseen by English Heritage to ensure it retains the authentic period features) and associated sites. The project is being developed in partnership with the Tenants and Residents Association, Lambeth Council, and a community development group called 'Together in Notre Dame'. The aim is to provide a new tenants hall and other community facilities for local people. In December 2001 a draft constitution for a trust to administer the development was produced and it is hoped that the new trust, called the 'Notre Dame Orangery Development Trust', will be in operation early in 2002.

The Orangery was originally in the garden of 39 South Side, one of two houses built by the wealthy merchant, Robert Thornton, which stood on the site of the present Notre Dame Estate. The garden ran to several acres and the Orangery was designed as a green-house for Thornton's exotic plants, but also as an entertaining venue and eye catcher within the heavily planted informal landscape. It may have been a memorial to his father, John Thornton, since a marble tablet inside (now lost) was inscribed with 19 lines from *The Task* written by John Thornton's friend, the poet William Cowper.

The Orangery in the early 20th century

The building was fully glazed and looked south over the gardens and lakes; to the east there was a mound and grotto. This idyllically rural setting was immortalised in contemporary images and later photographs. The gardens were famous for their beauty, and several visits by royalty are recorded.

The Thornton houses remained in domestic use until 1851, when both properties were bought for the Sisters of Notre Dame, a Belgian order of nuns who had arrived in England in 1845. They added two large gothic wings to either side of the main house. The Orangery was converted into St. Theresa's Hall and decorated with the symbols of the Order, whilst the gardens became more formalized in typical Victorian fashion.

On the land that was originally the Kitchen Garden to the rear of the Orangery, a girls' School was built (now St Mary's Primary School). This was subsequently extended at about the turn of the century and at the same time the laundry building was erected to the north of the Orangery to serve the Convent School. During World War II the Sisters returned to Belgium and the buildings were used by various bodies including General De Gaulle's Free French Forces. However, the buildings and estate fell into disrepair following bombing raids, which caused extensive damage in the area. In 1942 Wandsworth Council had purchased the estate to build social housing. The main buildings were pulled down in 1947 leaving only the Orangery and the laundry. Initially houses were built and then the flats between 1947-1952.

The Orangery was in poor condition and threatened with demolition, but in 1951 it was given a reprieve and after renovation work it was handed to the residents for use as a Youth and Social Club. However by 1954 it was proving inadequate for the estate's needs and the club was disbanded. The Orangery was rapidly vandalised – to a worse condition than that inflicted by wartime damage. It received listed building status in 1955, and the Council adapted it to provide a shelter for the adjacent children's play area. The rooms to the rear were demolished, the sash windows and other interior detail were completely removed and the wooden floor replaced by concrete.

The disused former laundry building was then adapted for the Tenants Association, and shared with the adjacent St. Mary's School. At some point in the late 1950s the northern end of the building was demolished in order to improve the junction between Worsopp Drive and Crescent Lane, and a small block added to the west façade to house toilet facilities. When St. Mary's school acquired Grant Maintained status, the building reverted to the Tenants Association.

Soon, we hope, the Orangery will be returned to active use again. Its motto, from Virgil's *Georgics*, inscribed on the entablature, will remain unchanged:-
'HERE IS PERPETUAL SPRING
AND HERE IS SUMMER
EVEN IN THE OTHER MONTHS'
LEE SEAMAN, 2002

*In 1998, Clapham Common made an unexpected, and
to Clapham people, unwelcome appearance in national politics when
the Cabinet Minister,* **Ron Davies**, *resigned as a result of a
"moment of madness" there. The Encyclopedia Britannica website
summarised the incident succintly under the entry:
Year in Review, United Kingdom: Domestic Affairs.*

THE LABOUR PARTY GOVERNMENT, which had been elected in May 1997, continued in 1998 its program of reforming the United Kingdom's constitution...

...One unexpected jolt to the government's constitutional program
occurred on October 27, when Ron Davies resigned as secretary of state for
Wales and, two days later, as Labour's candidate to be first secretary of the new
assembly for Wales. Davies admitted to a "moment of madness" the previous
night on Clapham Common, an area in south London often used by men seeking
casual gay sex. Davies's encounters resulted in the theft of his car and wallet
and an attempt to blackmail him. Rather than succumb to blackmail, he gave a
statement to the police and resigned from the Cabinet. In the media coverage
that followed this resignation, two members of Blair's Cabinet were publicly
identified as homosexuals. (A third gay minister had openly acknowledged his
sexuality more than a decade earlier.) Although considerable controversy
surrounded the media's actions, none attached to the ministers themselves,
who continued as Cabinet members with Blair's full support.

Davies was the first person to resign from Blair's Cabinet; ..

Extracted from the website BRITANNICA. COM

*Surfing the net in 2000 produced plenty of information
about* **Clapham Common.** *Time* **Out** *described it thus:*

A FLAT, GRASSY EXPANSE within a triangle of roads, **Clapham Common** is
somewhere between a park and a wild place; its bleak atmosphere has never
been more vividly evoked than in Graham Greene's *The End of the Affair*. After
dark, parts of the Common have gained a reputation as gay cruising grounds
(and brought to an end the career of Welsh Secretary Ron Davies who experienced
his ill-explained 'moment of madness' here in late 1998).

While Lambeth Council's website claimed:

Clapham Common is a vast green space which attracts visitors from across the world. Concerts, theatre, film shows and competitive sport are among its all-year-round events. It is probably the capital's most used recreational area.

It featured as a place for sport and entertainment

The London Ultimate League is a summer league for Ultimate teams in the London (England) area. The league welcomes players of all standards. Games take place on weeknight evenings, and the league typically runs from early May through until July...

The "final" is effectively being played next week (July 26), between Freak Show and Far Queue at Clapham Common (Alex, Wayne, let the list know in the unlikely event that you change the date - some of us are coming to watch). Both teams are undefeated, so it all boils down to this one. Should be a really exciting match. Good luck.

Australian football on the Common

The FSS Financial Pre-Season Cup was held on 15th April 2000 at Clapham Common in London. Matches were played with 14 a side, with 10 minute halves.

The following teams participated – West London Wildcats, Wandsworth Demons, Sussex Swans, London Gryphons, Bristol Dockers, Northern Volunteers, Clapham Demons, Bush Raiders, North London Lions, Wimbledon Hawks and the Dublin Demons.

A visitor to the Common witnessed urban games in August

Arrived Sunday at 10.00 am... Watched some street in the morning warm up and all looked good. Dirt started, riders all doing good and getting ready for the final. The dirt final went off pretty good until Shaun Eglington slammed real heavy on the third set, I really thought he was dead, a woman jumped in to see what she could do, he was seriously out cold, Paul Roberts called over the PA for the medics... The vert fianl [sic]was supposed to be next, got up on the ramp, swarming with boarders who decided they would run a jam instead, they had the PA so no one was informed about the street final running instead of the vert until about 15 minutes into it. When the street was finished the vert fianl was on. Wrong. Vert fianl consisted of a loose jam session and highest air which lasted for 20 minutes… After all this I needed a beer, guess what? "sold out".

It attracted interest well beyond Clapham

Le week-end du 4 au 6 août, Clapham Common, à Londres, s'est transformé en une gigantesque masse de jeunes, rassemblés pour un événement unique de sports urbains. Au programme du bmx et du skate pour la page des sports, mais aussi de l'art et du son avec des graffs, des DJ's, des break dancers, des virtuoses de capoeria et bien sûr, des concerts. Vous l'aurez compris, la foule de spectateurs – de jeunes riders, apprentis DJ's ou simples fans, n'a pas eu le temps de s'ennuyer. La véritable performance des riders n'est pas seulement dans leurs performances respectives, mais surtout dans le fait d'avoir enchaîné 11 heures non stop de spectacle.

On the Common. Linoprint, late 1980s

But the Common had a certain reputation

Can someone tell me some good places in London to go fly my power kite? I live just down from Tower Bridge and need somewhere relatively near to play.

among many suggestions

if u wanna find a good place to fly, try clapham common but remember not to fly when it gets dark and don't talk to any MPs

Extracted from various WEBSITES

As earlier chapters have shown, model boating on the Long Pond has always been popular. **Derek Cross**, *Chairman of the Clapham Model Yacht Club, describes the sport and its development over the century, to the problems of the present day.*

IT SEEMS LIKELY THAT MODEL BOAT SAILING has been more or less continuous on the Long Pond over the years since the mid 1880s apart from the periods of the two World Wars. A Club was formed to sail on the pond in 1870 and regular races were held on most Saturday afternoons. The current "Clapham Model Yacht Club" (CMYC) was formed in 1934 and has continued to the present day.

The sailing of model boats on the pond has always been an attraction to both sailors and those who watch. I have been told by those who remember the years between the wars that the pond was so popular on Sundays that sailors had to get there early in order to find space to launch a boat. Up to the late 1930s there were no facilities for members of the Club to store boats, although I understand there was a wooden hut erected in the post Second World War period which did allow some storage. It was removed later and replaced by a purpose built Clubhouse which does provide for boat storage and getting in out of the rain. The Clubhouse is in current use and indeed has its own address, No 1 Rookery Road; this is a great asset but, regrettably, has been vulnerable to attack by vandals and thieves, so much so that little equipment is now left in the building, but it is still a great place for rigging the boats and making tea.

Up to the 1970s racing yachts were "free sailing". That meant once the boat was launched the skipper had no control over it. As "racing" implies that a boat must be able to get from point A to point B more quickly than its competitor some control had to be devised that would automatically steer the boat, so that if the direction of the wind changed, the boat would respond and resume its correct course. Two systems of self steering gear were favour. From the early 1900s, the "Braine Gear", was used, by which the position of the sails was linked to the rudder. A more modern and sophisticated system is the "Vane Gear" in which there is a vane, or feather, linked direct to the rudder and which acts like a miniature sail. The boat is launched with the vane set parallel to the direction of the wind. If the boat turns off the wind the vane reacts to it, so turning the rudder and bringing the boat back on course.

The course that is set for these "free sailing" boats had to be straight up the length of the pond and back, the boat being re-trimmed for the return leg.

In the hands of an experienced skipper the boat would keep a very good course but on occasion would deviate and head for the bank, so explaining why an essential piece of equipment for the skipper was a pole with which to fend the boat off the bank. It helped to have a "mate" to do the same on the other side of the pond!

The 1970s brought the introduction of affordable radio control for model yachts. The possibilities then became endless. A yacht could be steered around a preset course and with the many radio frequencies available fleets of yachts could be sailed, as many as twelve yachts, or even more, sailing the course at the same time. Courses were preset and usually followed the full sized "Olympic" course of a basic triangle. The radio controls gave both rudder movement and sail adjustment so allowing boats to tack and round the marker buoys.

As would be expected, this new freedom of movement allowed a new dimension in model yacht sailing. The CMYC grew in membership and sailing on the Long Pond increased in frequency. A racing calendar was produced and competition with other Clubs, both home and away, was on the increase. As a spectator sport there was increased attraction as the public could now follow a proper race and be aware who was in the lead, and there was also a variety of boat classes to be seen of varying sizes. All in all the years of 1970 to the early 1980s were perhaps the most exiting for CMYC.

The modern model racing yacht is now Bermudan rigged and is designed as a pure racing machine. In some respects they are not as attractive as the pre-war designs but they are undoubtedly faster and, with the new materials of plastic and carbon fibre, very much lighter. As designers of model yachts pursued their objective of even greater speeds hull shapes became more extreme and keels became longer. This greater keel length brought its own problems on ponds which were previously adequate as regards depth of water; these now became less able to cope with the modern designs and this has been the case with the Long Pond.

Model yacht sailing on the Long Pond has always been dependent on the level of water and the amount of silt and débris built up in the pond. Up to the 1980s the Common and the ponds had been maintained by the London County Council and the Long Pond was drained and cleaned every other year, the last such cleaning being carried out in 1980. Since that date the maintenance of the Common and the ponds has become the responsibility of the London Borough of Lambeth and regrettably little has been done to keep the Long Pond in good condition. Sailing became difficult, so much so that the water depth was insufficient to allow the sailing of the most popular class of yacht. Fortunately, the Model

Yachting Association (our governing body, formed in 1911) had introduced a new class of yacht, the One Metre Class, which has a shorter keel and this class was adopted by the CMYC as its main fleet, so allowing racing to continue.

There was renewed hope in 1993 when the contract for the maintenance of the Common was let to a private contractor, Serviceteam. Part of that contract was that the Long Pond be drained and cleaned each year. An attempt was made in April 1993 to drain the pond but it was found that the pond drain had been damaged and the pond could not be drained. Later, in 1998, the fish were removed from the pond, a move that was to have a disastrous effect on the pond in that the weed growth increased rapidly and by 2000 racing on a regular basis had been abandoned, even the sailing of children's toy boats had become impossible. The whole surface of the pond was now covered in weed.

The service contractor changed in 1998 to TeamLambeth and the requirement for annual cleaning of the Long Pond was dropped from the new contract. It may have been due to the persistence of the CMYC in writing to the Council that an attempt was made to drain and clean the pond in 2001, but those local residents who saw the work being carried will know what a poor attempt it was.

Inside the clubhouse of the Clapham Model Yacht Club

The work was completed and the pond refilled, and promptly erupted in a new growth of weed. Little sailing was done in 2001. The commencement of 2002 brought a small change in the fortunes of model boating on the Long Pond and the CMYC. The further growth of weed has apparently been controlled by the fortuitous transfer of fish back into the pond.

The membership of the CMYC still being modest we have not yet regained the glory days of very large fleets of yachts racing on Sunday mornings, but we do have small fleets sailing on the first and third Sundays each month with different classes of yachts, and two or three times a year we host meetings of the Vintage Group on the pond. At these meetings you will see a range of elderly boats of all kinds, from clockwork Hornby speedboats to the toy "Star" sailing yachts much prized by small boys over past years as well as fine vintage hand built yachts from the 1920s, sometimes even earlier. There is still interest among the general public in the sight of a fleet of model yachts racing hard around the buoys and if we can keep the Long Pond in good condition, long may it continue.

DEREK CROSS, 2002

The ponds on Clapham Common have traditionally been used for fishing. In 1995, an anti-fishing group almost succeeded in stopping this. **Reg Gafoor** *was one of those who fought to preserve the ponds for fishing and secure their proper management.*

THE TWO FISHERIES ARE MOUNT AND EAGLE PONDS. They are stocked with common carp, mirror carp, linear carp, leather carp, tench, roach, perch and gudgeon. There are also crayfish (like mini-lobsters) in the water. The bird life is everything from Canada geese (too many, they do a lot of damage), coots, moorhens, to mallards, and tufted ducks. Cormorants come over and eat the fish. Swans come once or twice a year and stay for a month or so. There has even been a woodpecker in one of the trees by the Mount Pond.

The Clapham Angling Preservation Society was started when Lambeth Council shut the fishing down on Mount and Eagle Ponds after complaints from just a few people, who were linked to an anti-fishing group called PISCES. This was in 1995. A few of the anglers decided that this was very unfair, as no one had spoken to the anglers to hear their side of things, and so CAPS [Clapham Angling Preservation Society] was started. The first thing that had to be done was to pick a spokesman. This is where I came in, and another two anglers, Terry Peters and a disabled angler called John were also prepared to go up to the Town Hall and complain. We were told that the best way forward was to get a petition going, so this is what we did. We had all the anglers we knew going down Clapham High Street for signatures, and people from the Common backed us, such as the dog walkers.

While this was going on another person came on board to help. Dave Gray, an older angler, asked if I knew Tim Holdcroft, as he was going to go to the

Council to complain. I said I did not know him, but I had already got a petition up and Councillor Callahan from the Labour Group said he would help, and so I received a date to go to the Town Hall. This is when I met Tim Holdcroft. After the Council received our petition and heard that no one had spoken to the anglers, they decided to revisit the issue and get a report from Council officers. Meanwhile the anti-fishing group were getting people to write in, but we found out that these people did not even live in Lambeth.

CAPS realised that something had to be done to make a better fishery. The first thing they did was to ask for proper bins for discarded tackle, and then they proposed a bailiffing scheme. The anglers were prepared to take notice of other older anglers they respected, so CAPS asked Lambeth to let the anglers bailiff themselves. Lambeth thought this was not possible, but they were proved wrong, as we proposed that six bailiffs would be able to do the job.

In the end a full Council meeting was called and a free vote would be allowed. The galleries in the Town Hall were full, one side with anglers and children and the other with anti-fishing people. A spokesman from both groups would be able to put the case for and against. What the anti lobby did not know

Mark Artlett moves a carp between Clapham ponds in preparation for pond cleaning.

was that a person called Duncan Fairley from the specialist Anglers' Conservation Group had been able to help us, and had been informed that in the gallery that night was the General Secretary of PISCES, sitting next to the people who were complaining. I happened to mention this when I spoke, and this proved beyond doubt that the Clapham anglers were being singled out by an anti-angling group.

Since then CAPS have been running and bailiffing the fishing on Clapham Common. They have gone from strength to strength. They have built nesting boxes for the birds, and have restored park benches for people of the borough. They have built up a very good junior section and held fishing matches for them. They have also built up sponsorship from sheer hard work, and sponsors now number nearly forty, including many local big shops and also the Post Office. Included in these people are the previous Sports Minister Kate Hoey [MP for Lambeth Vauxhall] who attends the prize giving and open days and has backed us since the beginning of CAPS. Two Mayors of Lambeth, both Labour and Conservative, have attended these functions. There are many more things we have done, such as an aeration system for the ponds, and even bat nesting boxes – which I think is very unusual for a fishing club, but shows how hard we try.

We are very proud of what we have achieved and in 2001 have worked with Lambeth and the Environment Agency to get grants so that the desilting and planting of the ponds can take place, and the children of Lambeth and future generations of anglers will be able to keep on fishing on the Common.

REG GAFOOR, 2002

Dog walking has long been one of the most popular uses of Clapham Common. **Dave Fairbairn**, *a retired compositor for a national newspaper, has been walking his dog on the Common for many years.*

WHERE DOES ONE START on the subject of "Dog walking on Clapham Common since the 1980s"?

Having had the pleasure of walking my own dogs on Clapham Common over that period, my memories obviously must include the many friendships that they and Clapham Common have made for me over that period. The best way to highlight those memories must be to join us on a Monday morning's walk.

My present dog, Max, is a four-year-old working Border Collie with boundless energy, and is known by most users of 'The Common'. I say this with affection, because being born and bred in Battersea, as youngsters, we were either going up 'The Common' or down 'The Park'.

As usual we arrive at Mount Pond at 9.30 a.m. It's a sunny morning, and we observe the terrapins sunbathing for the second time this year, and wonder how they survive hibernation each winter. The first young coots and a single Canadian gosling are also at the water's edge, so Max must be kept on his lead. With it being the close fishing season, there's nobody fishing and it's noticeable that the carp are jumping in pairs. When Reg Gafoor meets his fellow wardens later for their usual Monday inspection, I'll ask him if they are mating.

Having fed the ducks, Max is let off his lead and immediately spots his friends – canine and human – near the bandstand and he's away. The bandstand café is not open on a Monday, so it will be coffee at The Windmill stall today. Walking towards the swings, Brian's house [in Windmill Drive] that he has converted from a bungalow – comes into view,

Dave Fairbairn

and I remember the hot summer evening in the late '80s when Brian had left his front door open. A small Border Collie, that he later named Pia, walked in and remained his pet until her death last year.

We have our coffee break with more of our friends, members of the 'Common Lottery' syndicate and realise we've no winnings again. We then make our way towards Long Pond, and by now Max is going in ever decreasing circles, rounding up his mates as usual. Anna's dog, Jamie, has spotted us, and he's haring towards us, leaving Anna a distant observer. I realise that it must have gone 10 o'clock and he's after his biscuits – a practice he's pursued for many years.

Jamie couldn't have done this when the last big event ruined the Common. His path would have been blocked by an eight-foot high metal fence, that entrapped all the users of the Common.

How times have changed. When the same area was used in 1985 for The Association of Combined Youth Clubs' Silver Jubilee – Festival of Youth – it was lightly fenced with free access. Princess Anne, being its patron, attended the event.

By now many of our friends have stopped for a chat but the bonus this morning is meeting Sid who informs me that he's 92 in June. I knew Sid when he had Rocky, a growing Staff, though he was really so soft. Nowadays every dog is 'My Luvly' to Sid. The Common is so user friendly for the old 'uns because it has plenty of seats where they can sit to have a breather, to assist them in keeping mobile. It's another attribute that makes the Common so special.

We now head for Battersea Woods (where my previous dog's ashes are scattered), passing the gap where a line of trees were flattened during the hurricane of 1987. The dogs were not the only ones disorientated by the new landscape that day.

Continuing towards the bandstand again I remember Ray Bailey, the famous cartoonist responsible for Dan Dare in the Eagle comic, who now lives in Canada. One morning in early 1996 he asked me to stand still and within a few minutes he had sketched me. The following morning he presented me with a coloured cartoon with the bandstand, my dog and a frightened squirrel in the background – signed (Rab –'96). It still hangs on my wall today.

By now it's 11.15 a.m. and true to form, Reg and his fellow wardens are on the jetty at Mount Pond. It's the very same jetty, where as a child I fished for tiddlers and had the pleasure of using the boats – canoe, paddle and rowing at 6d. for 30 minutes, and motor boats at 6d. for 10 minutes. Reg did confirm that the carp were mating.

One mustn't forget Maureen with Shadow, who returned to St.Andrew's, Scotland two years ago, and still 'phones to say how she misses the friendships of Clapham Common, because up here 'you just pass like ships in the night'.

DAVE FAIRBAIRN, 2002

Fenella Russell-Smith, Sales Manager of the Clapham branch of Hampton's International, gives an estate agent's view of the changes in Clapham over the 17 years she has worked in the area.

IN 1978 A FRIEND SAID SHE WAS BUYING A HOUSE IN CLAPHAM with her brother. My reaction was astonishment and "Where's Clapham!" Many years later she still owns the house and it is now 650% more valuable than it was. It was in the area now known as 'Between the Commons' but then unknown by anyone who lived elsewhere.

I have worked in the area for most of the last 17 years and the changes have been great. The open spaces, good schools, family houses and Underground links started a flow of people, who would formerly have considered South of the River to be another country, to come and live here.

Shops have changed to cater for the more affluent buyers and as braver friends of Chelsea and Fulham inhabitants have moved south they have been followed by others.

First to appeal were the roads off Northcote Road mainly because of the good local schools. The wider houses with bigger gardens off Abbeville Road then followed as families expanded and now many find it hard to move on as the shops and cafés along the road and the shared school runs make life so much easier for busy mothers. Schools in the Clapham Common area are also excellent and there is even a Montessori school on the North Side.

The big houses around Clapham Common were previously, in most cases, full of bedsits. Even the lovely Georgian houses of Crescent Grove had their low moments but are now beautifully cared for and lived in mainly as houses. Values have soared over recent years from around £500,000 to near £2,000,000 for the larger houses in the area.

The Old Town has changed dramatically as well in very recent times with many boutique shops following the greater wealth of the current inhabitants. Moens, the splendid butcher, whose window is often a work of meat art, has many exciting and unusual food items to tempt the jaded palates of local people whose tastes have changed over recent years. Dinner parties are held in the beautifully designed kitchens with their stylish open dining areas, a change from the days when kitchens were hidden away from the formal dining room.

Clapham Common provides a unique feeling of space, unlike any offered by the parks in more central areas. To get almost anywhere in Clapham involves driving past at least one side of it and it is one of the few places in London where you can watch the sun set over grass rather than concrete. In the summer the Common is the centre of local outdoor life. People of all ages and backgrounds get together and play, sit and chat over a pint of beer from the famous Windmill pub or enjoy long picnics and barbeques. The possibility for activity is endless and even stretches to a hatless, blond man occasionally seen exercising his shire horse bareback around the Common!

Clapham is a town and community within Greater London and yet only a short journey across the water from the West End, Fulham, Chelsea and the City. For those concerned with such things there are even certain parts of Clapham that remain in the dialling code area of '7' and not '8'. And the SW4 postcode is beginning to hold as much weight as SW6!

We were all thrilled when the Clapham Picture House arrived as it provides with its four screens an eclectic mix of mainstream and arthouse films. Formerly the site of the old snooker hall, the Picture House opened in December 1992 and has a café, an exhibition area, a Saturday Morning Kids' Club and is well-established for its cultural significance within Clapham's community.

I believe, as an estate agent, that the High Street and Clapham North are also excellent areas for investment. Development has started in the High Street and is moving northwards. We already have a superb Sainsbury's, Eco (arguably one of the best pizza restaurants in town), an Oddbins and a number of other shops and restaurants. We have a bookshop, Wordsworth, which it would be nice to see used more and a Marks & Spencer wouldn't go amiss – but it's all moving in the right direction. Eventually Clapham North is likely to become more and more attractive, particularly to those who require easy access to the City. With the vast and obvious improvements to the Northern Line, this is beginning to look like a distinct possibility.

In terms of health Clapham is well catered for by doctors, dentists and particularly the non-traditional methods. One might in the past have thought of the Clapham Common Clinic as bohemian and irregular, but with the surging trend for alternative therapies it can now be described as progressive and extremely well-placed. Described by *Time Out* as being 'the friendliest clinic in London' it provides a massive range of therapies; from aromatherapy to psychotherapy. The personnel are, as *Time Out* says, extremely friendly, relaxed and considerate.

Being such a desirable area these days, Clapham is bound to fall prey to the big health club chains such as Holmes Place who are looking for opportunities to make money. This fitness giant has taken advantage of our developing community and has jumped in with its contemporary style of building, its high-appeal marketing and relentless incentives for joining. As a member I am aware of its huge appeal to previously deprived Claphamites. This has rather led to queuing for equipment, waiting on lists for fitness classes and driving around endlessly looking for somewhere to park. The under fives' swimming time makes it especially popular with young families. It is my belief that the current fashion for fitness will bring in more of these establishments and the discreet and more modest new Soho Gym in the High Street will soon come into its own.

I am not sure that there is any other similar community so close to London. You can certainly find similar environments further out of London in areas such as Barnes, Richmond and Dulwich, but Clapham has an appeal of its own.

FENELLA RUSSELL-SMITH, 2002

When the century began, the electric railway was a novelty and the clergy were bewailing the effects of the bicycle. Clapham was going through a period of rapid change. The century ended in the era of the mobile phone and the internet. Surfing the net at the beginning of 2001 generally showed Clapham as young, trendy and well off, living well in the local restaurants and pubs. This is how **Time Out** *saw it.*

CLAPHAM HAS TWO CENTRES: **Clapham Junction** (technically part of Battersea) and **Clapham Common**. Until the railways arrived, Clapham Junction was a country crossroads, with **The Falcon** providing refreshment for travellers. Nowadays, the pub provides respite for shoppers: Clapham's own department store, **Arding & Hobbs**, opposite, has been serving the area since 1885. With more than 2,500 trains passing through every day, Clapham Junction is one of the busiest stations in the world.

Battersea Rise, leading towards the Common, is a somewhat arty stretch, with a huge choice of restaurants, including **La Pampa**, an Argentinian grill joint. **Northcote Road**, running at right angles to Battersea Rise, is a rapidly developing bar and restaurant alley that still (just) clings on to its street fruit and vegetable market. Beyond the junction with Bramfield Road is a stretch of antique shops. **The Hive**, at 53 Webb's Road (parallel to Northcote Road) [The Hive had moved to Northcote Road by 2002], is one of the most extraordinary shops in south London. Devoted entirely to bees and their products, it features a huge glass hive containing 20,000 live bees, linked to the outside world by a tunnel opening on to the street.

Battersea Rise eventually becomes Clapham Common North Side, the eastern reaches of which contain tall, stately houses with enviable views of the

Common…The streets around the north end of Clapham Common are transforming from down-at-heel to desirable at an extraordinary rate. A sure sign of this is the proliferation of good new bars and restaurants (try laid-back French **Gastro** at 67 Venn Street; the pizzas at trendy **Eco**, 162 Clapham High Street; or cheap Thai scoff at **Pepper Tree**, 19 Clapham Common South Side).

There's more than a whiff of snobbery about genteel **Clapham Old Town**, just north-east of the Common, but it's worth a visit, if only to take in the villagey atmosphere – especially at its central point, where eighteenth-century pubs face on to an approximate square (complete with a small, country-ish bus terminus). The 88 bus, rather self-consciously styled 'The Clapham Omnibus', starts its pleasantly circuitous route from here.

Famous for its lush setting on the edge of the common, **Holy Trinity Church** was well known in the nineteenth century as the headquarters of the Clapham Sect, a group of wealthy Anglicans who advocated 'muscular Christianity'; one of them was William Wilberforce, the anti-slavery campaigner. The church was rebuilt [restored] after being hit by a V2 in 1945. For breakfast, or a spot of afternoon tea, the determinedly camp **Tea-time** [renamed The Pavement in 2002], at 21 The Pavement, is recommended.

*School inspection reports by **OFSTED** showed a different picture.*

Glenbrook Junior School is set amid the Clapham Park Estate in the London Borough of Lambeth. The school is fully subscribed and there are 232 pupils who attend full-time, many of whom come from African-Caribbean families. English is the first language for most pupils but other languages spoken are various African languages, Portuguese and Spanish…

Most of the pupils attending live on the estate in poor housing conditions. There is a significant proportion of temporary housing accommodation and this means that some pupils only stay in the school for a number of weeks. The proportion of pupils eligible for free school meals (114) is well above the average.

Glenbrook Junior School is a secure and caring community where the needs of individual pupils are the prime concern of all who work there. Standards in English, mathematics and science are below the national average but overall, pupils make satisfactory progress. The provision for pupils with special educational needs and English as an additional language is a strength. Pupils' behaviour is good in class and other parts of the school. Sufficient time is given to literacy and numeracy and teaching is satisfactory overall. Leadership and management are satisfactory, with some strengths, notably the leadership provided by the headteacher. The school has continued to improve since the last inspection and the overall effectiveness of the school is satisfactory.

Clapham Manor Primary School is situated in Clapham Town Ward in the Borough of Lambeth. There are 385 full-time pupils on roll, with a further 15 full-time nursery places and 19 part-time. It is a popular school, with many pupils travelling a considerable distance, although the majority come from the local area. Most pupils live in local authority housing, with a small proportion from the private sector. Many are from poor socio-economic backgrounds, and include pupils of black Caribbean and African heritage, Indian, Bangladeshi, Chinese, and white European...

Clapham Manor is a very good school. Its success is built on the very strong foundations of mutual respect, celebration of diversity, and effective partnership between staff, home and community. No school in Lambeth has shown more improvement in the last year, and only six other London schools have improved more...

Macaulay Voluntary Aided Primary School is maintained by Lambeth education authority. It provides religious education according to the teaching of the Church of England, under the direction of the school's governors. At the time of the inspection, the number of full-time pupil was 204, plus 50 children who attend part-time in the nursery. The school is about the same size as other primary schools nationally. Its admissions policy states that 21 places are allocated to regular worshippers in a Christian Church and the remaining 9 places are open to the public. It is always over-subscribed.

Compared with 1900, religion had declined and become more diverse

The fifth annual South London Inter Faith Group Walk took place at the beginning of June. Sixty walkers started out with refreshments at 9.30am at Balham Mosque, learning something of how the mosque is used. The next port of call was the nearby Radha Krishna Hindu Temple – a small intimate mandir, unusually led by women. The numbers had swelled by then.

A twenty minute walk through Balham, carrying placards, and led by a Japanese Buddhist monk beating a hand drum, brought the pilgrims to Nightingale House, the largest Jewish Retirement Home in Europe where they joined the rabbi and residents for Kiddush – the prayers and sharing of bread and wine.

Ahead lay a long stint up the hill and across Clapham Common. Trinity Hospice was the picnic lunch stop, spread out on the grass around the pond in the gardens. The Chaplain talked about the work and the aims of the Hospice and ministering to the physical and spiritual needs of the terminally ill. An abiding image was of two Muslim walkers performing their midday prayers on the lawn.

As it was a good half hour walk along a busy main road to All Saints Battersea, some 'cheated' and climbed on a bus! By now some had dropped out but others had joined so the numbers stayed between 80 and 100.

At All Saints, the Vicar explained how the space was used for worship and community activities, an Indian priest led the singing and an African woman danced and prayed with many walkers inspired to follow in her footsteps.

Out in the sunshine again the walkers crossed Battersea Park to converge with other walkers at the Peace Pagoda and to see inside the Buddhist Temple where the custodian of the Pagoda lives, the monk who had led the Walk from Balham.

So, in true pilgrim style, some 200 set out on the last leg to Westminster Cathedral...

Extracted from THE BRIDGE,
the monthly paper of the Diocese of Southwark, September 2000

So what was Clapham like?
This was the Lambeth Council view

Clapham Old Town is renowned for its village-like atmosphere. There are many specialist shops, from the 60s and 70s designer shop **Places and Spaces** to the quality gift and furnishing store **Pyramid**. Recent additions include the designer mens wear shop **The Room**. There are several delicatessens including **Mise en Place** [closed in 2002 and replaced by an art gallery]. Nearby, **The Pavement** has attractions such as specialist butcher **Moen and Sons**, The Pavement tea rooms and the modern gift shop **Zeitgeist**, and **Kitschen Synq** [closed in 2002].

Pubs and restaurants in the Old Town such as the **Sun**, the **Prince of Wales**, and the **Polygon Bar and Grill**, attract large numbers. **Abbeyville** [sic] **Road** is also a popular shopping and restaurant area. **Tessa Fantoni's** two stores offer a tremendous range of gifts and furnishings, among many other quality shops within this most successful neighbourhood shopping area.

General shopping facilities are in the High Street. They include **Sainsbury's**,

Superdrug, major banks and building societies, **McDonalds**, **Burger King** [now closed] and many small retailers. The High Street lacked investment during the recession but new retail and residential developments are now in the pipeline.

With its bars and restaurants Clapham is the perfect meeting place. There is also the recently expanded **Picture House** independent cinema, **Southside Nightclub** [renamed in 2002]and the swimming pool and gym on Clapham Manor Street, run by Relaxion for Lambeth Council. **Bread and Roses** is an award-winning pub with excellent meeting facilities for hire. **Moxon's**, the locally well-known fish restaurant, is a 1999 Time Out award-winner [replaced in 2002 by **Thyme**]

Norman Marsh, President of the Clapham Society, and the Mayor of Lambeth planting a tree on Clapham Common in 1996

The town centre is within a Conservation Area, allowing the character of the area to be retained. Key buildings and open spaces in Clapham are benefiting from a successful Heritage Lottery funding bid. A number of key properties on The Pavement are due to be renovated. The buoyant residential and commercial property market reflects the unique qualities of the area, its proximity to central London and its excellent local facilities.

The **Clapham Society** works to protect the special character of Clapham, its conservation area, buildings and especially its most precious asset Clapham Common.

The main transport interchange is at Clapham Cross. Clapham is on the Northern Line tube and linked to main line rail services at the High Street. Bus Services are frequent. A main road artery, the A3, runs through Clapham and will become part of London's Red Route. The country's busiest rail station, Clapham Junction, lies outside Lambeth but within easy reach.

Extracted from various WEBSITES, 2001

A young **Kosovan immigrant** *from a farming community had not only to learn the language but also to adapt to a very different way of life when he arrived in England. He is now living independently, earning his living and training to be an electrician.*

I CAME TO CLAPHAM IN MAY 1998, from my father's farm in Kosovo. I was 15 years old. In my village the Serbs took the young Muslim boys and men away. My father asked an English lorry driver to bring me to England. My father offered many thousands of pounds. The lorry driver said: "It's OK mate – I don't want any money."

He took me to England and on the road just near Clapham South he left me. I spoke no English. I went down the tube, and I was there for six hours until I heard a man talk Albanian. He took me to the police, and then to the immigration and Wandsworth Social Services. In the Resource Centre I shut my door and learned English from a dictionary. Then I was sent to fostercarers in Clapham. I was happy. They are good people and explained about England – the Queen, Parliament, the police, shopping in Abbeville Road. I am surprised there are so many Indian shopkeepers.

I am surprised so many people go on the tube to offices every day. I did not understand where they worked or how they get food for all these people. I learned that the supermarkets get food from the country and from other countries.

I learnt the tube system and also buses and trains. In the tube during the Kosovo war one woman begs and says she is Kosovan. I shout at her and say she is not Kosovan. I know this because no Kosovan person would beg. It is not acceptable. We work or we die. We do not ask other people for money. I can find my way anywhere, but when I come out of the tube at Clapham I know I am home. It is good here, safe and no fighting.

I like the Common, but I do not really understand it. It is not like Kosovo. Not fields, just open for everyone. People fish for very small fish for many hours there. I fish in my country, but for big fish to eat. There are a lot of people for a small piece of land, which Clapham people like very much, and so do I. I like to watch football and go to the pub, but people do not talk much.

Abbeville Road is good – shops, a Post Office, police near and schools, more like a village. In England people do not go so often to each others' houses. Also they do not have so much family, people live just as father, mother and children – no grandmothers, cousins and aunts. Neighbours do not work together. In Clapham you do not shout into mobile phones outside gates, or make noises. There are many laws and Clapham is good area, you do things more correctly in some parts of London.

In the tube they do not believe me if I forget to buy my ticket even though I go every day. People do not recognise me at Clapham South or in the shops, or in the Post Office. This is not like Kosovo where I am known, my father is known and all speak to me, but I like Clapham very much – it is my second home.

KOSOVAN IMMIGRANT *interviewed by Celia Bibby*, 2001

So we reach the present, and **Conor Haselden,**
who is eight, describes his life in Clapham in 2002.
Those who described Clapham in 1900 at the beginning of this book
would recognise the Bandstand, football on the Common,
and Clapham Manor School, but would quite fail to understand
much of what a twenty-first century child regards as normal.
This is how we live now – how strange may our world
appear to those who read this book in years to come?

HOME. My earliest memory of living in Clapham is climbing on the bandstand on Clapham Common, playing a game. I live on a big road called Clapham Common North Side, right next to the Common so you can just cross the road and you're on the Common.

My house is in a block of flats called Okeover Manor. We have a front garden and a back garden which is joined onto the one next door. Sometimes it's annoying living in a flat because you have to share a garden, so if you want to build a treehouse or something the neighbours probably won't want you to. The good things are that it's a nice large flat and my own room is quite big so there's room for all my books and toys. I have lived in this flat all my life. We have a photo of my Mum watching as the kitchen is being rebuilt, while I am in her tummy.

SCHOOL. I go to Clapham Manor Primary School. I started going to the nursery there when I was 3 years old. Now I'm in year 4 and I think it's a wonderful school. I really like Literacy because I like writing stories, History is my second-favourite lesson and Maths is a bit boring. I enjoy the school events like the summer fair, the Christmas show and the Black History Month celebration and the parents enjoy it too. At the moment in History we are doing the Victorians and in Maths we are measuring angles and SATs [Standard Attainment Tests, a means of regularly assessing pupils' progress] are next week!

PLAY. Sometimes friends from school come round for tea and if it's nice we'll climb trees in the garden. I'm drawing knights, maps and spaceships a lot

Conor Haselden and other members of the Clapham Rovers football team, 2002

at the moment and I love watching *The Simpsons* on TV and playing my Gameboy. I like Clapham because there's lots of things I can do right next to my house, like watching great films at the Picture House, swimming in the leisure centre and playing on the Common. At weekends I play football with lots of my friends on Clapham Common. Our team is called Clapham Rovers under-9s (named after the FA Cup Winners in 1880).

MY FAMILY. Like me my Mum was born in St Thomas' Hospital. Her parents were living in Battersea then. My family on my Mum's side is quite big and I see them more because they live nearer than my Dad's family. When my Mum's family come round the living room is packed with aunties and cousins. My Mum's mum and dad were born in Kerry and Tipperary so I'm part Irish. We have been to Ireland but I can only remember a trip where we climbed a mountain and I got my foot stuck in a peat bog.

My Dad was born in Middlesex but now his family all live outside London. His mum lives in the middle of a village in Shropshire and his sister and her husband live near her in a house they built themselves where you can see the Welsh hills. My Dad's brother lives in Texas so I don't see him so often. His wife Teresa is Mexican and we hope they're coming to visit.

The furthest place I've been on holiday is Kalkan in Turkey where my aunt has a flat. We have also been to France, Ireland and the Isle of Wight.

I like going to other places but my favourite place is Clapham.

CONOR HASELEDEN, 2002

ACKNOWLEDGMENTS

THE CLAPHAM SOCIETY would like to thank all contributors, who are acknowledged, individually at the end of each piece. In particular we are grateful for the cooperation of copyright holders listed below in granting permission to print relevant extracts from published works. Whilst every effort has been made to trace copyright holders we regret that this has not always been possible.

Booth Papers, British Library of Political and Economic Science, London School of
   Economics. The Booth archive may be viewed on line (www.lse.ac.uk/booth)
Noël Coward, *Present Indicative,* Methuen Publishing Limited.
   © The Estate of Noël Coward
Frances Lloyd George, *The Years that are Past,* Hutchinson & Co.
Jack Hobbs, *My Life Story,* Hambledon Press
Norman Sherry, *The Life of Graham Greene,* Jonathan Cape.
   Used by permission of The Random House Group
Records of The South London Hospital for Women in the London Metropolitan
   Archives, by permission of the St.George's Hospital NHS Trust
Mike Phillips and Trevor Phillips, *Windrush: The Irresistible Rise of Multi-Racial
   Britain,* HarperCollins Publishers Ltd, © 1998 Mike Phillips and Trevor Phillips
John Walsh, *The Falling Angels,* HarperCollins Publishers Ltd. © 1999 John Walsh
Angela Carter, *Shaking a Leg, Journalism and Writings* © Angela Carter 1997
   Reproduced by permission of the Estate of Angela Carter
   c/o Rogers, Coleridge & White Ltd., 20 Powis Mews, London W11 1JN

Photographs

Leslie Ash 184
Clement Baptiste 182
Bernard Battley 17, 26, 27, 71, 84, 85, 116
Margaret Battley 12
Black Cultural Archives, 138, 139, 140
Brian Bloice 88
Clapham Society 22, 25, 159, 171
Bill Emmett 217
Dave Fairbairn 209
Friends of the South London
   Hospital 40, 193
Nigel Haselden 220
Holy Trinity Church 16
Imperial War Museum 45, 90, 91, 93, 94
Anna Jefferson Smith 205, 207

London's Transport
   Museum 30, 99,188
Patrick Loobey 3
Brian Luff 145, 148
Derrick McRobert 202
Moen & Sons 191
Bob Pethurst 72
QAS 174
Lee Seaman 198
Peter Skuse 123, 125, 128
Surrey County Cricket Club 34
Michael Surridge 11, 107
Arthur Tunesi 82
PamelaTurner 60
Brian Vincent 178

INDEX

THE CLAPHAM SOCIETY

Our aims

- We aim to improve the quality of life in Clapham and strengthen its identity and sense of community
- We seek to promote excellence in new developments as well as conservation of the best features of the past
- We want Clapham to be a vibrant, exciting and safe place to live, with job opportunities as well as shopping and leisure amenities

Our activities

- We fight to protect the special character of Clapham, its conservation areas and buildings of historic and architectural interest
- We consult on current planning and development proposals; and, if necessary, present evidence to formal planning enquiries
- We run a programme of monthly events, including talks on local and wider London topics, and walks around Clapham, which focus on new developments as well as local history
- We produce and distribute to members and key local people a regular newsletter giving information and opinions on current and impending issues and events
- We foster and maintain constructive relationships with Lambeth councillors and officers, including particularly the Clapham Town Centre Manager, in order to present effectively the views of the Society and its members
- We liaise and consult with other amenity groups
- We publish books about the area and its history, as well as guided walk leaflets and cards
- We organise parties for new members and social gatherings for members and their guests in houses and gardens of interest
- We run a local history group

Key areas of involvement

PLANNING: The local authorities have a statutory duty to consult us on planning and licensing matters. Our Planning Sub-Committee draws on a wealth of professional expertise and experience to comment on planning applications and developments and to give evidence at public enquiries.

THE COMMON: Our Common and Open Spaces Sub-Committee is dedicated to securing the future of Clapham's most precious asset. It advises on its maintenance and improvement for sport and wildlife and on the preservation of its character. We have developed a Code of Practice to improve the management of events on the Common, with a ban on those whose scale makes them inappropriate for this location.

ROADS AND TRANSPORT: Our Roads and Transport Sub-Committee reviews and, where necessary, challenges transport issues, taking into account the interests of people who live, work, walk, use public transport, cycle and drive in the area.

Join the Clapham Society...

....if you are interested in Clapham, its community, its businesses, its amenities and its buildings and are concerned to protect and enhance its character. We depend on our member' wide range of skills and experience, as well as their moral and financial support. We rely entirely on members' subscriptions and donations to pay for the newsletter and our administrative expenses.

For a Membership Application form please contact:

The Membership Secretary
Joyce Luck
15 Cavendish Road
London SW12 OBH

The following **Clapham Society** books
are in print and available from your bookseller
or from The Clapham Society
at the address shown in the front
of this book.

The Buildings of Clapham

A HISTORY OF THE DEVELOPMENT OF CLAPHAM and its buildings with street-by-street gazetteer giving date, builder, architect, noteworthy features of each building and information on interesting former residents. Illustrated with maps – old and new – archive photographs and drawings of architectural details. Detailed glossary and index. 236 pages. *Price* £11.95

The Story of Clapham Common

48 PAGES OF TEXT AND PHOTOGRAPHS about Clapham Common from early times up to the present. *Price* £5.95